THE EXISTENCE OF GOD

D0781086

Does God exist? What are the various arguments that seek to prove the existence of God? Can atheists refute these arguments? *The Existence of God: A Philosophical Introduction* assesses classical and contemporary arguments concerning the existence of God:

- The ontological argument, introducing the nature of existence, possible worlds, parody objections, and the evolutionary origin of the concept of God.
- The cosmological argument, discussing metaphysical paradoxes of infinity, scientific models of the universe, and philosophers' discussions about ultimate reality and the meaning of life.
- The design argument, addressing Aquinas's Fifth Way, Darwin's theory of evolution, the concept of irreducible complexity, and the current controversy over intelligent design and school education.

Bringing the subject fully up to date, Yujin Nagasawa explains these arguments in relation to recent research in cognitive science, the mathematics of infinity, big bang cosmology, and debates about ethics and morality in light of contemporary political and social events.

The book also includes fascinating insights into the passions, beliefs and struggles of the philosophers and scientists who have tackled the challenge of proving the existence of God, including Thomas Aquinas, and Kurt Gödel - who at the end of his career as a famous mathematician worked on a secret project to prove the existence of God.

The Existence of God: A Philosophical Introduction is an ideal gateway to the philosophy of religion and an excellent starting point for anyone interested in arguments about the existence of God.

Yujin Nagasawa is Senior Lecturer in Philosophy at the University of Birmingham, UK. He is author of *God and Phenomenal Consciousness* (2008), and editor/co-editor of *There's Something About Mary: Essays on Phenomenal Consciousness and Frank Jackson's Knowledge Argument* (2004), *New Waves in Philosophy of Religion* (2008) and *Scientific Approaches to the Philosophy of Religion* (2012).

THE EXISTENCE OF GOD

A philosophical introduction

Yujin Nagasawa

Routledge
Taylor & Francis Group

LONDON AND NEW YORK

This edition published 2011
by Routledge
2 Park Square, Milton Park, Abingdon, Oxon, OX14 4RN

Simultaneously published in the USA and Canada
by Routledge
711 Third Avenue, New York, NY 10017

Routledge is an imprint of the Taylor & Francis Group, an informa business
© 2011 Yujin Nagasawa

British Library Cataloguing in Publication Data
A catalogue record for this book is available from the British Library

Library of Congress Cataloging in Publication Data
Nagasawa, Yujin.
The existence of God : a philosophical introduction / by Yujin Nagasawa.
    p. cm.
    Includes bibliographical references and index.
    1. God--Proof. I. Title.
    BL200.N34 2011
    121'.6--dc22   2010043554

ISBN: 978-0-415-46588-5 (hbk)
ISBN: 978-0-415-46589-2 (pbk)
ISBN: 978-0-203-81862-6 (ebk)

Typeset in Joanna and Scala Sans
by Bookcraft Ltd, Stroud, Gloucestershire

To my parents Yonosuke and Yoko Nagasawa

CONTENTS

LIST OF FIGURES

LIST OF TABLES

PREFACE

I love standing in the dark on a moonless night and gazing up at the sky.
If the air is crisp and I manage to find a good spot, I can command a spec-
tacular view of the stardust above. Human eyes are more versatile than we
tend to think. They can, without a telescope, capture a view of the heavens
that stretches from the moon, which is approximately 1.3 light seconds
away from the earth, to the Andromeda galaxy, which is approximately 2.5
million light years away. A light second is the distance over which light
travels in a vacuum in one second, and a light year is the distance over which
it travels in a vacuum in one year. This implies two things. First, what I see
when I look up is really a very long way away indeed – an almost incon-
ceivably long way away. Second, the moon that I see when I look up does
not actually represent what it looks like now, as it were, but as it looked 1.3
seconds ago. Similarly, the Andromeda galaxy that I see represents its state
2.5 million years ago. Hence, by observing the stars at various distances I
can literally see millions of years of history at once, just above myself. When I
contemplate the vast scale of the universe, everything that bothers me in my
everyday life – no matter how important and troublesome it is for me, right
now – dissolves into triviality.

Philosophers are among those who have been deeply impressed, pain-
fully puzzled, and genuinely fascinated by the magnificent scale and breath-
taking elegance of the universe. When did the universe come into being?
What, if anything, created it? Where are we from and where are we going?

Why is there this universe rather than a different one? Why is there anything in the first place rather than nothing at all?

The history of philosophy, at least at its core, is, more or less, the history of philosophers' attempts to answer these fundamental metaphysical questions. In this book, I address these questions by focusing on one key notion: the existence of God. I introduce the endeavors of philosophers over thousands of years to prove God's existence and to explain the origin of everything by reference to it. I discuss, without presupposing any background knowledge of philosophy or science, a number of interesting arguments for the existence of God that philosophers have invented.

I try to situate my discussion in a richer context than is ordinarily provided in scholarly volumes and textbooks with occasional observations about the following:

1   The historical background – I explain the social and cultural conditions that have led philosophers to pursue specific ideas and arguments concerning the existence of God and I place them in the context of philosophical and scientific history broadly conceived.
2   The human side of the story – I illustrate philosophers' passions, beliefs, and struggles in tackling problems concerning the existence of God and related issues by introducing pertinent, often fascinating, episodes.
3   Wider implications of the arguments – I enrich our perspective on these arguments by explaining how philosophical discussion of the existence of God might bear on contemporary, real-life political controversies and disputes among scientists.

I believe that bringing historical context and contemporary relevance to philosophy by illuminating the lives and personalities of key figures will lead us to an intrinsically rewarding experience in our engagement with the subject matter.

Over the course of this book I hope to convince you that there are some arguments for the existence of God that are – even if they might not succeed ultimately – very impressive. Whether or not I realize that goal, I hope one thing will be clear when you close this book: philosophers' curiosity about the deep metaphysical problems, and their enduring efforts to solve them, are both genuine and remarkable.

ACKNOWLEDGEMENTS

This book project has been greatly benefited by discussion with students in my philosophy of religion courses at the University of Birmingham over the last five years. I would like to thank them all. John Hick and Daniel Hill provided me with some useful historical information. William Barnett, Andrei Buckareff, Todd Buras, Philip Goff, Graham Oppy, Alexander Pruss, and Naomi Thompson gave helpful comments. Tony Bruce and Adam Johnson of Routledge provided impeccable editorial support. I am grateful to all of them. I wrote this book as part of a research project that I conducted for the Cognition, Religion, and Theology Project at the University of Oxford, funded by the John Templeton Foundation. I would like to thank the Project and the Foundation for their generous support. I also thank anonymous reviewers for useful comments and constructive suggestions, and my colleagues in the School of Philosophy, Theology, and Religion at the University of Birmingham for general academic support. The views expressed in this book are my own and do not necessarily represent those of any organizations or individuals. Finally, I am grateful to my wife Asja Pörtsch, my parents Yoko and Yonosuke Nagasawa – to whom this book is dedicated – and my brother Naoe Nagasawa for their love and encouragement.

PART I

AN ARMCHAIR PROOF OF THE EXISTENCE OF GOD

[The ontological argument] is very beautiful and really very ingenious.

G. W. Leibniz

[The ontological argument is the] most famous of all fishy philosophical arguments.

Robert Nozick

Considered by daylight ... and without prejudice, this famous Ontological Proof is really a charming joke.

Arthur Schopenhauer

1 Gödel's secret project

On January 14, 1978, at the age of 71, the mathematician Kurt Gödel died in Princeton Hospital in New Jersey. In its obituary of Gödel, The Times (London) described him as 'the most influential mathematical logician of the century' and his incompleteness theorems as proofs that 'changed the whole philosophical view of the foundation of mathematics'.

Gödel published the incompleteness theorems in 1931, when he was 25 years old. The theorems show, roughly speaking, that (i) in any consistent axiomatic system of arithmetic there always exists a formula such that, ironically, its truth or falsity cannot be proved within the system itself (i.e., the system is not complete); and, on the other hand, (ii) if the truth or falsity of all the formulae in a system can be proved within that system (i.e., the system is complete), the system cannot prove the consistency of the system itself. Many scholars were astonished by Gödel's discovery, because they had believed that, however messy and chaotic the material world is, the world of mathematics was always complete and elegant. Gödel's theorems demolished such a naive view of mathematics. In 1999, *Time* magazine included Gödel in its list of the greatest scientists and thinkers of the twentieth century, along with Francis Crick, James Watson, Albert Einstein, Sigmund Freud, and Alan Turing.

Despite Gödel's glorious academic achievements his demise was little known outside mathematics, and the public memorial service for him was not very well attended. More shockingly, when he passed away he weighed only 65 pounds.

Gödel was an obsessed and paranoid genius. In the depths of winter, he wore warm clothes indoors and opened all the windows because he believed that someone was trying to kill him with poisonous gas. He refused to eat anything but what his wife Adele cooked because he believed that someone was attempting to poison his food. Allegedly, one of the primary causes of Gödel's death was that Adele became ill and could no longer cook for him. He preferred to die from starvation rather than eat what someone else had prepared.

Gödel met Adele in a night-club in Vienna in 1927, when he was 21. Gödel's parents disapproved of his relationship with her because she was a dancer, divorced, and six years older than he was. Adele, however, provided indispensable loving support to Gödel throughout his life. For his colleagues and students, Gödel was not always an easy person to work with; his eccentric behavior and bizarre opinions often puzzled people around him. However, he was always gentle and faithful to Adele, and he looked after her both financially and emotionally. He paid for virtually everything for her, and, apparently, she learned how to write checks only after his death.

A few years before his death, there was a rumor among mathematicians that Gödel was working on something odd, something distinctively different from his usual mathematical projects. More specifically, according to the rumor, he was devoting himself to a 'proof' of the existence of God.

Gödel left notes that are dated February 10, 1970 and filled with many mathematical symbols. The notes show that Gödel was doing research on a proof of the existence of God that is known among philosophers as the 'ontological argument' or the 'ontological proof'. The ontological argument, which was first clearly formulated in the Middle Ages, proposes that one can prove the existence of God simply by analyzing the concept of God. Gödel's aim was to reformulate and strengthen this medieval argument by adapting tools that were familiar to him from mathematical logic.

Gödel was a theist. In his answer to a sociologist's questionnaire that he filled in but never returned, he described his religious position as follows: 'Baptist Lutheran (but not member of any rel. cong.) My belief is theistic, not pantheistic, following Leibniz rather than Spinoza.'[1] However, Gödel's interest in the ontological argument seemed to be purely intellectual; it was not directly connected to his religious commitment. Some believe that Gödel did not publish his work on the ontological argument precisely because he did not want others to think that he had become deeply religious.[2]

So what is the ontological argument by which Gödel was absorbed near the end of his life? Why did he become interested in the argument if his interest was not motivated by his religious commitment? In order to answer these questions – and to appreciate the strength of the ontological argument – we must go back to the eleventh century.

2 Anselm's discovery

Some philosophers claim that the roots of the various ontological arguments can be traced to Ancient Greece.[3] However, there is a consensus among scholars that St. Anselm of Canterbury – one of the founders of scholasticism and one of the most influential medieval philosophers and theologians – invented the argument independently and formulated it clearly for the first time. Anselm introduced the argument in his book the Proslogion, which he wrote between 1077 and 1078.

Anselm was born in either 1033 or 1034 in Aosta, a city in the kingdom of Burgundy. Aosta is located in the Italian Alps and near the borders of what are now France and Switzerland. Anselm's father Gundulph was a Lombard who became a citizen of Aosta and his mother Ermenberga was from a traditional Burgundian family. Gundulph and Ermenberga were in great contrast with each other. Gundulph was a harsh and ill-tempered man and refused consent when his son, Anselm, expressed his desire to enter a monastery at the age of 15. Ermenberga, on the other hand, was a wise and virtuous woman who taught Anselm the joy of learning and thinking. After his mother's death, Anselm decided to leave home, because his father's harshness had become unbearable. He crossed the Alps, travelled to France and eventually arrived at Normandy, where he studied under Lanfranc, prior of the Benedictine abbey of Bec and a prominent theologian. At the monastery of Bec, Anselm devoted himself to scholarly work on theology. In 1060, he entered the abbey as a novice and in 1063, when Lanfranc was appointed abbot of Caen, Anselm was elected as prior. Anselm became abbot of Bec in 1078, upon the death of the founder and first abbot. At Bec, Anselm produced important works including the Monologion (1076) and the Proslogion (1077–8).

Archbishop Lanfranc, Anselm's old master, died in 1089, but England's King William Rufus held open the post of archbishop for four years in order to take the revenues for his own purposes. Rufus was not a committed Christian and he did not cooperate with efforts to reform the Church. Nevertheless, in 1093, Rufus finally decided to appoint Anselm Archbishop of Canterbury. Anselm was not very keen to take the position, as he sensed, given Rufus's attitude, that his tenure as archbishop would be difficult. Unlike his father, William the Conqueror, Rufus did not want to spend money on the Church and instead raided monasteries when he needed funds.

In 1097, when Anselm went to Rome without permission, Rufus forbade him to return. Rufus's successor, Henry I, invited Anselm to return. As it transpired, however, Henry was almost as enthusiastic as Rufus was about the idea of royal jurisdiction over the Church, and Anselm was exiled again, from 1103 to 1107. Two years later, in April 1109, Anselm died at the age of 76 among his monks in Canterbury. He was canonized in 1494 by Alexander VI and named a Doctor of the Church on his memorial day in 1720 by Pope Clement XI. Anselm's work did not attract much attention in his time. Some scholars ascribe this lack of interest to the style of Anselm's writings. While the works of most other influential theologians in the Middle Ages are systematically structured treatises, Anselm's works are mainly dialogues and tracts covering a variety of issues.

Anselm was a radical and controversial leader. He ordered priests, deacons, and canons to abandon their wives and prohibited sons from inheriting their fathers' churches. He claimed that some of the priests in England did not consider the spiritual needs of Christians sufficiently and spent too much time pleasing their patrons. Anselm is also said to have been the first in the Church to oppose the African slave trade. In 1102, Anselm obtained from the national ecclesiastical council at Westminster a prohibition of the slave trade. The council decreed, 'Let no one hereafter presume to engage in that nefarious trade in which hitherto in England men were usually sold like brute animals.'[4]

In his book the Monologion Anselm introduced several independent arguments that jointly support the existence of God. He was, however, not entirely satisfied. He wanted to accomplish what might be regarded as the dream of theistic philosophers: to discover a *single* proof that is so powerful that every rational person could not but admit the existence of God. In the preface of the Proslogion Anselm describes vividly and honestly what a struggle it was for him to search for such an argument. He writes:

> After I had published [the *Monologion*] ... I began to wonder if perhaps it might be possible to find one single argument that for its proof required no other save itself, and that by itself would suffice to prove that God really exists, that He is the supreme good needing no other and is He whom all things have need of for their being and well-being, and also to prove whatever we believe about the Divine Being.[5]

While Anselm believed firmly in God, it was extremely difficult for him to find such an argument for God's existence. Anselm describes the difficulty as follows:

> But as often and as diligently as I turned my thoughts to this, sometimes it seemed to me that I had almost reached what I was seeking, sometimes it eluded my acutest thinking completely, so that finally, in desperation, I was about to give up what I was looking for as something impossible to find.[6]

When we cannot find a solution to a problem, even though we have invested a lot of time and effort, often the best thing to do is try to shift our focus for a moment. Sometimes inspiration strikes us while our attention is elsewhere. Human nature does not seem to have changed over the last 900 years, because this trick worked for Anselm as well:

> However, when I had decided to put aside this idea altogether, lest by uselessly occupying my mind it might prevent other ideas with which I could make some progress, then, in spite of my unwillingness and my resistance to it, it began to force itself upon me more and more pressingly. So it was that one day when I was quite worn out with resisting its importunacy, there came to me, in the very conflict of my thoughts, what I had despaired of finding, so that I eagerly grasped the notion which in my distraction I had been rejecting.[7]

Anselm was so excited about his discovery that he decided to share it with the public:

> Judging, then, that what had given me such joy to discover would afford pleasure, if it were written down, to anyone who might read it, I have written the following short tract dealing with this question as well as several others, from the point of view of one trying to raise his mind to contemplate God and seeking to understand what he believes.[8]

What, then, is Anselm's ontological argument?

The first step in Anselm's ontological argument is to define God as 'that-than-which-no-greater-can-be-thought'. This definition seems acceptable to most traditional theists because, according to Judaeo-Christian-Islamic theism, God is a perfect being and no other creatures are superior to God. Unlike human beings, who are subject to many limitations, He[9] knows everything (He is omniscient), He can do anything that it is logically possible to do (He is omnipotent), and He is morally perfect (He is omnibenevolent). Anselm says that once this definition of God is accepted, we can prove that such a God exists merely by analyzing the concept of God alone.

It is sometimes thought, not only among atheists but also among theists, that the Anselmian concept of God, as that-than-which-no-greater-can-be-thought, is an unnatural, philosophical artifact of scholasticism. This is partly because the concept assumes individual divine attributes such as omniscience, omnipotence, and omnibenevolence, which are highly complex philosophical concepts. However, contemporary research in developmental psychology and cognitive science suggests that the Anselmian concept of God might not be an unnatural artifact after all. Some researchers in these fields maintain that the concepts of the divine attributes that are assumed by the Anselmian concept are naturally formed in childhood. The twentieth-century Swiss psychologist Jean Piaget hypothesized that children younger than seven years old ascribe omniscience and omnipotence to adults, especially to their parents. This makes sense because there is a survival advantage for young children in trusting adults unquestioningly. By utterly trusting adults, children can acquire knowledge and skills that are useful for securing food and shelter. Adopting a skeptical stance towards adults, on the other hand, is not beneficial to children at all in this respect. Piaget's hypothesis has been confirmed by recent empirical studies undertaken by cognitive scientists. These studies suggest that young children naturally first form a belief that adults are omniscient and omnipotent, and later, as they grow up, correct such a belief.[10] One might wonder if children also ascribe omnibenevolence, that is, moral perfection, to adults. The cognitive scientist of religion Justin L. Barrett contends that it might well be the case that, just as children overestimate the knowledge and power of adults, they might overestimate the morality of adults as well.[11] Cognitive science of religion is a very new field, but it is interesting to note that it provides empirical data which seem to imply that the Anselmian concept of God has cognitive and developmental origins. (See the next part of this book for more findings in the cognitive science of religion.)

Anselm calls a person who sincerely denies the existence of God 'the fool', a phrase that he presumably derived from the Bible: 'The fool says in his heart, "There is no God." They are corrupt, their deeds are vile; there is no one who does good' (Psalm 14:1).[12] Anselm says that even the fool agrees that God, defined as that-than-which-no-greater-can-be-thought, exists at least in the mind because anyone can understand the phrase 'that-than-which-no-greater-can-be-thought'. Here, for the fool, God, as that-than-which-no-greater-can-be-thought, is comparable to imaginary beings, such as unicorns and ghosts. Now Anselm asks, 'Does that-than-which-no-greater-can-be-thought exist only in the mind or does it exist both in the mind *and* also in reality?' In other words, is God, as that-than-which-no-greater-can-be-thought, more like unicorns and ghosts, which exist only in the mind, or is it more like the president of the United States and Mount Everest, which exist in the mind as well as in reality? Anselm says that if God exists only in the mind another being can be thought that is even greater than God. Such a being is thought to have all the characteristics that God has *and* it is also thought to exist in reality. However, Anselm says, it is contradictory to say that a being can be thought that is greater than God because we presupposed that God is, by definition, that-than-which-no-greater-can-be-thought, that is, that no being can be thought that is greater than God. It is impossible that a being can be thought that is greater than that-than-which-no-greater-can-be-thought (Figure I.1). Hence, it is impossible that God, as that-than-which-no-greater-can-be-thought, does not exist in reality and thus, Anselm concludes, God does indeed exist in reality

In order to appreciate the ontological argument fully we need to understand its distinctive features. The first distinctive feature is that the argument is formulated in such a way that anyone, even 'the fool', can follow it. This is because, in formulating the ontological argument, Anselm does not

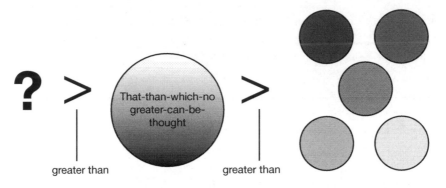

Figure I.1 Is it possible that a being can be thought that is greater than that-than-which-no-greater-can-be-thought?

appeal to any religious experience or concepts that only religious believers can accept. Whether or not it is ultimately successful, the argument tries to convince atheists by proposing a derivation of the existence of God without appealing to the existence of anything supernatural in its premises. The ontological argument does talk about God as that-than-which-no-greater-can-be-thought but it does not presuppose the existence of such a being. This kind of approach to the existence of God and other theological problems is called 'natural theology', as opposed to 'revealed theology'.

In order to illustrate the distinction between natural theology and revealed theology, let us move our clock forward to the seventeenth century for a moment. When the French mathematician and philosopher Blaise Pascal died in 1662 from stomach cancer his servant found, by pure coincidence, a note kept sewn to the inside of Pascal's coat. Obviously, this note was always with Pascal; every time he changed his coat he removed it from the old coat and sewed it into the new one. The note describes a religious experience that he had one night when he was 31 years old. Pascal experienced a mystical vision which he called a 'night of fire'. His note reads as follows:

> Memorial
> In the year of grace, 1654, on Monday, 23rd of November, Feast of St Clement, Pope and Martyr, and others in the Martyrology. Vigil of St Chrysogonus, Martyr, and others.
>
> From about half past ten in the evening until about half past twelve.

FIRE

God of Abraham, God of Isaac, God of Jacob,
Not of the philosophers and scholars.
Certitude. Certitude. Feeling. Joy. Peace.
God of Jesus Christ.
'Thy God and my God'.
Forgetfulness of the world and of everything, except God.
He is to be found only in the ways taught in the Gospel.
Greatness of the Human Soul.

'Righteous Father, the world hath not known Thee,
But I have known Thee'.

Joy, joy, joy, tears of joy.
I have separated myself from Him.
'They have forsaken Me, the fountain of living waters'.
'My God, wilt Thou leave me?'
Let me not be separated from Him eternally.

'This is eternal life, That they might know Thee, the only true God,
And Jesus Christ, whom Thou hast sent'.

Jesus Christ.
Jesus Christ.

I have separated myself from Him:
I have fled from Him,
denied Him,
crucified Him.
Let me never be separated from Him.
We keep hold of Him only by the ways taught in the Gospel.
Renunciation, total and sweet.
Total submission to Jesus Christ and to my director.
Eternally in joy for a day's training on earth.
'I will not forget thy words'.

Amen.[13]

Phrases that are placed in quotation marks are derived from the Bible. Pascal never seems to have mentioned this amazing religious experience to anyone, keeping it secret until his death. We could not have known about it had Pascal's servant not discovered the note. The most interesting part of this note is that Pascal says that what he experienced was the 'God of Abraham, God of Isaac, God of Jacob' and '[n]ot of the philosophers and scholars'.

The phrases 'the God of Abraham, God of Isaac, God of Jacob' and 'the God of the philosophers and scholars' correspond to revealed theology and natural theology, respectively. In revealed theology, philosophers and theologians try to understand the nature and the existence of God primarily through supernatural means. For example, revealed theology purports to bring to light the essence of God through religious experience and biblical revelation. The concept of God derived through this approach denotes what Pascal calls the God of Abraham, Isaac, and Jacob. This is the concept of God found in mystical experience and the Bible. In natural theology, on the other hand, philosophers and theologians try to understand the nature and the existence of God appealing only to thought and ordinary, as opposed to supernatural, experience, formulating the concept of God and deriving God's essence and existence through reason. The concept of God established by this approach is what Pascal calls the God of the philosophers and scholars. As its name suggests, this concept of God is more formal and scholastic than that of the God of Abraham, Isaac, and Jacob. It is controversial among philosophers of religion and theologians whether these two concepts of God are compatible. Some claim that the God of the philosophers and scholars is far-fetched and incompatible with the more intuitive and experiential God of Abraham, Isaac, and Jacob. Some claim that these two concepts are compatible because they merely represent two different ways of understanding the same God. Despite the fact that Pascal remarked that what he experienced was the God of Abraham, Isaac, and Jacob and not the God of the philosophers and scholars, he thought that ultimately we need both revealed theology and natural theology to understand God. In his seminal *Pensées* he writes, 'If we submit everything to reason, our religion will have no mysterious and supernatural element. If we offend the principles of reason, our religion will be absurd and ridiculous.'[14]

Move our clock back to the eleventh century. Anselm's ontological argument is a paradigm example of an argument in natural theology rather than revealed theology. Anselm does not try to prove the existence of God by appealing to personal religious experience or biblical revelation. He appeals to reason alone, hoping that his argument has the potential to convince even atheists who deny the authenticity of religious experience and biblical revelation.

Another distinctive feature of the ontological argument, distinctive even compared with other arguments in natural theology, is that it is a pure *a priori* argument. What does *a priori* mean? Take, for example, the statements, 'Napoleon died in 1821' and 'There are approximately 6.7 billion people in the world.' These statements are true *a posteriori*, that is, we can only confirm whether they are true on the basis of experience or empirical evidence. We need to conduct some historical study or demographic research in order to establish that these statements are true. This means that arguments for these statements have to be *a posteriori* as well. Consider, on the other hand, such statements such as 'A triangle is three sided' and 'Bachelors are unmarried men.' These statements are true *a priori* because, unlike *a posteriori* statements, we can confirm whether they are true on the basis of reason alone, without any experience or empirical evidence. All we need to do in order to confirm their truths is to analyze the sentences conceptually. This means that arguments for these statements also have to be *a priori*.

The distinction between *a priori* and *a posteriori* explains clearly why the ontological argument is so unique. Unlike other arguments for the existence of God, the ontological argument says that the conclusion that God exists is an *a priori* statement and, hence, can be derived solely through *a priori* reasoning. As we shall see in Parts II and III of this book, almost all other arguments for the existence of God adopt *a posteriori* reasoning by appealing to observations regarding the external world, such as the complexity of biological organisms or the origin of the universe. The ontological argument is, in this sense, a pure 'armchair proof'; it claims that we can prove the existence of God through mental exercise alone.

Having in mind the above unique feature, we can speculate about why Gödel was fascinated by the ontological argument rather than other theistic arguments; perhaps it was because the ontological argument derives the existence of God *a priori* just as mathematical proofs derive mathematical theorems *a priori*. Apparently, Gödel believed that *a priori* reasoning in mathematics is more reliable than *a posteriori* reasoning in natural science, as one episode suggests: when the astrophysicist John Bahcall introduced himself as a physicist at a faculty dinner Gödel's response was: 'I don't believe in natural science.'[15]

3 Descartes's ontological argument

The ontological argument was discussed and criticized by Thomas Aquinas and other medieval theologians, but it did not receive the attention it deserved for a long time. It was revived, however, in 1641 by the French philosopher René Descartes in his seminal work *Meditations on First Philosophy*. The argument was already over 560 years old by then.

Descartes is commonly regarded as the father of modern philosophy and science. He was born in 1596 in La Haye, which is now called Descartes in his honor, in the Touraine region of France. In 1606 or 1607, he was sent to the Jesuit Collège Royal Henry-Le-Grand at La Flèche. After graduation, following his father's wishes, he studied law at the University of Poitiers and was awarded his degree on November 10, 1616. November 10 was a key date for Descartes; as he himself realized, many important events in his life took place on this date.[16] On *November 10, 1618*, while travelling, he met an amateur Dutch scientist called Isaac Beeckman. Some think that Beeckman indirectly changed the course of the history of philosophy and science, because it was he who opened Descartes's eyes to these subjects. Although they spent only a few months together, Beeckman introduced several intellectually challenging problems to Descartes and convinced him that he should engage in solving them. Descartes was so grateful to Beeckman that he dedicated the *Compendium Musicae*, his earliest surviving book, to him. Exactly one year later, that is, again, *November 10, 1619*, he had a series of dreams, three in fact, that convinced him to devote the rest of his life to philosophy, science, and mathematics.

Descartes's dreams were described in a small notebook that he carried around while he was travelling in Europe between 1619 and 1622.[17] The dreams that Descartes had were mysterious but the notebook itself in which he recorded them was also mysterious. A French scholar, Adrien Baillet, saw the notebook, wrote down Descartes's descriptions of the dreams, and paraphrased them in his biography of Descartes. No one knows, however, where the original notebook is; it seems to have been lost. The notebook cannot have been a fiction contrived by Baillet because it was later discovered that Leibniz also had a copy of it.

Descartes was 23 years old when he had the series of three dreams in 1619. In a stove-heated room he fell asleep, filled with great excitement that he had discovered the foundations of a 'marvelous science'.

In the first dream Descartes imagined himself walking on an extremely windy day.[18] He felt a pain in his right side and could not walk straight. He struggled to continue making his way towards his destination. He entered a college with open gates, hoping to pray in a chapel there. He was thrown against the wall of the chapel by the strong wind. He then saw a person in the courtyard. He suggested that Descartes see Mr N., who would have something to give him. For some reason, Descartes in his dream assumed that the object was a melon from a foreign country. Descartes was still struggling to stay upright against the wind, but surprisingly, people who started gathering around him did not seem to have any problem in standing upright. The wind finally started calming down and Descartes woke up. His pain remained and he worried that the dream was created by an evil spirit. He turned over on his right side and prayed for God. He contemplated good and evil for a couple of hours and then fell asleep again.

In the second dream Descartes heard a very loud noise, which he guessed was a thunder-clap. The awful weather in the first dream seemed to have come back but Descartes was not so frightened this time. He opened his eyes to find many fiery sparks filling his room.

A moment later the third dream started. This dream was different from the previous ones because there was nothing frightening in it. Descartes was sitting at his desk and discovered a book on it; it was a dictionary. He was not sure who had left it but thought that it might be quite useful. When he tried to reach the dictionary he found another book entitled the *Corpus Poetarum*. He opened a random page and found a poem by Decius Magnus Ausonius, an ancient Roman poet and rhetorician. The first line of the poem was, 'What path shall I take in life?' Then a man whom Descartes did not know appeared in the room showing him another verse from another book, beginning with the words 'Yes and No'. Descartes knew that it was also written by Ausonius, so he told the man that Ausonius is one of the poets whose work was in the *Corpus Poetarum* on his desk. Descartes tried to find the book but he had difficulty locating it. He thought that the book had vanished but eventually it reappeared. He was proud that he knew the order and arrangement of the book perfectly. However, he could not find the 'Yes and No' poem in the book, so he told the man that he could show him instead a more beautiful passage from Ausonius beginning with the phrase, 'What path shall I take in life?' The man said that he wanted to see it but at that point he and the books vanished.

The three dreams now count among the most often-discussed dreams in history. Sigmund Freud was once asked to analyze Descartes's dreams but declined. He mentioned, however, that the dreams were likely derived not from the deep unconscious but from conscious processes.[19] Perhaps it was unnecessary for Freud to analyze the dreams because Descartes himself had already done so. Surprisingly enough, Descartes claimed that he could analyze the dreams while he was having them. He said that the melon in the first dream represented the charms of solitude. The strong wind that pushed him against the wall of the church represented an evil spirit. The loud noise and fiery sparks of the second dream represented the spirit of truth that came to possess him. Descartes thought that the dictionary in the third dream represented 'all the sciences gathered together', the Corpus Poetarum represented philosophy and wisdom in unity, and the 'Yes and No' poem represented truth and falsity. Descartes thought that the third dream was particularly important because it represented the wish of the spirit of truth that the treasures of all the sciences should be unlocked for him. The night of November 10, 1619 marks a monumental event in his life, as well as in the history of philosophy and science.

Descartes is best known for the phrase, 'Cogito, ergo sum' ('I think, therefore I am'), which he reached through his attempt to discover what, if anything, he could know with certainty to be true.[20] In order to find such a truth, he decided to try to doubt absolutely everything he could. He thought that if anything at all remained after his persistent exercise of doubting, that would be the ultimate truth. He tried to doubt, for instance, the reality of everything around him, such as tables, chairs, people, and so on. He even tried to doubt the existence of his own body. He could doubt the existence of these objects because what he thought he saw could have been mere illusions created by an evil spirit. Similarly, he could doubt what he heard, what he smelt, what he tasted, what he touched, and so on. It is extremely unlikely that there is an evil spirit that creates such illusions purposefully, but at least such a scenario is a logical possibility. Descartes discovered, however, that there was one thing that he could never doubt: his own existence. The more he doubted the more certain it was that he existed. He wrote:

> I have convinced myself that nothing in the world exists – no sky, no earth, no minds, no bodies; so am not I likewise non-existent? But if I did convince myself of anything, I must have existed. But there is some deceiver, supremely powerful, supremely intelligent, who purposely always deceive me. If he deceives me, then again I undoubtedly exist; let him deceive me as much as he may, he will never bring it about that, at the time of thinking (quamdiu cogitabo) that I am something, I am in

fact nothing. Thus I have now weighed all considerations enough and more than enough; and must at length conclude that this proposition 'I am', 'I exist', whenever I utter it or conceive it in my mind is, necessarily true.[21]

Descartes's approach is most commonly interpreted as an instance of 'methodological doubt'. He did not doubt everything sincerely but only methodologically; he tried to doubt whatever he could in order to reach the ultimate truth.

Descartes was a private and eccentric figure. Although he left his intellectual autobiography, *Discourse on Method*, the details of his life are for the most part unknown. He moved to Holland in 1629 and lived in seclusion, moving frequently from one place to another for almost 20 years until his death. The contemporary philosopher A. C. Grayling speculates that Descartes might even have been a spy, engaging in intelligence activities or secret work during the period of his military service and travels.[22]

One anecdote in particular illustrates Descartes's eccentricity. In 1649, one year before his death, Descartes travelled to Sweden to tutor 20-year-old Queen Christina there. On the ship he told others that his daughter Francine was travelling with him. They thought that was strange because they never saw Descartes accompanying a child. Out of curiosity, they decided to search Descartes's quarters. While they did not find any person, they found a strange box sitting there. They were so curious that they could not resist. They opened the box quickly before Descartes came back. They were shocked by what they found in the box. It was a doll of a girl that moved like a living human![23]

The authenticity of the above anecdote is unconfirmed. However, Descartes *was* interested in automata and once tried to build a dancing man, a flying pigeon, and a spaniel chasing a pheasant.[24] Moreover, even though he was never married, he did have a daughter called Francine with a servant, Hélène Jans. Francine died of scarlet fever at the age of five, which Descartes remarked was the greatest sorrow of his life.

Since childhood Descartes had a tendency to be weak and was not fond of waking up early. When he was a student at college he even had privileges to sleep late and not to be obliged to attend classes in the mornings. However, when he arrived in Sweden at the age of 53, his tutee, Queen Christina, woke him up early every day, often at 5 a.m. The unaccustomed sleeping cycle and the cold northern European winter caused Descartes to develop pneumonia. He died in the spring of 1650 without seeing his motherland again.

Descartes was first buried in Stockholm, but his remains were later exhumed and taken to Paris. In 1819, when they were laid in the church of Saint-Germain-des-Prés, the skull was missing. A Swedish chemist, Jöns Jacob Berzelius, later bought what he believed to be Descartes's skull and asked to place it with the rest of the remains. Today, however, the skull is still separated from the rest of Descartes's body, being displayed at the Musée de l'Homme in the Palais de Chaillot.

In his *Meditations*, the work that introduced the *cogito* argument, Descartes provided two versions of the ontological argument that are distinct from Anselm's. Descartes describes the first version as follows:

> Now if it follows, from my mere ability to elicit the idea of some object from my consciousness (*cogitatione*), that all the properties that I clearly and distinctly perceive the object to have do really belong to it; could not this give rise to an argument by which the existence of God might be proved? I assuredly find in myself the idea of God – of a supremely perfect being – no less than the idea of a figure or a number; and I clearly and distinctly understand that everlasting existence belongs to his nature, no less than I can see that what I prove of some figure, or number, belongs to the nature of that figure, or number. So, even if my meditations on previous days were not entirely true, yet I ought to hold the existence of God with at least the same degree of certainty as I have so far held mathematical truths.[25]

The above argument can be summarized as follows: if I clearly and distinctly perceive some property to pertain to the nature of an object, then that property pertains to the nature of the object; I clearly and distinctly perceive eternal existence to pertain to God's nature; therefore, eternal existence pertains to God's nature; therefore, God exists eternally.

As Descartes himself says, the above argument is more comparable to mathematical axioms than ordinary philosophical arguments because what it asserts essentially is that the existence of God is a self-evident truth. Just as we can immediately grasp mathematical axioms, according to Descartes, we can immediately grasp the nature of God as an eternal existence.

Descartes's second version of the ontological argument, on the other hand, is comparable to conventional philosophical arguments:

[T]here is indeed no necessity for me ever to happen upon any thought of (*cogitationem de*) God; but whenever I choose to think of (*cogitare de*) the First and Supreme Being, and as it were bring out the idea of him from the treasury of my mind, I must necessarily ascribe to him all perfections, even if I do not at the moment enumerate them all, or attend to each. This necessity clearly ensures that, when later on I observe that existence is a perfection, I am justified in concluding that the First and Supreme Being exists. In the same way, it is not necessary that I should ever imagine any triangle; but whenever I choose to consider a rectilinear figure that has just three angles, I must ascribe to it properties from which it is rightly inferred that its three angles are not greater than two right angles; even if I do not notice this at the time. When, on the other hand, I examine what figures can be inscribed in circles, it is in no way necessary for me to think all quadrilaterals belong to this class; indeed, I cannot even imagine this, so long as I will admit only what I clearly and distinctly understand. Thus there is a great difference between such false suppositions and my genuine innate ideas, among which the first and chief is my idea of God. In many ways, I can see that this idea is no fiction depending on my way of thinking (*cogitatione*), but an image of a real and immutable nature. First, I can frame no other concept of anything to whose essence existence belongs, except God alone; again, I cannot conceive of two or more such Gods; and given that one God exists, I clearly see that necessarily he has existed from all eternity, and will exist to all eternity; and I perceive many other Divine attributes, which I can in no wise diminish or alter.[26]

This version can be summarized as follows: when I think of God I am necessitated to ascribe all perfections to Him; existence is a perfection; thus I am necessitated to ascribe existence to God; therefore, God exists. Contrary to the first version, this version is not comparable to mathematical axioms because it is not a mere expression of a self-evident truth. It is based on an inference from God's perfection to His existence.

While Descartes appears to think that the first version is more powerful, the second version is more widely known. In fact the second version is what is commonly referred to as the 'Cartesian ontological argument'. 'Existence is a perfection' is a famous key phrase in the argument, which has been, as we shall see, a target of criticism.

Descartes's two versions are different from Anselm's version. First, unlike Anselm's version, they do not appeal to the definition of God as that-than-which-no-greater-can-be-thought. Anselm's definition of God as that-than-which-no-greater-can-be-thought can be construed as a relational definition because it is based on the idea that no other beings are greater than God, and thus trades on the 'greater than' relation between God and other beings. Descartes's definition of God, however, is not (at least explicitly) relational. It states simply that God is a supremely perfect being. Second, while Anselm's version appeals to the comparison between two beings, that-than-which-no-greater-can-be-thought existing only in the mind and the same being existing both in the mind and reality, Descartes's versions do not appeal to any comparison. Descartes's first version derives the existence of God directly from our clear and distinct idea of God's nature, and the second version derives it indirectly from God's perfection. Nevertheless Descartes's versions are properly construed as forms of the ontological argument because, just like Anselm's version, they purport to prove the existence of God on the basis of *a priori* reasoning alone.

Descartes describes God's existence as everlasting and eternal. What does he mean by these phrases? There are two interpretations of Descartes's description. The first is that he thinks that God exists eternally in a temporal sense. A being is eternally existent in this sense if it exists always. That is, unlike ordinary beings like human beings, there is no beginning and no end for an eternal being. There is no point on a time-scale where an eternal being comes into existence or ceases to exist. The second interpretation of Descartes's description, which is arguably more important in this context, is that he thinks that God exists necessarily. In order to see what necessary existence is, consider, first, things that do not exist necessarily, that is, things that exist only *contingently*. Something exists contingently and not necessarily if it is possible for that thing not to have existed. Consider the history of the world. There is only one actual history but it could have run differently in many ways. For example, Socrates might never have existed. It could have been the case that his parents had never met, or that one of them died before Socrates came to be conceived. Similarly, the Great Wall of China might never have been built. It could have been the case that China had not had enough labor to build it, or that China had been conquered by the Mongols before anyone had the idea of building the wall. Anything like this, such that it might not have existed, exists only contingently. By contrast, anything that exists necessarily is such that it is not possible for it not to have existed. There is no logically possible state of affairs in which a necessarily existent thing does not exist. Hence, if God exists necessarily, He does not exist merely by chance; unlike the existence of Socrates or the Great Wall of China, God's existence is always guaranteed. Many theists think that God exists necessarily because it is impossible for God, as that-than-which-no-greater-can-be-thought, or as a supremely perfect being, not to exist, because being necessarily existent is greater or superior to being only contingently existent.

Contemporary philosophers often put the above points in terms of 'possible worlds'. The Great Wall of China and Socrates are contingent beings because while they exist in the actual world, they do not exist in some other possible worlds, any of which could have turned out to be actual. On the other hand, if God is a necessary being, then He exists not only in the actual world but in all other possible worlds; there is no possible world in which God does not exist (Figure I.2). Since necessary existence and temporal eternal existence seem to be mutually consistent, many theists ascribe both of them to God.

Another unique form of existence that is often attributed to God is omnipresence. An omnipresent being exists everywhere in space in a given possible world. Thus, if God is such a being, then, in a relevant sense, we can find Him everywhere. All the three forms of existence we have

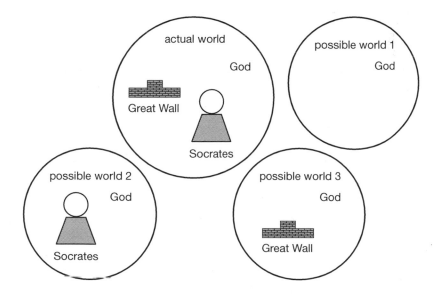

Figure I.2 Socrates and the Great Wall of China are contingent beings because they do not exist in some possible worlds. On the other hand God is a necessary being because He exists in all possible worlds.

seen, that is, omnipresence, temporal eternity, and necessary existence, are comparable to one another: omnipresence is the property of existing everywhere in space in a given possible world; eternity is the property of being everywhere on a time-scale in a given possible world; necessary existence is the property of existing in all possible worlds. Precisely which form of existence Descartes had in mind when he presented the above argument is a matter of dispute.

A seventeenth-century German philosopher, Gottfried Leibniz, was impressed by the ontological argument. He remarks, 'what Descartes has borrowed from Anselm, Archbishop of Canterbury, is very beautiful and really very ingenious'. He continues, 'This celebrated archbishop, who was without doubt one of the most able men of his time, congratulates himself, not without reason, for having discovered a means of proving the existence of God *a priori*, by means of its own notion, without recurring to its effect.'[27] Nevertheless, Leibniz was not entirely satisfied with the ontological argument. He contends that in the argument 'there is still a gap therein to be filled'.[28] Leibniz says that the ontological argument does not prove what it claims to prove:

    i   God exists.

Instead, according to Leibniz, it proves something slightly less impressive:

    ii   If it is *possible* for God to exist, then He exists.

If the ontological argument proves only (ii), then it cannot be said to be a proof of the existence of God because (ii) is compatible with the non-existence of God. One can hold (ii) and, for example, the following consistently:

    iii   If it is not possible for God to exist, then He does not exist.

In fact, (iii) seems to be trivially true. If God's existence is not possible, then there is no way that He exists. Thus one could accept (ii) while denying the existence of God by saying, 'If it is *possible* for God to exist, then He exists. However, it is *not* possible for Him to exist, and, thus, God does not exist.' In order to eliminate the non-existence of God we need to show that it is possible for God to exist – the antecedent of (ii) – or, equivalently, it is false that God's existence is not possible – the negation of the antecedent of (iii).

It is often overlooked that Leibniz is not the first one to make this point. Marin Mersenne, a French philosopher, theologian, and mathematician who was a contemporary of Descartes, made essentially the same point in his reply to Descartes's *Meditations*.[29] Mersenne writes as follows:

> Now it does not follow from this [ontological argument] that God in fact exists, but merely that he would have to exist if his nature is possible, or non-contradictory. In other words, the nature or essence of God cannot be conceived apart from existence; hence, granted the essence, God really exists.[30]

Just like Leibniz, Mersenne says that the ontological argument proves at most (ii), rather than (i). What distinguishes Leibniz is not that he reconfirmed Mersenne's point but that he provided a supplementary argument, which aims to show that it is indeed possible for God to exist.[31] That is, Leibniz introduced a sub-argument that fills the 'gap' in the ontological argument.

Leibniz claims that it is possible for God to exist because the concept of God does not contain any contradiction. God, as a supremely perfect being, has only perfections, which Leibniz defines as properties that are simple and purely positive. Being simple and purely positive, no perfection can contradict any other perfection. The concept of God, hence, is not contradictory and, therefore, Leibniz concludes, it is possible for God to exist. Leibniz claims that his supplementary argument for the claim that it is possible for God to exist completes the ontological argument and gives it 'mathematical certainty'. Leibniz's supplementary argument is important because, as explained below, it is the basis of Gödel's version of the ontological argument.

4 Objections to the ontological argument

Some philosophers find the ontological argument compelling. For example, Bertrand Russell, one of the greatest philosophers of the twentieth century, writes in his autobiography that when he was an undergraduate student at the University of Cambridge he was convinced by the argument: 'I had gone out to buy a tin of tobacco, and was going back with it along Trinity Lane, when suddenly I threw it up in the air and exclaimed: "Great God in boots! – the ontological argument is sound!"'[32] Later Russell abandoned theism and argued against it throughout his life. Nevertheless, he always acknowledged the force of the ontological argument. When he was in his seventies he wrote, 'it is easier to feel convinced that [the ontological argument] must be fallacious than it is to find out precisely where the fallacy lies'.[33]

Yet most philosophers find the ontological argument unpersuasive. Theodore M. Drange writes, for instance, 'Most philosophers regard [the ontological argument] as either cognitively meaningless or as a kind of play on words, a semantic puzzle to sort out if one has some extra time.' He continues, 'There is hardly anyone who is a theist on the basis of the ontological argument. I taught philosophy to thousands of students, and not a single one of them ever put any stock in it.'[34] While some might disagree with Drange's remark, it is undeniable that when we follow the ontological argument, at least initially, we cannot but feel that we have been tricked by it somehow. Critics are not, however, justified in dismissing the argument without explaining how it fails. In what follows, therefore, we review several prominent objections to the argument. Most are equally applicable to distinct versions of the argument including Anselm's, Descartes's, and others that we discuss later. We will see that locating a flaw in the argument is not as easy as it initially appears.

Objection 1: existence is not a predicate

Immanuel Kant, an eighteenth-century German philosopher who is regarded as the last major figure of the Enlightenment, provided a number of objections to the ontological argument, one of which is particularly well received.

According to Kant, the ontological argument fails because it is based on one crucial, but false, assumption. The assumption in question is that existence is a predicate. Predicates are words that refer to properties of things. Consider, for example, the statement 'Hannah is tall.' The phrase 'is tall' is a predicate because it refers to Hannah's property of being tall. Consider, to take another example, the statement 'Matt has a headache.' The phrase 'has a headache' is a predicate because it refers to Matt's property of having a headache. The ontological argument seems to treat existence as a predicate by construing the statement 'God exists' as 'God has the property of being existent'. God, as that-than-which-no-greater-can-be-thought, or as a supremely perfect being, has such a property because, the argument seems to assume, it is one of many 'great-making properties', properties that contribute to the greatness of God.

Kant says, however, that the phrase 'is existent' is not comparable to ordinary predicates such as 'is tall' and 'has a headache'. When we express that Hannah has the property of being tall and Matt has the property of having a headache, we do not need to say, 'Hannah has the property of being tall *and* she exists' and 'Matt has the property of having a headache *and* he exists', because the possession of a property entails the existence of the possessor. Conversely, it does not make sense to say that 'Hannah is tall but she does not exist' or 'Matt has a headache but he does not exist.' These observations show that existence is not a predicate or a property. Therefore, Kant concluded, the ontological argument fails.

Kant's objection is closely related to Bertrand Russell's important contribution to the philosophy of language. Russell's main interest is to distinguish between the surface structure of language and the logical structure that underlies it. Consider, for example, the proposition 'The present king of France is bald.' Is this proposition true or false? If the proposition is true, then the present king of France is bald. If the proposition is false, then it is not the case that the present king of France is bald. Neither seems correct because there is no such person as the present king of France in the first place! According to Russell's theory of descriptions, which is regarded as one of the most important contributions to the philosophy of language in the twentieth century, this proposition can be analyzed as a set of the following three propositions:

1   There is an x such that x is a present king of France.
2   There is no y, other than x, such that y is a present king of France.
3   x is bald.

Propositions (1) and (2) entail that there is an object that is uniquely the present king of France and (3) says that the object in question is bald. Russell's verdict is that the statement 'The present king of France is bald' is false because (1) is false. There is no being that is a present king of France.

Russell agrees with Kant that existence does not ascribe any property to an object. The phrase 'exists' is not comparable to 'eats' or 'reads', and the phrase 'is existent' is not comparable to 'is tall' or 'is bald'. It is a mistake to construe the above proposition (1) as saying that x has the property of being existent and the property of being a present king of France. It only says that there is something in the world that the concept of a present king of France refers to. Thus, when we say that God exists we do not mean that God has the property of being existent just like He has the property of being omniscient or the property of being omnibenevolent. What we really mean is that there is an object that satisfies the concept of God as that-than-which-no-greater-can-be-thought, or as a supremely perfect being. That is why in symbolic logic there is a special symbol for existence, called an existential quantifier, '∃', while there are no special symbols for predicates. Existential claims are symbolized with existential quantifiers, while other claims about predicates are symbolized with ordinary alphabets. For example, 'an x exists' is symbolized as '∃x' while 'an x is tall' or 'an x is bald' are symbolized as 'Tx' and 'Bx', respectively. Russell concludes, '[God's] existence, in fact, quite definitely is not a predicate.'[35] It is interesting to realize that Kant's objection to the ontological argument seems to have anticipated Russell's theory, which was developed more than 120 years later.

Does Kant's objection succeed in refuting the ontological argument? In order for it to succeed, the following two conditions have to be met: (i) existence is not a predicate, and (ii) the ontological argument presupposes that existence is a predicate. However, both (i) and (ii) are controversial. Regarding (i), there are a number of philosophers who deny that existence is not a predicate. Colin McGinn and Barry Miller, for example, argue that existence is a predicate at least in certain contexts.[36] They claim that, contrary to what Kant and Russell say, existence could indeed be a property that characterizes its possessor. This suggests that in order to defend Kant's objection critics need to solve first the controversial issues concerning existence in the philosophy of language, and that is not an easy task. Suppose, however, that critics of the ontological argument manage to establish that existence is indeed not a predicate. Does that mean that Kant's objection succeeds in refuting the ontological argument? That is not obvious, either, because (ii), that is, the claim that the ontological argument presupposes that existence is a predicate, is also controversial. No version of the ontological argument has a premise saying explicitly that existence is a predicate. This means that if the ontological argument assumes (ii) it has to assume it only implicitly. As mentioned above, Descartes's second version of the ontological argument is based on the key phrase 'existence is a perfection', which does seem to entail implicitly that existence is comparable to other predicates like tallness or baldness. Descartes's first version, however, does not make such an assumption. That version is based on the idea that the existence of God is a self-evident truth, which is analogous to mathematical axioms. If so, Descartes does not need to make the above assumption, or indeed any assumption at all, to derive the existence of God. It is also far from clear that Anselm's version of the ontological argument is based on (ii). Anselm says that that-than-which-no-greater-can-be-thought exists not only in the mind but also in reality because if it does not exist in reality, then we can conceive of a being that is greater than that being, which is contradictory. Here Anselm's argument seems to remain intact even if we assume that existence is not a predicate. This is because even if we give up the idea that existence is a predicate it still seems to make sense to say that the being in question, if it exists, is greater than if it does not. And we can and we do commonly make a comparison between what exists and what does not (e.g., 'it is better for there to be a beautiful flower than nothing').

The dispute concerning whether existence is a predicate might even be irrelevant to the cogency of the ontological argument. This is because even if existence is not a predicate, *necessary* existence, which is also normally ascribed to God by theists, seems to be a predicate. Again, necessary existence is existence in all possible worlds. This clearly seems to be a property because a property is, by definition, an attribute that characterizes its possessor. Necessary existence does certainly seem to be an attribute that characterizes the uniqueness of God; it is a property that many, if not most, other existent beings do not have. According to Norman Malcolm, the assumption that necessary existence, rather than existence *simpliciter*, is a predicate is in fact what Anselm makes in the *Proslogion*.[37] Anselm says, 'if that, than which nothing greater can be conceived, can be conceived not to exist, it is not that than which nothing greater can be conceived'.[38] Malcolm interprets this as saying that the logical impossibility of non-existence is a perfection, which is equivalent to saying that necessary existence is a perfection.

Many critics regard Kant's objection as a knock-down objection to the ontological argument, but we have seen that it is not so easy to defend it.

Objection 2: question-begging

A nineteenth-century philosopher, Arthur Schopenhauer, remarked, 'Considered by daylight … and without prejudice, this famous Ontological Proof is really a charming joke.'[39] According to him, the ontological argument is comparable to a magician's trick. When a magician produces a rabbit from his hat, he smuggles the rabbit into a convenient place from which it can be retrieved while diverting the attention of his audience somewhere else.[40] Similarly, Schopenhauer claims, Anselm and Descartes smuggle the very conclusion that God exists into the premises of the argument and then produce it in a dramatic manner, as if something significant had been discovered. If the conclusion is already contained in the premises, the onto-logical argument is as trivial as a simple magic trick. Schopenhauer makes the same point by saying that what the ontological argument does is the same as what 'the chicken does within the egg that has been long brooded over'.[41] When a chick hatches out it does not emerge miraculously from an empty eggshell; it already exists within the shell. Similarly, when the existence of God is derived by the ontological argument it does not emerge miraculously from the premises; it already exists within them.

What Schopenhauer says here is that the ontological argument commits the fallacy of question-begging. An argument commits this fallacy when the conclusion is presupposed in its premises. According to the objection in question, the ontological argument commits the fallacy because the definition of God as that-than-which-no-greater-can-be-thought, or as a supremely perfect being, implicitly presupposes that God exists. It is not surprising at all, therefore, that the argument can 'derive' the existence of God from the premises. Consider the following argument, which is clearly question-begging:

> An 'ExFlyingPig' is defined as an existent flying pig. Does an ExFlyingPig exist? Of course it does because an ExFlyingPig is, by definition, a flying pig that exists. It is contradictory to say that an ExFlyingPig does not exist as much as it is contradictory to say that a triangle is not three-sided. Therefore, an ExFlyingPig exists.

The objection in question says that the ontological argument is compa-rable to the above argument. The purpose of the above argument is to show that an ExFlyingPig exists but it is presupposed in the definition of an ExFlyingPig that it does exist. Similarly, the purpose of the ontological argument is to show that God exists but it is presupposed in the definition of God that He exists.

Is the objection in question cogent? That is far from obvious. Consider Anselm's version of the ontological argument. Anselm says that that-than-which-no-greater-can-be-thought must exist because if it does not then we can think of a being that is greater, which is logically impossible. Here, contrary to what the objection says, Anselm does not define God in a ques-tion-begging manner. Anselm does not derive God's existence simply by presupposing that He exists.

Descartes's first version of the ontological argument does not seem vulner-able to this objection either. That version says, again, that the existence of

God is a self-evident truth, which is comparable to mathematical axioms. If it is indeed true that the existence of God is comparable to mathematical axioms, then it is no more question-begging than mathematical axioms. It is in fact trivially true that the first version is not vulnerable to the objection in question because that version is not really an argument; it is just an expression of what Descartes regards as a self-evident truth. The fallacy of question-begging can be committed only by an argument.

On the other hand, Descartes's second version does seem to have the appearance of question-begging. That version defines God as a supremely perfect being and concludes that such a being exists because existence is a perfection that needs to be possessed by the being. Consider, however, the following parallel argument:

1   God is, by definition, a supremely perfect being.
2   Omniscience is a perfection.

Therefore,

3   God is omniscient.

Should we say that the above argument is unsuccessful because it is question-begging? It is not very clear that we should. The argument is informative enough, the two premises seem reasonable, and the conclusion follows from the premises. If so, it is not very obvious that Descartes's second version, which has the same structure as that of the above argument, is question-begging.

It is known that rejecting deductive arguments, such as the above argument and the ontological argument, by appealing to the fallacy of question-begging is not always easy. A (valid) deductive argument is one in which it is *impossible* for the conclusion to be false if the premises are true. (For example: 'All men are mortal; Socrates is a man; therefore, Socrates is mortal.') That is, the conclusion follows *necessarily* from the premises. An inductive argument is, on the other hand, one in which the conclusion is supported by the premises in such a way that it is *improbable* that the conclusion is false if the premises are true. (For example: 'All wild rabbits we have seen in this region so far are grey; therefore, all wild rabbits in this region are grey.') That is, the conclusion follows *probably* from the premises.

It is often difficult to refute a deductive argument by appealing to the fallacy of question-begging because it is a feature of any valid deductive argument that the conclusion is entailed by the premises. Otherwise, the argument cannot imply its conclusion as a matter of necessity. Conversely, if the premises do not entail the conclusion the argument cannot imply the conclusion via valid deduction.

Objection 3: the island parody

When Anselm introduced the ontological argument in the *Proslogion* in the eleventh century it soon attracted a response entitled, 'A Reply to the Foregoing by a Certain Writer on Behalf of the Fool'. That 'certain writer' was Gaunilo of Marmoutiers. The reply is the only known work of Gaunilo's and nothing much is known about this Benedictine monk. In the reply Gaunilo introduced arguably the most distinctive objections ever raised against the ontological argument.

As a theist, Gaunilo accepts the conclusion of the ontological argument that God exists. However, he disagrees with Anselm that the argument succeeds in proving the existence of God. That is why he puts forward an objection to Anselm on behalf of 'the fool', by which he means the atheist. Gaunilo purports to undermine the argument by advancing the following claim: the ontological argument must contain a flaw because if it were successful in proving the existence of God, there would be parallel parodies that are equally successful in proving the existence of absurd entities.

As an example, Gaunilo introduces a parody which purports to prove the existence of 'the greatest possible island': consider an island-than-which-no-greater-island-can-be-thought. Such an island exists at least in the mind because anyone can understand the phrase 'an island-than-which-no-greater-island-can-be-thought'. Now does such an island exist only in the mind or does it exists both in the mind *and* also in reality? If that island exists only in the mind another island can be thought that is even greater than that island. Such an island is thought to have all the characteristics that the original island has *and* it is also thought to exist in reality. However, it is contradictory to say that an island can be thought that is greater than the island in question. That is, it is impossible that an island can be thought that is greater than the island-than-which-no-greater-island-can-be-thought. Hence, it is impossible that the island-than-which-no-greater-island-can-be-thought does not exist in reality and, therefore, such an island does indeed exist in reality. However, as Gaunilo says, we all know that there is no such island in reality.

Gaunilo's purpose is not to ridicule Anselm. His purpose is rather to show that, given that we can concoct the absurd island parody, there must be something wrong with the ontological argument somewhere. Gaunilo's parody objection is often regarded as only a second-class, supplementary objection to the ontological argument or as a mere curious consequence that one can derive from it. In fact many critics treat the parody objection as a supplement to a more substantial objection to the ontological argument.[42] Few critics regard it as something that could constitute a serious objection. Yet the parody objection has a number of virtues that other objections lack.

First, unlike many other objections, the parody objection does not dispute any of the ontological argument's controversial metaphysical assumptions.[43] This becomes evident when comparing the parody objection with the first objection discussed above, according to which the ontological argument is based on the false assumption that existence is a predicate. We saw above that that objection is not easy to defend because, in order to defend it, one has to prove not only that the ontological argument presupposes that existence is a predicate – which is controversial in its own right – but also that existence is, indeed, not a predicate – which is even more controversial, independently of the debate over the ontological argument. The parody objection, on the other hand, does not involve this sort of complication. The parody objection accepts, at least for the sake of argument, all the premises of the argument and all the assumptions that it makes. It then constructs a parallel argument that reveals an apparent absurdity entailed by the ontological argument. In this sense, the parody objection is as metaphysically and dialectically sympathetic as possible to the ontological argument, until the last stage, where it purportedly reveals its absurdity. The parody objection is also distinct from the second objection discussed above, according to which the ontological argument is question-begging. Even if we assume that the ontological argument is not question-begging we can still construct the island parody, which, again, seems to show that there is something wrong with the ontological argument.

Another virtue of the parody objection is that it is applicable to multiple versions of the ontological argument. Consider again the first objection to the argument. That objection was introduced by Kant mainly to refute Descartes's second version of the ontological argument. The objection seems to refute the second version because that version appears to assume that existence is a predicate when it states 'existence is a perfection'. It is, however, far from obvious that the same objection applies to Anselm's version and Descartes's first version because, as we saw above, they do not seem to be committed to the claim that existence is a predicate. Unlike Kant's objection, the parody objection does seem applicable to all versions of the ontological argument because a parody argument can be constructed merely by rephrasing relevant components of *any* version of the ontological argument. As I mentioned above, Gaunilo uses the objection to undermine Anselm's version of the ontological argument; Gassendi, Descartes's contemporary, uses it to undermine Descartes's version of the argument (by appealing to a parody argument for the existence of a 'perfect Pegasus');[44] and Graham Oppy uses it to undermine even Gödel's modal version of the argument mentioned below.[45]

Of course, the parody objection is not almighty. One main drawback of the objection is that even if it is successful it does not pinpoint exactly what is wrong with the ontological argument. If the objection is successful it shows only that there is *something* wrong *somewhere* in the argument.[46] So, borrowing Schopenhauer's analogy, the parody objection can show only that the magician's production of a rabbit is a trick without specifying exactly where the rabbit is hidden. However, while it would be interesting to know exactly what is wrong with the ontological argument, the parody objection alone potentially is sufficient to refute the argument.

Is the island objection then successful in refuting the ontological argument? The answer, unfortunately, seems to be no, as it appears to exhibit several flaws. First, the island objection fails because the island parody is not strictly parallel to the ontological argument. The purpose of the island objection is to construct a parody argument such that (i) it is exactly parallel to the ontological argument; and (ii) it entails an absurd conclusion that the greatest possible island exists in reality. The island argument fails to satisfy (i) because the scope of the island argument is not the same as that of the ontological argument. While the ontological argument is concerned with the set of all possible beings, the island argument is concerned with a significantly smaller subset of it, namely, the set of all possible *islands*. Consider a parallel example. Suppose that we construct an argument that is concerned with all possible people. We then construct its parallel parody that is concerned with all possible weightlifters, which, of course, constitute a subset of the set of all possible people. It is far from obvious that the fact that a parallel argument about all possible weightlifters entails an absurd conclusion tells us anything about the plausibility of the original argument about all possible people.

Second, the island argument is based on an assumption to which proponents of the ontological argument are not committed. The ontological argument is based on the implicit assumption that there are intrinsic maxima for properties traditionally attributed to God as that-than-which-no-greater-can-be-thought.[47] So, for example, it assumes implicitly that there is a maximum amount of knowledge that God, or any being, can have. Similarly, the island argument is based on the implicit assumption that there are intrinsic maxima for properties that an island can have. So, for example, it assumes implicitly that there is a maximum number of beautiful palm trees or pleasant beaches that any island, in particular, an island-than-which-no-greater-island-can-be-thought, can have. However, proponents of the ontological argument, who are committed to the assumption that there are intrinsic maxima for God's properties, such as knowledge, are not committed to the assumption that there are intrinsic maxima for an island's properties. Moreover, there is an obvious reason to reject such an assumption about an island's properties: For any island i it is always possible to make i greater by adding, for example, one more beautiful palm tree or one more pleasant beach.[48]

The island objection is, therefore, unsuccessful. It is not strictly parallel to the ontological argument because its scope is too narrow and it makes an assumption about intrinsic maxima that the ontological argument does not make.

Objection 4: the devil parody

Critics of the ontological argument have tried to improve on the parody objection. In the early twentieth century Albert A. Cock introduced a new parody objection, which appeals to an argument for the existence of the worst possible being, rather than the greatest possible island.[49]

Let us call that-than-which-no-*worse*-can-be-thought 'the devil'. The devil exists at least in the mind because anyone can understand the phrase 'that-than-which-no-worse-can-be-thought'. Now does the devil exist only in the mind or does it exist both in the mind *and* also in reality? If the devil exists only in the mind another being can be thought that is even worse than the devil. Such a being is thought to have all the characteristics that the devil has *and* it is also thought to exist in reality. However, it is contradictory to say that a being can be thought that is worse than the devil. That is, it is impossible that a being can be thought that is worse than that-than-which-no-worse-can-be-thought. Hence, it is impossible that that-than-which-no-worse-can-be-thought does not exist in reality and, therefore, the devil does indeed exist in reality. However, as Cock says, we all know that there is no such being as the devil.

The appeal to the devil parody can be regarded as an attempt to overcome the above-mentioned two difficulties that Gaunilo's island objection faces. In response to the first difficulty, the devil parody maintains the same scope as that of the ontological argument. The scope of the devil parody is no wider or narrower than that of the ontological argument, namely, all possible beings. In response to the second difficulty, the devil parody assumes nothing more about intrinsic maxima than does the ontological argument. This is because, unlike the island argument, it is not concerned with the upper limit of any property.

Unfortunately, however, the devil objection seems to fail because the devil parody is not in fact parallel to the ontological argument. In particular, it adopts a different sense of greatness from that which the ontological argument adopts. Consider the following four different senses of greatness:

A   *Great for oneself*: for example, the property of being smart is great for a criminal to have because it benefits the criminal.

B   *Great for the world and others*: for example, the property of being smart is not great for a criminal to have because it is not beneficial to the world and others.

C   *Great in one's character/capacity*: for example, the property of being sharp is great for a knife to have *qua* knife.[50]

D   *Great intrinsically*: for example, the properties of being knowledgeable, powerful, benevolent, beautiful, and so on, are great in themselves, regardless of their greatness in the above three senses.

Which sense of greatness does Anselm have in mind when he formulates the ontological argument? While he does not explain it clearly in the *Proslogion* he writes as follows in the *Monologion*:

> We have found, then, that there is something supremely good (because all good things are good through some one thing, namely that which is good through itself). But in the same way we arrive at the necessary conclusion that there is something supremely great, since whatsoever is great is great through some one thing, namely that which is great through itself. I do not mean great in terms of size, like some sort of body; but something which, the greater it is, the better or more valuable it is, like wisdom. And since only that which is supremely good can be supremely great, it is necessary that there is something that is best and greatest – i.e. of everything that exists, the supreme.[51]

Anselm's use of the phrase 'great through itself' seems to suggest that what he has in mind is the fourth sense of greatness, which is indeed what most theistic philosophers tend to adopt when considering the ontological argument. Descartes also seems to have the fourth sense of greatness in mind when he formulates his versions since, again, he remarks that existence is a perfection, which is normally construed as being intrinsically great.

The devil parody is not an exact parallel of the ontological argument because it is based on the second, rather than the fourth, sense of greatness. The devil parody presupposes that it is worse for the devil to exist than not because the existence of the devil is not beneficial to the world or to people. If we have in mind the fourth sense of greatness, however, we obtain a different result. Existence is great intrinsically regardless of its bearer because here we are not concerned with its impact on the world and people. This means that a closer parallel of the ontological argument must be an argument for the non-existence of the devil; for the devil, that is, that-than-which-no-worse-can-be-thought, must lack everything that is intrinsically great, including existence.[52]

However, the argument for the non-existence of the devil does not seem to constitute a powerful objection to the ontological argument for several reasons. First, it is difficult to see that such an argument shows the absurdity of the ontological argument. This is because it is known that we *can* derive *a priori* the non-existence of some beings (e.g., a square circle, a married bachelor, etc.). Second, the non-existence of the devil does not seem to be theologically problematic. Many theists would happily accept the conclusion that the devil does not exist. The non-existence of the devil is certainly much less troublesome than the *existence* of the greatest possible island or of the devil.

One might claim at this point that a parody argument does not have to parallel the ontological argument exactly because, after all, it is just a parody. The purpose of the parody objection is, one might say, to show that there is something wrong with the ontological argument by presenting an absurd parody argument, which is comparable to, but not necessarily strictly parallel to, the ontological argument.

If this claim is correct, however, the parody objection is too weak. As we saw above, while the parody objection does not pinpoint exactly what is wrong with the ontological argument it is meant to be sufficient to refute it. If, however, a parody argument is not even parallel to the ontological argument, the parody objection is far from sufficient. Its being true merely that the ontological argument and a parody argument are *similar* and that the parody argument is absurd does not entail that the ontological argument is also absurd.

5 Hartshorne's discovery

Many philosophers in the early twentieth century, including those who defended theism, neglected the ontological argument and treated it as a relic of the Middle Ages and the Enlightenment. However, in the second half of the twentieth century, the argument was revived once again.

In 1923, 26-year-old Harvard University student Charles Hartshorne submitted a doctoral thesis in which he defended Anselm's ontological argument. In the thesis, he described the argument as 'an incomparably brilliant and cogent course of reasoning'.[53] Defending the ontological argument at the time was very unfashionable and few took his thesis seriously. Hartshorne himself rejected what he said in the thesis not long after submitting it. Thirty years later, however, Hartshorne, then a professor at the University of Chicago, attracted philosophers' attention by revealing his new discovery regarding the ontological argument. In *Philosophers Speak of God*, which he published with his student William L. Reese in 1953, Hartshorne revealed that there is a hitherto unknown version of the ontological argument in Chapter 3 of Anselm's *Proslogion*.[54]

Philosophers had taken it for granted that, in the *Proslogion*, Anselm defends only one version of the ontological argument. However, Hartshorne claimed that there was a second version of the argument, now called the 'modal ontological argument', hidden in Anselm's subtle text. Norman Malcolm made the same point in his paper, 'Anselm's Ontological Argument', published in 1960, and Hartshorne discussed the modal ontological argument in detail in his paper, 'The Logic of the Ontological Argument', published in 1961. Hartshorne and Malcolm opened up a new phase in the debate over the argument.

Anselm's presentations of the ontological argument in the *Proslogion* and his response to Gaunilo are highly intractable. There have been many alternative interpretations of the texts and many alternative forms of the argument have been derived from them. Some even contend that Anselm provides three[55] or four[56] distinct versions of the ontological argument. (Yet the prominent theologian Karl Barth goes so far as to claim that Anselm does not, in the *Proslogion*, attempt to provide any deductive argument for the existence of God; rather, he provides an expression of faith, which *presupposes* the existence of God.[57]). Whether or not Anselm really means to advance the modal ontological argument in Chapter 3 of the *Proslogion* remains contentious. Even Malcolm himself, who derives the modal ontological argument from Chapter 3, writes, 'There is no evidence that [Anselm] thought of himself as offering two different proofs.'[58] Nevertheless, as we see below, it is clear that the modal ontological argument is an ingenious and powerful argument, and one that is distinct from any of the versions of the ontological argument discussed so far.

Hartshorne had a long life. He was born in Kittanning, Pennsylvania in 1897 and died in 2000 at Austin, Texas at the age of 103. His last articles in an academic journal were published in 1998, when he was 101.[59] Even after his death at least eight articles, which are based on his notes and lectures, were published. He said that the secret of longevity was to take a nap after lunch.

Hartshorne worked not only on philosophy and theology, but also on something that appears completely distinct: the study of birdsong. Ever since he had bought a pocket-sized bird guide and a pair of field glasses at the age of 16, he was fascinated by the lives of wild birds.[60] He conducted serious field research on birdsong in diverse areas in Europe, Australia, India, and Japan, many of which he visited for philosophy lectures and conferences. He even published a book entitled *Born to Sing: An Interpretation and World Survey of Bird Song*[61] and over 20 articles on birdsong. Daniel Dombrowski remarks that Hartshorne was 'the first philosopher since Aristotle to be an expert in both metaphysics and ornithology'.[62] In *Born to Sing*, Hartshorne proposed an interesting, if not extraordinary, hypothesis about birdsong: some bird species have acquired, through the process of evolution, not only the ability to sing for mating but the ability to appreciate melody and sing for pure joy. The book, which contained a 'world list of superior singers', attracted a lot of attention, just as did his work on the ontological argument. Once when Hartshorne went to Australia for a philosophy meeting, he encountered at the airport a group of ornithologists who were familiar with his work on birdsong. They were so excited to see him that they took him to their own ornithology conference, which was being held in the same area. The philosophers who were expecting him had to search high and low to locate him.

Philosophers are fond of discussing modal concepts, such as possibility and necessity. For example, they are interested in knowing whether it is *possible* to create a physical duplicate of a human being that does not have inner conscious experience, including pain and pleasure – philosophers call such a being a 'zombie'.[63] Given our technological limitations, it is practically impossible for us to create such a being. However, it is contentious whether it is *necessarily* impossible to create it. To take another example, philosophers are interested in knowing whether it is possible that Socrates is an alligator instead of a human being.[64] It is controversial whether Socrates' body *could have been* entirely that of an alligator; it may be necessarily true that Socrates' body is not entirely an alligator's. The version of the ontological argument that Hartshorne and Malcolm found in Chapter 3 of the *Proslogion* is commonly called the 'modal ontological argument' because it is also concerned with possibility and necessity.

While there are many subtly different versions of the modal ontological argument, a prominent version can be described as follows: in general, if something is conceivable, then it is at least possible for that thing to exist. Consider, for example, flying pigs. We can conceive of flying pigs and from this fact we can conclude that it is at least possible for them to exist. We know that there are no such animals in reality, but they could have existed perhaps had the laws of nature been slightly different or had pigs evolved in a different way. Similarly, even if we are atheists, we can conceive of God, as that-than-which-no-greater-can-be-thought, or as a supremely perfect being, and from this fact we can conclude that it is at least possible for Him to exist. There is no contradiction in saying that God can exist, just as there is no contradiction in saying that a flying pig can exist. It is controversial whether God *actually* exists, but apparently everyone can agree that it is at least possible that God exists. Now the modal ontological argument reminds us that God is traditionally defined as a necessary being. So by agreeing that it is possible for God to exist we agree that it is possible that God's existence is necessary. The modal ontological argument at this point invokes a principle that is widely accepted among logicians and philosophers: if it is possible that something is necessary, then that thing is simply necessary. In order words, we can omit the phrase 'it is possible that' from the phrase 'it is possible that something is necessary'. So, for instance, if it is possible that 'Agatha Christie is a human being' is necessary, then simply, 'Agatha Christie is a human being' is necessary. If we apply this principle to what we have derived so far, namely, that it is possible that God's existence is necessary, we can conclude that God's existence is necessary. If God's existence is necessary, moreover, then it is also actual, because the necessity of something entails the actuality of that thing. In sum: from the conceivability of God we can derive the possibility of God; from the possibility of God, as a necessary existence, we can derive the necessity of God; from the necessity of God we can derive the actuality of God. The modal ontological argument concludes, therefore, that God actually exists.

Let us restate the modal ontological argument in terms of possible worlds: it is conceivable that God exists, which entails that there is at least one possible world in which God exists. Given that God is a necessary existence this means that there is at least one possible world in which God's existence is necessary. However, by agreeing that there is at least one such possible world, we are committed to the claim that God's existence is necessary, that is, God exists in all possible worlds. If God exists in all possible worlds, then He exists, in particular, in the actual world. Therefore, God exists in the actual world (Figure I.3).

Alvin Plantinga modifies the modal ontological argument slightly and formulates it in terms of 'maximal excellence' and 'maximal greatness'.[65] Maximal excellence in a given possible world entails omniscience, omnipotence, and omnibenevolence in that world, and maximal greatness entails maximal excellence in all possible worlds. Plantinga's formulation is as follows: it is possible that maximal greatness is exemplified, that is, it is possible that there is a being that is maximally great. This means that it is possible that, necessarily, there is a maximally excellent being. Therefore, it is necessary that there is a maximally excellent being. Therefore, there is a

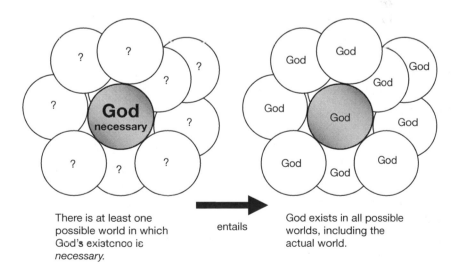

There is at least one possible world in which God's existence is *necessary.*   entails   God exists in all possible worlds, including the actual world.

Figure I.3 From the possibility of God's necessary existence the modal ontological argument derives the existence of God in all possible worlds, including the actual world.

maximally excellent being in all possible worlds. Therefore, there is a maximally excellent being in the actual world. Therefore, there is an omniscient, omnipotent, and omnibenevolent being in the actual world. Therefore, God exists. It is a unique feature of Plantinga's formulation that it does not rely on the assumption that God exists necessarily. Instead, it relies on the idea that maximal greatness is maximal excellence in all possible worlds.

Hartshorne's discovery of the modal ontological argument caused a heated debate among philosophers of religion. The argument gained some prominent supporters but also a number of critics.

6 Objections to the modal ontological argument

Anselm introduced the ontological argument more than 900 years ago, and Descartes introduced his own two versions more than 350 years ago. Nevertheless, debates over these arguments continue to this day. It is not surprising, then, that the debate over the modal ontological argument, which was introduced only about 50 years ago, is far from over. We saw above several objections to Anselm's and Descartes's versions and possible responses to them. Many of them are equally applicable to the modal ontological argument. Here we review some other objections that are specifically directed to the modal ontological argument.

Objection 1: factual necessary vs. logical necessary

John Hick tries to reject the modal ontological argument by invoking the distinction between 'logical necessity' and 'factual necessity'.[66] As we have seen, the argument relies on the concept of God as that-than-which-no-greater-can-be-thought, or as a supremely perfect being, and ascribes necessary existence to it. Necessary existence is often associated with the theological notion of divine independence, or 'aseity'. According to this notion, God is a self-existent being that does not depend on anything else. That is, God does not derive His existence from any external being and He always exists on His own. Hick calls the necessity of this kind of existence 'factual necessity'. According to Hick, however, a later stage of the modal ontological argument appeals to a different kind of necessity. The argument says that, given that the existence of God is possible, He must exist in all possible worlds, including the actual world. Hick calls the necessity of this kind of existence 'logical necessity'. He says logical necessity is different from factual necessity because it is concerned with the logically possibility and impossibility of God's existence, rather than the factual possibility and impossibility of it. Hick, therefore, concludes that the modal ontological argument equivocates on the notion of necessity.

Hick's objection is slightly puzzling because it is not clear in what sense it can be construed as a refutation of the modal ontological argument. Proponents of the argument could accept Hick's distinction between factual necessity and logical necessity and claim that the modal ontological argument is concerned with God as a logically necessary being rather than as a factually necessary being. So, they could argue that even though the argument might not prove the existence of God as a factually necessary being it does prove the existence of God as a logically necessary being. Alternatively, they could also argue that God is both factually and logically necessary. Indeed, if God is that-than-which-no-greater-can-be-thought, or a supremely perfect being, it seems reasonable to ascribe both types of necessity to Him. Unless it is shown that factual necessity and logical necessity are mutually inconsistent, there is no reason for theists to refrain from ascribing both to God.

Objection 2: conceivability does not entail possibility

In order to derive the statement that God's existence is possible, the modal ontological argument, or at least the version introduced above, appeals to the conceivability of the existence of God. It says that since it is conceivable that God exits, it is possible that God exists. One might reject the modal ontological argument by rejecting the general principle that if something is conceivable then it is at least possible for that thing to exist. In fact the tenability of the principle has been disputed among philosophers. Some claim that conceivability is not a reliable guide at all to determining what is possible. Some others claim that while conceivability is a reliable guide to determining what is *logically* possible, it is not a reliable guide to determining what is *metaphysically* possible. That is, according to them, conceivability can be used to find out whether something is logically contradictory but not much more than that.

We defer further discussion of the technical dispute among philosophers over conceivability and possibility to another occasion. It should be noted, however, that the above principle concerning conceivability was not introduced in an *ad hoc* manner in order to construct the modal ontological argument. It is a principle that has been accepted by many philosophers independently of the modal ontological argument. Furthermore, several strategies have been introduced to construct the modal ontological argument without appealing to this principle. For example, as we see below, Gödel borrows Leibniz's supplementary argument mentioned earlier to show that God's existence is possible. Gödel relies on the idea that, since God has only positive properties, the concept of God does not contain any contradiction. This allows us to derive the possibility of God's existence without referring to its conceivability. To take another example, Alexander R. Pruss defends a novel way of showing that the existence of God is probably possible.[67] His argument is based on a principle according to which a propositional belief that is at the motivational centre of a flourishing life is probably possibly true. Pruss argues that given this principle, and given the fact that there are flourishing lives at whose motivational centre is the proposition that God exists, we can conclude, without referring to the conceivability of God's existence, that God's existence is probably possible. (If we adopt Pruss's strategy, then the conclusion of the ontological argument turns out to be slightly weaker: probably God exists.) To take a further example, Todd Buras and Mike Cantrell try to show that God's existence is possible by appealing to the notion of natural desire. They claim that, since natural desires are a guide to possibility and human beings naturally desire at least one state of affairs for which the existence of God is a necessary condition, it is possible that God exists.[68]

In addition to the principle about conceivability the modal ontological argument is also based on a principle about possibility and necessity. The principle says, as we have seen, that if it is possible that something is necessary, then that thing is simply necessary. This principle is entailed by the axioms of a system of modal logic called 'S5'. However, there are some logicians and philosophers who find the system untenable. If S5 is untenable, then the modal ontological argument is unlikely to be sound. Still, defending such an objection to the ontological argument would be quite difficult because S5 is the oldest and the most widely used system of modal logic. It is accepted as the standard system. Indeed, proponents of the modal ontological argument would be pleased if rejection of the standard system of modal logic were the only plausible way of undermining the argument.

Objection 3: Findlay's paradox

The eighteenth-century philosopher David Hume famously claimed that there is no being whose non-existence implies a contradiction. The twentieth-century philosopher J. N. Findlay introduced an interesting objection to the modal ontological argument by appealing to Hume's claim. The objection, which is often called 'Findlay's paradox', says that from the failure of the modal ontological argument we can actually prove the non-existence of God.[69] Findlay's paradox runs as follows: if Hume is right, even the non-existence of God entails no contradiction. That is, God's existence is not (logically) necessary but only contingent. God's existence cannot be contingent, however, because a being that merely happens to exist is not worthy of worship. This means that God's existence can be neither necessary nor contingent. Findlay concludes, therefore, that God does not exist.

Hartshorne remarks that Findlay's objection is '[t]he most important contribution since Kant to the Anselmian controversy, on its skeptical side'.[70] Findlay's objection does not, however, seem to be successful. First, Hume's claim is not forceful enough to positively refute the modal onto-logical argument (or any other versions of the ontological argument). What Hume says is that, for any being, whether it is a person, a book, a car, or even God, it is never necessarily false that that being does not exist. This is merely a bald negation of a premise of the modal ontological argument. One cannot refute an argument merely by asserting the negation of its premise; one must explain why the premise is false. Second, Findlay's claim that if God is a contingent being He is not worthy of worship is controver-sial. While some theists claim that God's perfection, which includes neces-sary existence, is the basis of His worship-worthiness, others claim that God's worship-worthiness is based on other things, such as the fact that He created the universe and all the creatures in it.[71]

7 Gödel's ontological argument

At the start of World War II Gödel and his wife decided to flee Nazi Europe for the United States. They left Vienna for Princeton, New Jersey, where Gödel was offered an academic position at the Institute for Advanced Study. Their journey was long and exhausting. They took the Trans-Siberian Railway to go through Russia, sailed from Russia to Japan and then from Japan to San Francisco. When they arrived in San Francisco they crossed the United States by train to reach Princeton.

Gödel's sponsors for his application for American citizenship could not have been more prominent: Albert Einstein, one of the greatest physicists of all time, and Oskar Morgenstern, a distinguished economist who, with John von Neumann, founded game theory. It was, of course, very important for Gödel to pass the citizenship test, but obviously he took it too seriously. Morgenstern describes how much effort Gödel put in preparing for the test:

> Since [Gödel] is a very thorough man, he started informing himself about the history of the settlement of North America by human beings. That led gradually to the study of the history of American Indians, their various tribes, etc.[72]

Gödel also studied thoroughly his local area, Princeton, and asked Morgenstern about the mayor, the township council, and election procedures. Morgenstern told Gödel that these issues were not relevant to the test and that most questions would be easily answerable.

One day, after studying the US constitution, Gödel made a confession to Morgenstern. Gödel said that he had discovered that there was a logical loophole in the constitution and that he could prove that a dictatorship could be legally installed in the United States! Morgenstern was disturbed by this claim and told Gödel that he should not, under any circumstances, talk about it at the test. Morgenstern relayed this to Einstein, who was 'horrified that such an idea had occurred to Gödel'. Einstein tried to calm Gödel down and told him that he should not worry about these things.

The day of the citizenship test finally came. Morgenstern picked up Gödel and Einstein by car. In Morgenstern's car Einstein asked Gödel, 'Now, Gödel, are you really well prepared for this examination?' This question upset Gödel terribly and Einstein was amused to see the worry on Gödel's face. Witnesses were normally questioned separately from the candidate, but because of Einstein's fame all three were allowed to sit together. The examiner asked, 'Mr Gödel, where do you come from?' Gödel answered, 'Where do I come from? Austria.' The examiner continued, 'What kind of government did you have in Austria?' Gödel answered, 'It was a republic, but the constitution was such that it finally was changed into a dictatorship.' The examiner responded to Gödel's answer, 'Oh! This is very bad. This could not happen in this country.' Gödel got excited about this response and exclaimed 'Oh yes, I can prove it!' Einstein and Morgenstern were mortified but, fortunately, the examiner responded calmly, 'Oh, God, let's not go into this.' Gödel passed the test and was granted US citizenship. After the test Einstein said to Gödel, 'Now, Gödel, this was your last but one examination.' Gödel immediately started worrying, 'Goodness, is there still another one to come?' Einstein responded, 'Gödel, the next examination is when you step into your grave.' Gödel said, 'But Einstein, I don't step into my grave.' And

Einstein said, 'Gödel, that's just the joke of it!' All three were relieved that this affair was over.

Despite the age difference of 27 years that existed between them, Einstein and Gödel cherished their friendship. Einstein once remarked that he went to Gödel's office every evening after work 'just to have the privilege of walking home with him'. Einstein did not have a chance to see Gödel's ontological argument because he died in 1955, many years before Gödel started working on it. However, Einstein might have been interested in it, because he himself left a number of remarks on the existence of God. In response to the question 'Do you believe in God?' Einstein famously responded, 'I believe in Spinoza's God, who reveals Himself in the lawful harmony of the world.' On the other hand, Gödel remarked, as noted earlier, 'My belief is theistic, not pantheistic, following Leibniz rather than Spinoza.'[73]

Graham Oppy summarizes Gödel's ontological argument as consisting of the following three definitions and six axioms:[74]

Definition 1: x is God-like if and only if x has as essential properties those and only those properties which are positive.

This seems to be consistent with a standard theistic notion of God. God has only positive properties, such as the properties of being omniscient, omnipotent, and omnibenevolent, and He does not have any non-positive properties, such as being ignorant, powerless, and morally imperfect.

Definition 2: A is an essence of x if and only if for every property B, x has B necessarily if and only if A entails B.
Definition 3: x exists necessarily if and only if every essence of x is necessarily exemplified.

These two definitions entail that God exists necessarily if and only if all of His attributes, such as omniscience, omnipotence, and omnibenevolence, are instantiated in all possible worlds.

Axiom 1: if a property is positive, then its negation is not positive.

Consider, for example, the property of being omniscient, which is a positive property. The negation of this property, that is, the property of not being omniscient, is not positive.

Axiom 2: any property entailed by – that is, strictly implied by – a positive property is positive.

Suppose that the property of being omnibenevolent is a positive property and that that property entails the property of being kind. It then follows that the property of being kind is also a positive property.

Axiom 3: the property of being God-like is positive.

Definition 1 suggests that the property of being God-like subsumes only positive properties, such as the properties of being omniscient, omnipotent, and omnibenevolent. This seems to be consistent with the axiom that the property of being God-like itself is also positive.

Axiom 4: if a property is positive, then it is necessarily positive.

So, for example, if the property of being omniscient is positive, then it is necessarily, that is, in every possible world, positive.

Axiom 5: necessary existence is positive.

This seems consistent with what we have seen: necessary existence contributes to the greatness of God as that-than-which-no-greater-can-be-thought, or as a supremely perfect being.

Axiom 6: for any property P, if P is positive, then being necessarily P is positive.

If, for example, being omniscient is a positive property, then being necessarily omniscient, that is being omniscient in all possible worlds, is also positive. Notice that this axiom is different from Axiom 4.

From these axioms and definitions, Gödel says, we can prove the existence of God. First, we can derive that if a property is positive, then it is consistent and thus possible to exemplify it. Given that the property of being God-like is positive, moreover, we can conclude that it is possible to exemplify that property. That is, it is possible for God to exist. Recall that this is what Leibniz's argument and the modal ontological argument also try to demonstrate. We can then show that if any being is God-like, the property of being God-like, which subsumes necessary existence, is an essence

of that being. This follows that the property of being God-like is exemplified, which is equivalent to saying that God exists in all possible worlds,
including the actual world. We can conclude, therefore, that God exists.

Gödel's ontological argument is interesting because it combines features
of various distinct versions of the ontological argument we have seen.
Structurally, it is based on Leibniz's version of the argument. It also borrows
the notion of positive property from Leibniz's version. Gödel's definition of
God-likeness, on the other hand, reminds us of Anselm's definition of God
as that-than-which-no-greater-can-be-thought and Descartes's definition of
Him as a supremely perfect being. And, finally, Gödel's appeal to the notion
of modality reminds us of the modal ontological argument.

Gödel completed his ontological argument in late 1970 and told Oskar
Morgenstern with great excitement that he was fully satisfied with it. He
knew that his death was approaching and wished to ensure that his notes
would not be destroyed when he died. However, he also hesitated to publish
them. Gödel's argument was not, therefore, widely known when he was alive.

Gödel died in 1978. In the early 1980s his colleague Dana Scott started
circulating among mathematicians three pages of handwritten notes entitled, 'Gödel's Ontological Proof', based on Gödel's original notes from the
1970s. Scott's notes were finally published in 1987 – almost 20 years after
Gödel wrote the original notes – as an appendix to a paper written by the
philosopher Jordan Howard Sobel.[75]

As we have seen, the ontological argument has a long history; it was formulated clearly for the first time in the eleventh century and since then many
renowned philosophers in every period have scrutinized it. However, the
debate over the argument remains very much alive. As to Gödel's version
of the argument, which is one of the most recent, philosophers have
begun considering it only relatively recently. Sobel's Logic and Theism (2003)
and Oppy's Arguing about Gods (2006) provide critical analyses of the argument, but it will certainly take many more years for the debate to mature.
Even Anselm's original version is still discussed. One of the most prominent philosophy journals, Mind, published in 2004 a major paper by Peter
Millican, in which he claims that he has discovered a fatal flaw in Anselm's
argument.[76] The paper has prompted new debate over the argument.[77] Even
among critics, there is still no consensus as to exactly where a flaw lies in
Anselm's reasoning. Philosophers still have not found the rabbit in Anselm's
magic act – if it exists at all.

PART II

'FOLLOW THE EVIDENCE WHEREVER IT LEADS': EVOLUTION VS. INTELLIGENT DESIGN

Saying that you don't believe in evolution is almost saying for us, well, we don't believe that the civil war ever took place in the United States.

Robert Eshbach (science teacher at Dover Area High School)

The chance that higher life forms might have emerged in this way [through evolution] is comparable with the chance that a tornado sweeping through a junk-yard might assemble a Boeing 747 from the materials therein ... I am at a loss to understand biologists' widespread compulsion to deny what seems to me to be obvious.

Fred Hoyle

1 Professor Flew's conversion

On December 9, 2004, major television networks and newspapers reported a rather unusual news story: An 81-year-old British philosopher, who had been well known for his defense of atheism for over 50 years, had declared that he now believed in the existence of God:

Famous Atheist Now Believes in God

Dec. 9, 2004 – A British philosophy professor who has been a leading champion of atheism for more than a half-century has changed his mind. He now believes in God more or less based on scientific evidence, and says so on a video released Thursday.

At age 81, after decades of insisting belief is a mistake, Antony Flew has concluded that some sort of intelligence or first cause must have created the universe. A super-intelligence is the only good explanation for the origin of life and the complexity of nature, Flew said in a telephone interview from England. (ABC News)[1]

Despite his conversion from atheism to theism, Flew did not become a member of any religious body. He said that his position was best described as deism, which is usually regarded as being incompatible with such traditional religions as Christianity, Judaism, and Islam. Deism is the doctrine that, while God created the universe, He does not interact with His creation. He does not communicate with His creatures or intervene in human affairs. God created the universe but He has done nothing since then. Flew wrote, 'while reason … assures us that there is a God, there is no room either for any supernatural revelation of that God or any transaction between that God and individual human beings'.[2] So Flew came to believe in the existence of a God 'who or which leaves [n]ature and its creatures (including human creatures) entirely to their own devices'.[3] God is, according to Flew, purely an impersonal prime mover.

Flew contended that throughout his career in philosophy, he was guided by Socrates' principle: 'Follow the evidence wherever it leads.' Thus he said that he had defended atheism for more than a half-century not because he was predisposed to it but simply because he thought that the evidence he had led to it. Similarly, on his own admission, he converted to theism, not because he started having sentiment toward theism but simply because he thought that the latest discoveries in science had led to theism.

While Flew's conversion was surprising news for many people, it did not happen completely out of the blue. In 2001, it was rumored on the World Wide Web that Flew had converted to theism, more specifically to Christianity, which, among other traditional religions, he had been criticizing for many years.[4] In response to this rumor, Flew wrote a small article for *The Secular Web*, a website dedicated to secular humanism. The title of the article was explicit enough to dispel the rumor: 'Sorry to Disappoint, but I'm Still an Atheist!'[5] In that article, Flew contended that the only possible source of the rumor that he could conceive of was a piece that he had written a little while ago, which contained arguments that 'could well disturb atheists'. Flew argued there that it was perfectly reasonable for theists to accept some important scientific discoveries without giving up their religious commitment. Consider, for example, the big bang. Many atheists think that there is a non-supernatural, scientific explanation of this event. They further think that even if a full explanation is beyond the reach of their capacities, the event does not entail the existence of God. However, at the same time, according to Flew, theists can rationally accept the big bang as an event that *confirms* their theistic understanding of the universe. Theism says that there was such an event, the beginning of the universe, initiated by God, and the big bang theory confirms that, indeed, the universe did have a beginning. A version of atheism that allows in this way that some theists are rationally justified in believing in the existence of God is called 'friendly atheism'.[6] Friendly atheism is based on the idea that being rationally justified in believing proposition p does not always entail or require that p is true. Suppose, for example, that my flight crashes into the sea and that after one week no one finds any survivors. Here my family is justified in believing that I am dead by now. However, suppose further that I am miraculously alive, floating on the sea waiting to be rescued. I am, then, of course, justified in believing that I am alive. This example shows that different people can be justified in believing in propositions that contradict each other. Friendly atheists say that while God does not exist and they are justified in believing that fact, there are some theists who are justified in believing that God does exist. Friendly atheism disagrees with 'unfriendly atheism', according to which no one is rationally justified in believing in the existence of God.

On another occasion, there was a rumor that Flew had converted to theism because he was convinced by one of the traditional arguments for the existence of God.[7] According to the rumor, Flew wrote in a private letter to a fellow philosopher that he was convinced by the 'Kalām cosmological argument'. As we will see in the next part of this book, the Kalām cosmological argument purports to prove the existence of God, as a personal cause of the universe, through philosophical, mathematical, and cosmological reasoning. Flew later said that he did not remember having written such a letter and that he did not find the Kalām cosmological argument convincing.

The rumor about his conversion popped up again in 2003. This time, again, Flew denied it. When people heard the same rumor again in 2004, they naturally expected that Flew would deny it soon. This time, however, he confirmed the rumor.

Some theists regard the conversion of one of the most prominent atheists as a great triumph for religious believers. For example, J. P. Moreland, a Christian philosopher, even says that Flew's conversion is an event that itself supports belief in the supernatural.[8] On May 11, 2006, Biola University, where Moreland teaches, awarded Flew the Philip E. Johnson Award for Liberty and Truth. The award is named after a retired law professor who is regarded as the father of the contemporary 'intelligent design' movement, which promotes the idea that 'certain features of the universe and of living things are best explained by an intelligent cause, not an undirected process such as natural selection'.[9] According to the university, the award was given to Flew for his 'lifelong commitment to free and open inquiry and to standing fast against intolerant assaults on freedom of thought and expression'.

Atheists, on the other hand, claim that Flew's conversion is far from a triumph for religious believers, because his deism is incompatible with traditional Judaeo-Christian-Islamic theism, nearly as much as atheism is. The only thing that deism and traditional theism share is the idea that some extraordinary being created the universe; they disagree on almost every other theological and metaphysical issue.

In 2007 Flew published, with Roy Abraham Varghese, a book entitled *There Is a God: How the World's Most Notorious Atheist Changed His Mind*. In that book Flew explained his new commitment to deism. He also expressed in the book some sympathy for Christianity, which many find perplexing because, again, deism is known for being incompatible with it. Subsequently, the *New York Times* published an article by Mark Oppenheimer, which questions the authenticity of the book.[10] According to Oppenheimer, Flew did not remember some of the people that he mentions in the book. Oppenheimer points out that the book was not actually written by Flew himself even though it is presented as a first-person account of his life and philosophy. According to Oppenheimer, nearly the whole book was written by the co-author, Varghese. Flew did not deny this. He said openly, 'This is really Roy's doing', and 'He showed it to me, and I said OK. I'm too old for this kind of work!' Varghese himself admits that the book was his idea and that he wrote a substantial part of it. Moreover, Bob Hostetler, an evangelical pastor and author, helped them in rewriting many passages to make the book more accessible.

Flew, however, rejected the criticism that he was manipulated by evangelical Christians:

> My name is on the book and it represents exactly my opinions. I would not have a book issued in my name that I do not 100 per cent agree with. I needed someone to do the actual writing because I'm 84 and that was Roy Varghese's role. The idea that someone manipulated me because I'm old is exactly wrong. I may be old but it is hard to manipulate me. That is my book and it represents my thinking.[11]

Whatever the truth is behind the publication of the book Flew seemed to be clear about one thing: his conversion was triggered by discoveries in recent biological sciences. He came to subscribe to theism because he was convinced that the origin of certain biological features in nature can be explained only by reference to the acts of an intelligent agent rather than to undirected evolutionary processes. In this respect Flew's conversion can be regarded as showing an affinity for the world-wide intelligent design movement. In fact Flew is one of those scholars who signed a letter in 2006 to demand that Tony Blair, then prime minister of the United Kingdom, include intelligent design in the science curriculum.

Flew died in 2010 without retracting his conversion to theism.

2 Battles over evolution

Dover is a town in south central Pennsylvania with a population of about 2,000 people. Until 2005 no one could have anticipated that this small American town would attract attention from scientific and religious communities all over the world.

In 2004 the Dover Area School District made an announcement that astonished many local teachers, students, and parents. Their press release said that from January 2005 teachers would be required to read the following statement in their ninth-grade biology class at Dover Area High School:

> The Pennsylvania Academic Standards require students to learn about Darwin's Theory of Evolution and eventually to take a standardized test of which evolution is a part.
>
> Because Darwin's Theory is a theory, it continues to be tested as new evidence is discovered. The Theory is not a fact. Gaps in the Theory exist for which there is no evidence. A theory is defined as a

well-tested explanation that unifies a broad range of observations. Intelligent Design is an explanation of the origin of life that differs from Darwin's view. The reference book, *Of Pandas and People*, is available for students who might be interested in gaining an understanding of what Intelligent Design actually involves.

With respect to any theory, students are encouraged to keep an open mind. The school leaves the discussion of the Origins of Life to individual students and their families. As a Standards-driven district, class instruction focuses upon preparing students to achieve proficiency on Standards-based assessments.

As mentioned above, intelligent design, which this statement introduces as an alternative to evolution, is the idea that certain features of nature are best explained by reference to an intelligent cause, rather than to an undirected process. Intelligent design has been promoted since the early 1990s by theistic scientists and philosophers, particularly those at the Discovery Institute. The Discovery Institute is a conservative think tank in Seattle founded in 1990 by former politician, diplomat, and journalist Bruce Chapman, the writer and political activist George Gilder, and a philosopher, Stephen C. Meyer.

Three school board members in Dover who voted against the above statement about evolution and intelligent design resigned in protest and teachers refused to read the statement on the basis of the Pennsylvania code of education, according to which teachers cannot present information they believe to be false. When the teachers refused to read the statement an administrator came into the classrooms and read it instead. In December 2004, the American Civil Liberties Union filed a lawsuit in federal court in Pennsylvania on behalf of 11 parents in Dover, who claim that the introduction of intelligent design by the Dover school board violated their constitutional rights. The suit was brought in the US District Court for the Middle District of Pennsylvania. By that time people in Dover had realized that they were being involved in something reminiscent of the long, exhausting battles over evolution and creationism that had taken place in the 1980s.

In 1981 the governor of Arkansas signed into law the 'Balanced Treatment for Creation-Science and Evolution-Science' Act (Act 590). The act explains the requirement for what it regards as a balanced treatment as follows:

Public schools within this State shall give balanced treatment to crea-tion-science and to evolution-science. Balanced treatment to these two models shall be given in classroom lectures taken as a whole for each course, in textbook materials taken as a whole for each course, in library materials taken as a whole for the sciences and taken as a whole for the humanities, and in other educational programs in public schools, to the extent that such lectures, textbooks, library materials, or educational programs deal in any way with the subject of the origin of man, life, the earth, or the universe.

Act 590 defines creation science as 'the scientific evidences for creation and inferences from those scientific evidences'. The 'scientific evidences' and related inferences that creation science includes are, according to the act, the following:

(1) Sudden creation of the universe, energy, and life from nothing; (2) The insufficiency of mutation and natural selection in bringing about development of all living kinds from a single organism; (3) Changes only within fixed limits of originally created kinds of animals and plants; (4) Separate ancestry for man and apes; (5) Explanation of the earth's geology by catastrophism, including the occurrence of a worldwide flood; and (6) A relatively recent inception of the earth and living kinds.

In 1982, however, US District Court Judge William R. Overton ruled that Act 590 was unconstitutional in light of the Establishment Clause of the First Amendment, which reads, 'Congress shall make no law respecting an establishment of religion, or prohibiting the free exercise thereof …'. Judge Overton concluded that creation science is not science because it fails to meet the following essential characteristics of science: (i) it is guided by natural law; (ii) it has to be explanatory by reference to natural law; (iii) it is testable against the empirical world; (iv) its conclusions are tentative, i.e., are not necessarily the final word; (v) it is falsifiable.

By (i) and (ii) the judge means that creation science, despite its name, is not a scientific theory because it is not formulated in terms of the laws of nature. Creation science tries to explain the origin of nature by appealing to supernatural intervention, which is fundamentally different from anything that standard scientific research addresses. By (iii) the judge means that creation science does not qualify as a scientific theory because it is impossible to test its validity empirically. There is no established scientific method to determine whether or not the universe and things in it were created by an intelligent agent that transcends the nature. By (iv) and (v) the judge means that, unlike scientific theories and hypotheses, creation science is not open to revision and falsification. It is often said that one of the most distinctive features of scientific theories is that they are always open to being revised in accordance with counter-evidence. Creation science, however, does not seem to share such a feature with conventional science.

The defeat in Arkansas did not stop creationists. In 1982 the state of Louisiana passed the 'Balanced Treatment for Creation-Science and Evolution-Science in Public School Instruction Act', which prohibits the teaching of evolution in the public schools without also teaching creation science. In response to the act, 72 Nobel Prize laureates, 17 state academies of science and 7 other scientific organizations filed an *amicus curiae* brief stating that teaching creationism 'misleads our youth about the nature of scientific inquiry'. The brief claims, first, that the act does not define creation science. The act does mention 'scientific evidences of creation' as the focus of creation science but that is a circular definition of creation science. The brief also criticizes the claim of the act that creation science and evolution science are mere theory rather than 'proven scientific fact'. (It is interesting to note that the state- ment of the Dover Area School District mentioned earlier presents the same idea when it says, 'Because Darwin's Theory is a theory, it continues to be tested as new evidence is discovered. The Theory is not a fact.') According to the brief, such a claim creates a false impression that since evolution is 'only a theory' it is not an established fact. In science, according to the brief, a fact is a 'property of a natural phenomenon', while a theory is a 'natural explanation for a body of facts' and hence the label of evolution as a theory by no means implies that it is not an established fact.

In a seven-to-two decision written by Justice Brennan in 1987, the US Supreme Court ruled that the act is unconstitutional because, again, it violated the Establishment Clause of the First Amendment. The state had claimed that the act was necessary for maintaining academic freedom for teachers. The court ruled, however, that such an act was unnecessary because teachers had always been allowed to introduce more than one theory. The act, by making it compulsory for teachers to teach creationism along with evolution, would ironically limit teachers' academic freedom to teach what they think is appropriate. The court did not rule out in principle the educa- tional merit of teaching about a controversy, saying, '[T]eaching a variety of scientific theories about the origins of humankind to schoolchildren might be validly done with the clear secular intent of enhancing the effectiveness of science instruction.' This did not save the act, however, as the court ruled that it supports specific religious views.

3 Intelligent design

Critics claim that intelligent design is nothing but 1980s creationism in disguise. Proponents of intelligent design maintain, however, that it is fundamentally distinct from creationism. What are the differences between creationism and intelligent design?

Perhaps the most characteristic feature of intelligent design is that it relies specifically on recent research in biological sciences, particularly molecular biology. When Darwin introduced the theory of evolution these areas of biology were virtually non-existent. Scientists at his time simply did not have the technology needed to investigate organisms at the molecular level. Even those involved in the dispute over evolution and creationism in the 1980s did not know as much as we do now about the subject. Proponents of intelligent design believe that the most recent developments in these new areas of biology have revealed gaps in Darwin's theory of evolution which motivate intelligent design. In his seminal work *On the Origin of Species by Means of Natural Selection, or the Preservation of Favoured Races in the Struggle for Life* Darwin invited critics to challenge his theory by putting forward the following claim: 'If it could be demonstrated that any complex organ existed, which could not possibly have been formed by numerous, successive, slight modifications, my theory would absolutely break down. But I can find out no such case.'[12]

Michael Behe, a biochemist at Lehigh University, challenges Darwin's theory and defends intelligent design by introducing the notion of 'irreducible complexity'. Behe characterizes an irreducibly complex system as 'a single system which is composed of several interacting parts that contribute to the basic function, and where the removal of any one of the parts causes the system to effectively cease functioning'.[13] Consider, for example, a mousetrap. A typical mousetrap consists of a catch, a hammer, a spring, a hold-down bar, and a platform, each of which contributes to its basic function, trapping a mouse. Behe says that a mousetrap is an example of an artificial object that is irreducibly complex because none of its parts can be eliminated while preserving its proper function (Figure II.1). The fact that a mousetrap is irreducibly complex also means that it does not have a functional precursor that consists entirely of a subset of its parts.

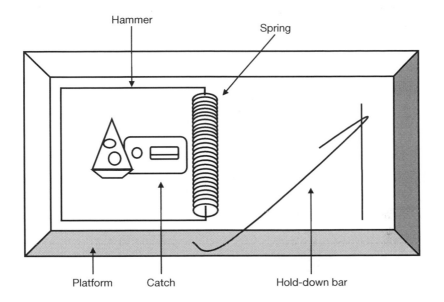

Hammer

Spring

Platform   Catch   Hold-down bar

Figure II.1 A mousetrap is said to be irreducibly complex because none of its parts can be eliminated while preserving its proper function.

What Darwin says in the above invitation to challenge his theory, according to Behe, is that the theory of evolution would collapse if it were shown that there is an irreducibly complex system in biology that is analogous to a mousetrap. An irreducibly complex biological system, if there is any, cannot be formed by numerous, successive, slight modifications because, just like a mousetrap, such an organism does not have a functional precursor consisting entirely of a small subset of its parts.

Behe claims that there indeed are irreducibly complex biological systems in nature. The most prominent example that he gives is the bacterial flagellum. The bacterial flagellum is a rotor that enables a bacterium to swim. The flagellum consists of many parts, such as a universal joint, a propeller, a drive shaft, and so on.[14] According to Behe, the flagellum is so perfectly structured that dropping any of its parts makes it unable to function as a rotor (Figure II.2). Looking at this structural elegance, the biologist Howard Berg describes the bacterial flagellum as 'the most efficient machine in the universe'.[15] Contrary to what Darwin's theory of evolution predicts, Behe says, the bacterial flagellum cannot possibly be formed by numerous, successive, slight modifications because it is irreducibly

Figure II.2 Behe claims that the bacterial flagellum is an irreducibly complex biological system.

complex. Behe, therefore, concludes that the theory of evolution is at best incomplete.

If we wish to support intelligent design we need to detect design in nature. However, since intelligent design aims to be a rigorous scientific theory, it is not optimum to rely entirely on our intuitive judgment in detecting it. We all know that our intuition is not always reliable. We know, for example, that people used to think mistakenly that some natural phenomena, such as thunder and earthquakes, were caused by a supernatural intelligence. We also know that even now we could make a misjudgment and think that a stain on a wall or a random pattern on a ceiling are drawn or imprinted by someone.

In fact, recent research in the emerging field of the cognitive science of religion suggests that humans, especially children, are naturally predisposed to see purpose and intelligence in nature. The psychologist Deborah Kelemen's empirical study of elementary school children in the United States suggests that they are intuitively inclined to explain the properties of living and non-living natural objects in teleological terms.[16] That is, they try to explain the properties of objects in terms of their purposes. Kelemen has extended her research to schoolchildren in the United Kingdom, where religion is culturally less influential than in the United States. Her results reveal that British children exhibit the same tendency to appeal to teleology, even if in a slightly different way.[17] She even contends that children might be 'intuitive theists', who are naturally predisposed to view natural phenomena as being caused by a non-human designer.[18] The psychologist Margaret E. Evans asked questions specifically about the origin of species to children and mothers in Christian fundamentalist and non-fundamentalist school communities in the United States. Their answers indicate that children between 8 and 10 years old are exclusively creationist, regardless of their communities.[19]

Anthropomorphism

The anthropologist Stewart Guthrie argues that religion arises from our tendency to attribute human characteristics to natural objects and events. While this tendency creates many false beliefs it is, or for a long time was, beneficial to our survival. If we see the shadow of an object in the woods it is better for our survival to recognize it as a predator. If it turns out to be something harmless, then that is not a big loss – it is better safe than sorry. Guthrie tries to explain away the prevalence of religion by appealing to such a cognitive tendency. The cognitive scientist Justin L. Barrett calls the cognitive system responsible for detecting intelligent agency the 'hyperactive agency detection device' (HADD). Empirical studies suggest that all people have the HADD and that it is already active in the first five months of life.[20]

If we are naturally predisposed to detect design, then we cannot fully rely on our intuitive judgment about whether a given object is designed by an intelligent being. William Dembski, a philosopher and mathematician at Southern Baptist Theological Seminary and a member of the Discovery Institute, therefore attempts to establish a rigorous mathematical method that makes it possible to detect design. The most fundamental idea behind his method is that we can detect design by eliminating chance through small probabilities. Dembski appeals to the notion of 'specified complexity' to formulate this idea.[21] The short string of letters 'ME', for example, is specified (because it has a meaning) but it is not complex. The longer string of letters 'CWOMSPOLLJFLDJFLEJSVILSCXODL ...' is complex but not specified. It is just a random string of many letters. However, we can confidently tell that a Shakespearean sonnet is formed by the guided process of an intelligent designer, namely Shakespeare himself, rather than by a random, unguided process, because it is both complex and specified. Suppose that you look up to the sky and clouds form a string of letters displaying a Shakespearean sonnet verbatim. It would then be unreasonable, or even irrational, to say that they were formed by chance. Such a pattern would have to have been formed by an intelligent being. Dembski concludes that specified complexity is a good measure of eliminating chance and detecting intelligence.

Dembski tries to reveal gaps in the theory of evolution by finding biological information that is both specified and complex. His example is, again, the bacterial flagellum.[22] Dembski claims that since the flagellum is a discrete combinational object, the probability of obtaining it can be determined by the following calculation: the probability of originating the building blocks required for the system, multiplied by the probability of locating them in one place once the building blocks are given, multiplied by the probability of configuring them once the building blocks are given and located in one place. In short:

$$P_{dco} = P_{orig} \times P_{local} \times P_{config}.$$

Dembski says that the flagellum cannot be a product of a random, unguided process because an analysis of the structure and the composition of the flagellum shows that P_{dco} for the flagellum falls below 10^{-150}, the number which Dembski labels the 'universal probability bound'. The universal probability bound is a probabilistic threshold that Dembski uses to eliminate chance. Dembski says 'any specified event of probability less than 1 in 10^{150} will remain improbable even after all conceivable probabilistic resources from the observable universe have been factored in'.[23] What he means here is that an event does not occur by chance even over the entire history of the universe until now, if the probability of its occurring is below 10^{-150}. He derived the number 10^{150} through the following calculation:

$$10^{80} \times 10^{45} \times 10^{25} = 10^{150}$$

where 10^{80} represents the number of elementary particles in the observable universe, 10^{45} the maximum number of transitions in physical states can occur in one second (the inverse of the Planck time), and 10^{25} the age of the universe in seconds multiplied by one billion. Dembski contends that because the probability of the assembly of the flagellum by chance is lower than 10^{-150} it is reasonable to conclude that it is a product of intelligent design rather than of a random, unguided process.

Intelligent design is often regarded as a pseudoscientific venture comparable to astrology or flat earth theory. In order to refute such an allegation Dembski cites SETI, the 'Search for Extraterrestrial Intelligence', a scientific program depicted in the movie *Contact*. Scientists in SETI projects observe millions of transmission signals from outer space to see if they exhibit any sign of intelligence. Dembski says that in SETI projects irreducible complexity plays a crucial role. The SETI scientists filter out signals that are random and hope to receive ones that are both specified and complex. If they find a signal that contains complex specified information, they can reliably conclude that the signal was transmitted by extraterrestrial intelligence. (Unfortunately, they have not found such a signal yet!) Whether or not there really exists extraterrestrial intelligence that transmits signals, the SETI program is widely regarded as a rigorous scientific project. If so, Dembski claims, whether or not there really is an intelligent designer behind nature, intelligent design is a rigorous scientific project.

Appeals to molecular biology and probability theory are not the only noteworthy features of intelligent design. Proponents of intelligent design also emphasize the fact that, unlike creationism, their theory does not presuppose the existence of God. Creationism traditionally has its foundations in a literal reading of the biblical book of Genesis, which is typically construed as saying that the earth was created by God only a few thousand years ago. That is the primary reason that critics label creationism as a religious, rather than scientific, project. Intelligent design, on the other hand, does not demand any religious commitment. In fact, it is formulated in such a way that one can consistently assert intelligent design while denying the existence of God. Behe says:

> The most important difference [between my intelligent design argument and William Paley's traditional design argument for the existence of God] is that my argument is limited to design itself; I strongly emphasize that it is not an argument for the existence of a benevolent God, as Paley's was. I hasten to add that I myself do believe in a benevolent God, and I recognize that philosophy and theology may be able to extend the argument. But a scientific argument for design in biology does not reach that far.[24]

If the intelligent designer is not God, what else could it be? Behe says that it could be 'an angel – fallen or not; Plato's demiurge; some mystical new-age force; space aliens from Alpha Centauri; time travelers; or some utterly unknown intelligent being'.[25] In fact there are people who seriously believe in space aliens, or extraterrestrials, as intelligent designers. According to the Raëlian Movement, a UFO religion founded by the French journalist Claude Vorilhon, all living creatures, including human beings, were created with advanced genetic engineering by aliens called the 'Elohim'. Raëlians believe that the Elohim are beings that were recognized by ancient people as angels and gods, and throughout history they have sent religious leaders such as Jesus and Moses to help humanity on earth.

Proponents of intelligent design claim that the existence of God might be demonstrated if we add further philosophical arguments to the theory. All that intelligent design says empirically, however, insofar as it is advanced as a scientific theory without making any religious or theistic presuppositions, is that at least some organisms were created by an intelligent designer rather than arising through an undirected evolutionary process.

Many critics maintain that there is nothing substantially new about intelligent design. They believe that it is merely a new gimmick that religious believers use to promote creationism. There certainly are important similarities between the promotion of creationism in the 1980s and that of intelligent design today. First, promoters of these theories have similar backgrounds. Most vigorous proponents of these theories are conservative Christians. As the Discovery Institute often emphasizes, there *are* some non-Christians who defend intelligent design, but there are very few of them. Second, they try to introduce creationism and intelligent design into school curricula in a similar way. In both cases they try to advance what appears to be a humble proposal: They do not want schools to eliminate evolution from the biology curriculum; they only want schools to teach that there is a controversy over evolution. On the face of it, this proposal seems easy to swallow because it is generally regarded as a good practice for children to learn different opinions on a given topic and discuss their merits and demerits. It certainly *sounds* better than introducing only one theory and making children accept it blindly.

Matt Duss was a part-time employee at the Discovery Institute. It was his job to photocopy documents. One day in 1999 he was asked to photocopy an internal memorandum that seemed slightly unusual. The document was entitled 'The Wedge' and stamped 'TOP SECRET' and 'NOT FOR

DISTRIBUTION'. Since Duss was curious, he made an extra copy for himself. He then gave it to Tim Rhodes, who put the whole document on the World Wide Web.[26] This is how the Discovery Institute's secret strategy to promote intelligent design was leaked.

The Wedge document describes a long-term political, social, academic, and educational campaign organized by the institute's Center for the Renewal of Science and Culture (later renamed the 'Center for Science and Culture'). The goal of the campaign is to defeat scientific materialism, which the institute believes has 'infected virtually every area of our culture, from politics and economics to literature and art'. Scientific materialism is, according to the document, defended by 'thinkers such as Charles Darwin, Karl Marx, and Sigmund Freud', who 'portrayed humans not as moral and spiritual beings, but as animals or machines who inhabited a universe ruled by purely impersonal forces and whose behavior and very thoughts were dictated by the unbending forces of biology, chemistry, and environment'. The document continues, 'Discovery Institute's Centre for the Renewal of Science and Culture seeks nothing less than the overthrow of materialism and its cultural legacies.' While, as mentioned earlier, proponents of intelligent design often try to present it as a scientific theory detached from any religious commitment, the document says that 'Design theory promises to reverse the stifling dominance of the materialist worldview, and to replace it with a science consonant with Christian and theistic convictions.'

Where does the title 'Wedge' come from? The Wedge document explains it as follows: 'If we view the predominant materialistic science as a giant tree, our strategy is intended to function as a "wedge" that, while relatively small, can split the trunk when applied at its weakest points.' This idea was introduced by Philip E. Johnson, the aforementioned father of the contemporary intelligent design movement and the author of the book *Darwin on Trial*. The Wedge strategy consists of three distinct phases. In the first phase, Discovery Institute members conduct research on intelligent design and publish academic work on the topic. This is, according to the document, 'the essential component of everything that comes afterwards'. In the second phase they try to prepare for the popular reception of intelligent design. They 'seek to cultivate and convince influential individuals in print and broadcast media, as well as think tank leaders, scientists and academics, congressional staff, talk show hosts, college and seminary presidents and faculty, future talent and potential academic allies'. The third phase is most directly relevant to public education. The document describes this phase as follows:

Once our research and writing have had time to mature, and the public prepared for the reception of design theory, we will move toward direct confrontation with the advocates of materialist science through challenge conferences in significant academic settings. We will also pursue possible legal assistance in response to resistance to the integration of design theory into public school science curricula. The attention, publicity, and influence of design theory should draw scientific materialists into open debate with design theorists, and we will be ready.

The central campaign for the third phase is what the Discovery Institute calls 'Teach the Controversy'. This campaign aims to teach schoolchildren that evolution is a 'theory in crisis', that is, a theory in which many scientists find serious gaps. As mentioned above, making students aware of controversies among scientists, rather than making them accept established facts, *appears* to have educational merit.

The Discovery Institute has put significant effort into presenting evolution as a theory in crisis. Since 2001 the institute has published what they call 'A Scientific Dissent from Darwinism', which comprises the following statement and a list of scientists who endorse it: 'We are skeptical of claims for the ability of random mutation and natural selection to account for the complexity of life. Careful examination of the evidence for Darwinian theory should be encouraged.' According to the August 2008 update, 761 scientists have endorsed this statement. (Since 2006 a non-profit organization, the Physicians and Surgeons for Scientific Integrity, which is associated with the Discovery Institute, has also published 'Physicians and Surgeons who Dissent from Darwinism', which has attracted more than 260 signatories.) The Discovery Institute is particularly proud of having such well-known scientists as Stanley N. Salthe (Professor Emeritus of Biology at Brooklyn College, City University of New York and the author of a biology textbook), Henry F. Schaefer, III (Professor of Chemistry at the University of Georgia and the sixth most cited chemist from 1981 to 1997), and Giuseppe Sermonti (Professor Emeritus at the Genetics Institute of the University of Perugia in Italy).[27]

A science reporter for the New York Times, Kenneth Chang, criticizes 'A Scientific Dissent from Darwinism'. According to him, random interviews with 20 signatories and a review of what a dozen others have expressed publicly reveal that many of them are evangelical Christians. Moreover, he says, only one quarter of the signatories are biologists. Chang believes that this suggests that their doubts about evolution stemmed from their religious beliefs rather than from genuine scientific research.[28]

Take a look at the statement for 'A Scientific Dissent from Darwinism' again: 'We are skeptical of claims for the ability of random mutation and natural selection to account for the complexity of life. Careful examination of the evidence for Darwinian theory should be encouraged.' Critics claim that this statement is ambiguous, perhaps deliberately so in order to cover as many views of individual scientists as possible. They also point out that the petition does not prove that there is a serious scientific controversy over evolution among scientists in relation to intelligent design because the statement does not deny evolution and, moreover, it does not even mention intelligent design.

Critics of intelligent design decided to take action in response to 'A Scientific Dissent from Darwinism'. In order to prove that evolution is not a 'theory in crisis', they have organized counter-petitions. The first is a parody called 'Project Steve',[29] which is named in honor of evolutionary biologist Stephen Jay Gould. This is an attempt to make a list of scientists named 'Steve' (or any its variations, such as 'Stephen', 'Stefan', 'Steven', and 'Stephanie') who support evolution. This was conducted by the National Center for Science Education (NCSE), an anti-creationist organization in California. The pro-evolution statement that Steves are asked to endorse reads as follows:

> Evolution is a vital, well-supported, unifying principle of the biological sciences, and the scientific evidence is overwhelmingly in favor of the idea that all living things share a common ancestry. Although there are legitimate debates about the patterns and processes of evolution, there is no serious scientific doubt that evolution occurred or that natural selection is a major mechanism in its occurrence. It is scientifically inappropriate and pedagogically irresponsible for creationist pseudo-science, including but not limited to 'intelligent design,' to be intro-duced into the science curricula of our nation's public schools.

A 'Steve-o-meter' on their website shows that as of August 9, 2010 the list included 1,140 signatories. Since, according to NCSE, Steves are estimated to comprise about 1 per cent of all scientists, the fact that there are as many as 1,140 scientists named Steve supporting evolution suggests that there are at least tens of thousands of scientists supporting evolution. The fact that a mere 761 people signed the anti-evolution petition does not, according to NCSE, prove that evolution is a 'theory in crisis'.

Another prominent pro-evolution petition is 'A Scientific Support for Darwinism and for Public Schools Not to Teach "Intelligent Design" as Science',[30] which was organized by an archaeologist R. Joe Brandon for only four days, from September 28 to October 1, 2005. The pro-evolution statement he prepared was the following:

> We, as scientists trained in fields that utilize evolutionary theory, do not consider Intelligent Design to be a fact-based science appropriate for teaching in public schools because it is theistic in nature, not empirical, and therefore does not pass the rigors of scientific hypothesis testing and theory development. As such, we petition that Intelligent Design not be presented in public schools as a viable science within the scientific curriculum.

On the Discovery Institute's list under 'A Scientific Dissent from Darwinism' only about 17 per cent of the signatories actually work in fields that are directly relevant to evolution. Brandon, on the other hand, tried to have as signatories for his petition only scientists in relevant fields. His initial plan was to have 400 signatories within four hours, but he was about 75 signatories shy at the four-hour mark. Hence he extended it to four days, which resulted in 7,733 signatories.[31]

In response to these counter-petitions, Bruce Chapman, the president of the Discovery Institute, says, 'How many does it take to be a noticeable minority – 10, 50, 100, 500? ... there is a minority of scientists who disagree with Darwin's theory, and it is not just a handful'. He also contends, 'We never claimed we're in a fight for numbers.'[32]

In order to present evolution as a theory in crisis Stephen C. Meyer, a co-founder of the Discovery Institute, also made an annotated bibliography of 44 papers in peer-reviewed science journals that he thinks point to serious gaps in evolution. The NCSE contacted the authors of all these papers and asked them whether they considered their work as providing any scientific evidence for intelligent design. Twenty-six of the authors, who wrote 34 out of the 44 publications on the list, responded and all denied that their studies support intelligent design. For example, according to the NCSE, one of the authors, David D. Williams, said, 'No, certainly not. How could it possibly?' In obvious reaction to these responses the Discovery Institute added the following disclaimer to the annotated bibliography: 'The publications are not presented either as support for the theory of intelligent design or as indicating that the authors cited doubt evolution.'[33]

The Discovery Institute has tried to make such a list because peer-reviewed publications are generally highly respected in science. When a science journal receives a paper from a researcher its editor normally sends it to peer-reviewers who are experts in a relevant field. These experts examine the paper and explain to the editor their judgments as to whether the paper makes an important contribution to the field and whether it merits being published. In order to ensure objectivity this is usually done as a double-blind process, that is, neither the author nor the reviewers know one another's identity. On the basis of the referees' recommendations the editor decides whether to publish the paper. This process ensures that journal publications satisfy high standards. Many critics of intelligent design often maintain that intelligent design is not science because virtually no peer-reviewed paper defending intelligent design has ever been published in mainstream science journals. We should not teach, they claim, a theory that cannot even survive the standard editorial process of scientific publications.

The 'teach the controversy' campaign did not succeed in impressing the majority of scientists. Nevertheless it was successful enough to win over one of the most powerful people in the world. On August 1, 2005 George W. Bush, then president of the United States, participated in a roundtable interview with reporters from Texas newspapers:

Reporter: I wanted to ask you about the – what seems to be a growing debate over evolution versus intelligent design. What are your personal views on that, and do you think both should be taught in public schools?

Bush: I think – as I said, harking back to my days as governor – both you and Herman are doing a fine job of dragging me back to the past. (Laughter). Then, I said that, first of all, that decision should be made to local school districts, but I felt like both sides ought to be properly taught.

Reporter: Both sides should be properly taught?

Bush: Yes, people – so people can understand what the debate is about.

Reporter: So the answer accepts the validity of intelligent design as an alternative to evolution?

Bush: I think that part of education is to expose people to different schools of thought, and I'm not suggesting – you're asking me whether or not people ought to be exposed to different ideas, and the answer is yes.[34]

The 'teach the controversy' campaign would make educational sense if the controversy over evolution were genuine. As we have seen, however, critics claim that the alleged controversy is not genuine at all; it is an illusion crafted purposefully by proponents of intelligent design. Evolution remains, according to the critics of intelligent design, one of the most reliable theories in all areas of science. The philosopher Daniel C. Dennett characterizes the strategy of proponents of intelligent design as follows. First, they misuse or misdescribe some scientific work on evolution and wait for proponents of evolution to respond. Once they respond and try to correct the misuse or the misdescription, the proponents announce that this is another piece of evidence that there is a controversy surrounding evolution that should be taught in schools.[35]

Nick Matzke at NCSE remarks, 'Intelligent design is just a new label for creationism ... It is just the latest legal strategy for creationism. It evolved in 1987 right after the Supreme Court ruled against creationism and said that that was unconstitutional.'[36] Jonathan Witt, a proponent of intelligent design at the Discovery Institute responds, however, that '[Matzke's] assertion is demonstrably false' because '[t]he idea of intelligent design reaches back to Socrates and Plato, and the term "intelligent design" as an alternative to blind evolution was used as early as 1897'.[37] Witt's criticism, however, misses Matzke's point. Matzke says explicitly that the intelligent design movement is the latest *legal* strategy to have emerged following the Louisiana case; thus whether the scientific and philosophical foundations of intelligent design can be traced back before the 1980s is beside the point. Nevertheless, it is important to emphasize that the controversy over intelligent design is not entirely legal, political, or educational in nature. Its core is indeed rooted in a perennial dispute over the apparent conflict between religious and naturalistic worldviews. In order to understand this fully it is necessary to review the history of the design argument for the existence of God.

4 History of the design argument

Picture the most beautiful natural phenomenon you have seen. Is it a colorful rainbow after the rain? Or a magnificent sunset seen on a tropical island? When we think of these amazing phenomena it is hard to believe that they are mere products of random natural processes, even if we are perfectly aware of their underlying physical mechanisms. It is difficult not to imagine an intelligence or purpose behind them. Immanuel Kant claims that seeing a designer in nature like this is 'the oldest, the clearest, and the best suited to ordinary human reason'.[38] The plausibility of this eighteenth-century claim has been confirmed by a number of recent empirical studies in the cognitive science of religion, some of which we saw above.

The philosophical origin of the design argument can be traced back to Ancient Greece. In the *Laws*, Plato's last and longest dialogue, one of the characters, 'the Athenian', whose name is not given but whose character seems similar to that of Socrates, discusses two arguments that motivate belief in gods. The one appeals to the eternity and divinity of the soul and the other appeals to design. The Athenian explains the argument that appeals to design as follows:

> [The argument is] based on the systematic motion of the heavenly bodies and the other objects under the control of reason, which is responsible for the order in the universe ... if a man goes in for such things as astronomy and the essential associated disciplines, and sees events apparently happening by necessity rather than because they are directed by the intention of a benevolent will, he'll turn into an atheist.[39]

While this argument can also be construed as a form of the cosmological argument, which will be discussed in the next part of this book, it certainly has an essential element of the design argument as well; it purports to find the purpose and intention of a designer through observation of the universe. What is amazing is that, according to the argument, the universe is not random and chaotic but ordered and systematic.

Cicero, a Roman orator and statesman of the first century BCE, provides an even clearer and more sophisticated formulation of the design argument:

> When you look at a picture or a statue, you recognize that it is a work of art. When you follow from afar the course of a ship, upon the sea, you do not question that its movement is guided by a skilled intelligence. When you see a sundial or a water-clock, you see that it tells the time by design and not by chance. How then can you imagine that the universe as a whole is devoid of purpose and intelligence, when it embraces everything, including these artifacts themselves and their artificers? Our friend Posidonius as you know has recently made a globe which in its revolution shows the movements of the sun and stars and planets, by day and night, just as they appear in the sky. Now if someone were to take this globe and show it to the people of Britain or Scythia would

a single one of those barbarians fail to see that it was the product of a conscious intelligence?[40]

It is interesting to see that Cicero's argument anticipates Paley's argument, which we discuss below, and the contemporary intelligent design argument, which would be introduced approximately 1,850 years later. The most crucial aspect of Cicero's argument is that it appeals to analogy. On the one hand, theists want to prove that God, as a designer of the universe and its inhabitants, exists. On the other hand, however, it is impossible for us to observe God's process of creating them directly. Cicero's argument overcomes this difficulty by invoking an analogy: We know that a sundial and a water-clock are designed by an intelligent being. The systematic movements of the sun and planets seem analogous to the movements of a sundial and a water-clock. Therefore, we can conclude that the movements of the sun and planets, as well as of the universe as a whole, are also designed by an intelligent being.

As we saw above, William Dembski, a contemporary proponent of intelligent design, presents his theory as an attempt to infer the existence of an intelligent designer by eliminating chance through small probabilities. Cicero also anticipated this probabilistic aspect of detecting design. He writes:

Is it not a wonder that anyone can bring himself to believe that a number of solid and separate particles by their chance collisions and moved only by the force of their own weight could bring into being so marvelous and beautiful a world? If anybody thinks that this is possible, I do not see why he should not think that if an infinite number of examples of the twenty-one letters of the alphabet, made of gold or what you will, were shaken together and poured out on the ground it would be possible for them to fall so as to spell out, say, the whole text of the Annals of Ennius. In fact I doubt whether chance would permit them to spell out a single verse!

So how can these people bring themselves to assert that the universe has been created by the blind and accidental collisions of inanimate particles devoid of color or any other quality? And even to assert that an infinite number of such worlds are coming into being and passing away all the time. If these chance collisions of atoms can make a world, why cannot they build a porch, or a temple, or a house or a city? A much easier and less laborious task.[41]

Paley is usually regarded as the one who anticipated intelligent design most clearly, but Cicero's argument seems to contain most of the essential elements of the contemporary theory of intelligent design. The only crucial difference between Cicero's argument, on the one hand, and Paley's argument and intelligent design, on the other, is that Cicero's argument does not concentrate on the apparent design of biological organisms. He focused on the order of the universe in general.

In his *Summa Theologica* the thirteenth-century philosopher and theologian Thomas Aquinas introduces 'Five Ways' to prove the existence of God. Among them, the fifth way is usually regarded as a version of the design argument (as explained in the next part of this book, the first three ways are regarded as versions of the cosmological argument and the fourth way as a version of the argument from perfection). Aquinas says that in nature even things that do not have intelligence or consciousness act for some end or for a purpose so as to obtain the best result. However, Aquinas says, nothing can act towards the end or for a purpose unless it is under the direction of an intelligent and conscious being. Therefore, Aquinas concludes, God, or at least an intelligent conscious governor of the universe, exists. In *Quaestiones Disputatae de Veritate* Aquinas, just like Cicero, addresses the probabilistic aspect of the detection of design:

> [W]hatever does not have a determinate cause happens by accident. Consequently, if [everything arises by chance] all the harmony and usefulness found in things would be the result of chance. This was actually what Empedocles held. He asserted that it was by accident that the parts of animals came together in this way through friendship – and this was his explanation of an animal and of a frequent occurrence! This explanation, of course, is absurd, for those things that happen by chance, happen only rarely; we know from experience, however, that harmony and usefulness are found in nature either at all times or at least for the most part. This cannot be the result of mere chance; it must be because an end is intended. What lacks intellect or knowledge, however, cannot tend directly toward an end. It can do this only if someone else's knowledge has established an end for it, and directs it to that end. Consequently, since natural things have no knowledge, there must be some previously existing intelligence directing them to an end, like an archer who gives a definite motion to an arrow so that it will wing its way to a determined end.[42]

Here Aquinas not only discusses the probabilistic aspect of the detection of intelligent design but also anticipates the modern debate on evolution. Aquinas rejects Empedocles' naturalistic account of the origin of parts of animals that appeals to friendship and chance. Aquinas maintains that the parts cannot come together without an intelligent designer who directs their developments. As we shall see below, Darwin's theory of evolution explains this very point without appealing to the existence of an intelligent designer.

William Paley is arguably the most prominent proponent of the design argument, which he defended in his book *Natural Theology or Evidences of the Existence and Attributes of the Deity, Collected from the Appearances of Nature*. He was also one of the most influential British thinkers in the late eighteenth and early nineteenth centuries.

Paley was born in 1743 in Peterborough, England. His father, a minor canon of the cathedral church, was later appointed headmaster of the free school in the Yorkshire parish of Giggleswick. After studying at his father's school Paley moved on to Christ's College at Cambridge. Observing the intelligence of Paley his father once said, 'My son ... will turn out a great man – very great indeed – I am certain of it, for he has by far the clearest head I ever met with in my life.'[43] Paley's dress and manner were clumsy and his fellow students at Cambridge found his accent provincial, yet they came gradually to be impressed by his intelligence. In 1763 he graduated as Senior Wrangler (an honor bestowed on the highest scorer in the bachelor's mathematics exam). After teaching Latin at Bracken's Academy in Greenwich, he was elected a fellow, and later tutor, of Christ's College. The clarity of his lectures was praised by his students and he earned a reputation as the best lecturer at Cambridge. While teaching there he was ordained and also acquired a master's degree. At Cambridge Paley also joined the Hyson Club, which was involved in the controversy over subscription to the thirty-nine articles. The articles, which were written in 1571, are statements that define the main doctrinal position of the Church of England. In 1774 Bishop Edmund Law published an anonymous pamphlet suggesting a simplification of the thirty-nine articles. This pamphlet was attacked in another anonymous pamphlet published by Thomas Randolph at Oxford. Subsequently, Paley published yet another pamphlet defending Bishop Law's original pamphlet. Paley's pamphlet was, just like the others, anonymous, but its style made clear the identity of the author. This pamphlet created many enemies for Paley. Paley resigned from Christ's College and married Jane Hewitt in 1776. He had a series of ecclesiastical positions throughout his life but because of his controversial views they did not necessarily reflect his impressive accomplishments.

In 1785 Paley published *Principles of Moral and Political Philosophy*, which was based on his lectures at Cambridge. The publisher paid him £1,000 even though he was a new author. This turned out to be a good deal for the publisher. The book became a standard ethics textbook at Cambridge and went through 15 editions in his lifetime. The book has a unique chapter criticizing slavery.[44] Paley was in fact a vocal opponent of the slave trade and was a major spokesman for the anti-slavery movement in the United Kingdom in the late eighteenth century. Paley's wife died in 1791 after a long battle with illness, and he married Catherine Dobinson in 1795.

Paley enjoyed fishing throughout his life. When the Bishop of Durham asked Paley how his manuscript *Natural Theology* – his last and most important work – was going, Paley replied, 'My Lord, I shall work steadily at it when the fly-fishing season is over.'[45] Paley managed to publish *Natural Theology* in 1802 but he was aware that his life was approaching its end. His kidney disease prevented him from carrying out his pastoral duties. Until his death in 1805, however, he was confident in himself. Even a few hours before his death he managed to lift a large pitcher of water to his mouth. He then desired to have his posture changed, but his doctor told him that he would be in danger of death under such an attempt. He responded to the doctor with great calmness and resignation, 'Well, try – never mind.' After some severe convulsions Paley died.[46] He was buried next to his first wife.

In *Natural Theology* Paley introduces the so-called watchmaker analogy:

> In crossing a heath, suppose I pitched my foot against a *stone*, and were asked how the stone came to be there; I might possibly answer, that, for any thing I knew to the contrary, it had lain there for ever: nor would it perhaps be very easy to show the absurdity of this answer. But suppose I had found a *watch* upon the ground, and it should be inquired how the watch happened to be in that place; I should hardly think of the answer which I had before given, that, for any thing I knew, the watch might have always been there.[47]

Paley continues that one can easily know that a watch, unlike a stone, is created by an intelligent designer because it consists of parts that are put together for a specific purpose and the parts are made with materials appropriate for the watch's specific movement. He writes:

> [I]f the different parts had been differently shaped from what they are, of
> a different size from what they are, or placed after any other manner, or
> in any other order, than that in which they are placed, either no motion
> at all would have been carried on in the machine, or none which would
> have answered the use that is now served by it.[48]

Paley's point can be simplified as follows: If its parts had not been
arranged in a specific manner, the watch would not have functioned
properly. Philosophers call this kind of conditional with the following
form a 'counterfactual': if p had (not) been the case q would (not) have
been the case. Paley claims that because the above counterfactual is true
and because a watch does function properly, we can infer the existence of a watchmaker. He maintains further that a parallel argument
can be constructed to prove the existence of an intelligent designer of
the universe. If its parts had not been arranged in a specific manner,
the universe and its inhabitants would not have functioned properly. 'In
every nature, and in every portion of nature', he says, 'we find attention bestowed upon even the minutest parts.' For example, '[t]he hinges
in the wings of an *earwig*, and the joints of its antennæ' are elaborately
designed 'as if the Creator had nothing else to finish'. Because the above
counterfactual is true and because the universe and its inhabitants do
function properly, we can infer the existence of an intelligent designer
(Figure II.3). Paley concludes that it is 'Under this stupendous Being we
live. Our happiness, our existence, is in his hands ... We have no reason
to fear, therefore, our being forgotten, or overlooked, or neglected.'[49]
Paley's work is unique because, unlike Cicero and Aquinas, he formulates his argument by reference to very specific biological features of the
world. That is why Paley's argument is widely regarded as an immediate
precursor to contemporary intelligent design.

Robert Chambers, a nineteenth-century author and publisher, claims,
however, that the watchmaker analogy is not Paley's invention. He advocates
that Paley stole the idea from a book written by Bernard Nieuwentyt, a
Dutch mathematician and physician.[50] Chambers tries to prove his claim by
comparing Paley's and Nieuwentyt's sentences:

Nieuwentyt: So many different wheels, nicely adapted by their teeth to each
other.

Paley: A series of wheels, the teeth of which catch in and apply to each
other.

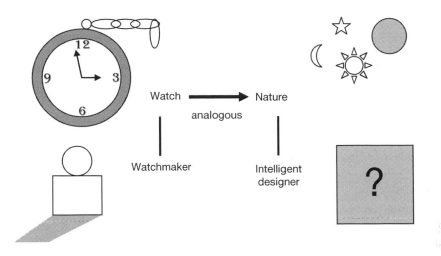

Figure II.3 Paley derives the existence of an intelligent designer of nature by appealing to the watchmaker analogy.

Nieuwentyt: Those wheels are made of brass, in order to keep them from rust; the spring is steel, no other metal being so proper for that purpose.

Paley: The wheels are made of brass, in order to keep them from rust; the spring of steel, no other metal being so elastic.

Nieuwentyt: Over the hand there is placed a clear glass, in the place of which if there were any other than a transparent substance, he must be at the pains of opening it every time to look upon the hand.

Paley: Over the face of the watch there is placed a glass, a material employed in no other part of the work, but in the room of which if there had been any other than a transparent substance, the hour could not have been seen without opening the case.

Some claim that perhaps Paley did not even mean to introduce the watch-maker analogy as his own invention. Paley was renowned for his excellence in presenting existing theories in clear language rather than developing revolutionary ideas. This is manifest in the fact that many of his major works are textbooks which were widely read by students for a long time. Whatever the truth, as we have seen, Cicero had defended essentially the same point more than 1,800 years earlier by referring to an example of a sundial

and a water-clock, which are sufficiently similar to a watch in Paley's and
Nieuwentyt's examples.

Until 1919, more than a century after Paley's death, all students entering
the University of Cambridge were required to pass exams in Greek, Latin,
and mathematics as well as on Paley's *A View of the Evidences of Christianity*. In
fact, as a Cambridge student, Darwin himself was no exception. Darwin is
the one who later effectively refuted Paley's design argument by introducing
the theory of evolution in his *On the Origin of Species*. However, he describes, in
his autobiography, how much he enjoyed reading Paley's work:

> I am convinced that I could have written out the whole of the 'Evidences'
> [by Paley] with perfect correctness, but not of course in the clear language
> of Paley. The logic of this book and, as I may add, of his 'Natural
> Theology', gave me as much delight as did Euclid. The careful study of
> these works, without attempting to learn any part by rote, was the only
> part of the academical course which, as I then felt and as I still believe,
> was of the least use to me in the education of my mind. I did not at that
> time trouble myself about Paley's premises; and taking these on trust,
> I was charmed and convinced by the long line of argumentation. By
> answering well the examination questions in Paley, by doing Euclid well,
> and by not failing miserably in Classics, I gained a good place among the
> oi polloi or crowd of men who do not go in for honours.[51]

Even in a letter that he sent in 1859, only nine days before he published
On the Origin of Species, in which Darwin introduced the theory of evolution,
he wrote, 'I do not think I hardly ever admired a book more than Paley's
"Natural Theology". I could almost formerly have said it by heart.'

5 Objections to the design argument

The eighteenth-century Scottish philosopher David Hume introduced a
number of powerful objections to the design argument in his book *Dialogues
Concerning Natural Religion*.

Hume was born in 1711 in Edinburgh, Scotland. His surname was originally Home but he changed it in 1734 so that it would be easier for the
English to pronounce. He studied law at the University of Edinburgh but
did not find the subject exciting. When he was eighteen Hume had a physical and psychological breakdown, which lasted for nearly five years. In
1734 he wrote a long letter to a physician in London, asking for help. In

this letter he mentions not only his symptoms but also his intellectual life. Hume scholars find the letter interesting because it seems to suggest that Hume discovered the foundation of his philosophical system around that time. Hume's discovery is comparable with the inspiration about a 'marvelous science' that Descartes had, also in his adolescence (see Part I of this book). In the letter to the physician Hume wrote:

> You must know then that, from my earliest infancy, I found always a strong inclination to books and letters. As our college education in Scotland, extending little further than the languages, ends commonly when we are about fourteen or fifteen years of age, I was after that left to my own choice in my reading, and found it incline me almost equally to books of reasoning and philosophy, and to poetry and the polite authors. Every one who is acquainted either with the philosophers or critics, knows that there is nothing yet established in either of these two sciences, and that they contain little more than endless disputes, even in the most fundamental articles. Upon examination of these, I found a certain boldness of temper growing in me, which was not inclined to submit to any authority in these subjects, but led me to seek out some new medium, by which truth might be established. After much study and reflection on this, at last, when I was about eighteen years of age, there seemed to be opened up to me a new scene of thought, which transported me beyond measure, and made me, with an ardour natural to young men, throw up every other pleasure or business to apply entirely to it.[52]

What exactly the phrase 'a new scene of thought' refers to is disputed among Hume scholars. Some of them claim that it refers to the core of the theory of causation that Hume would develop later; others claim that it refers to the new inductive and experimental, as opposed to deductive and conceptual, way of thinking; and some others claim that it refers to the discovery that the idea that judgments of value are based on feeling, rather than rational insight or evidence, can be applied to the theoretical domain as well.[53] In the same year that he wrote this letter, Hume moved to La Flèche in France and wrote his first book, *A Treatise of Human Nature*. It is interesting to note that La Flèche is where Descartes had studied in the previous century.

Hume returned in 1737 and published the *Treatise* subsequently. It was not a success. He writes, 'Never literary attempt was more unfortunate than my

"Treatise of Human Nature". It fell *dead-born from the press*, without reaching such distinction, as even to excite a murmur among the zealots.' It did not take, however, a long time for Hume to recover from the disappointment. '[B]eing naturally of a cheerful and sanguine temper, I very soon recovered the blow, and prosecuted with great ardor my studies in the country.'[54] Ironically, the *Treatise* is today regarded as one of the best philosophy books written originally in English. The following two volumes, *Essays: Moral and Political*, were more successful than the *Treatise* but did not help him to secure a chair at the University of Edinburgh in 1745. Ministers at Edinburgh blocked the appointment, claiming that Hume was an atheist.

Hume revised and expanded the ideas presented in the *Treatise* and published them in two volumes: *An Enquiry Concerning Human Understanding* and *An Enquiry Concerning the Principles of Morals*. Ironically, however, what attracted people's attention to him most was not these philosophical works but his other book project: *The History of England*. This work consists of a massive six volumes, totaling over a million words, which took Hume 15 years to complete.

Hume was never married and lived many years as a tutor, a librarian, and a diplomat. In addition to finding no position at the University of Edinburgh, Hume was rejected in his application to be appointed to a chair at the University of Glasgow. However, he achieved fame and wealth towards the end of his life. The Scottish author and lawyer James Boswell visited Hume near his death and managed to have the last interview with him. As Boswell describes him, '[Hume] was lean, ghastly, and quite of an earthy appearance ... He was quite different from the plump figure he used to present ... He seemed to be placid and even cheerful. He said he was just approaching to his end.' Boswell wondered and asked Hume if he would reject the possibility of an afterlife even with the prospect of death before his eyes. Hume's answer was that while it is 'possible that a piece of coal put upon the fire would not burn' it is 'a most unreasonable fancy that we should exist for ever'. Boswell also asked Hume if the thought of annihilation never gave him any uneasiness. Hume responded, 'not the least; no more than the thought that [I] had not been'. Boswell continued, 'Well, Mr Hume, I hope to triumph over you when I meet you in a future state; and remember you are not to pretend that you was joking with all this infidelity.' 'No, no', said Hume. 'But I shall have been so long there before you come that it will be nothing new.'[55] Hume died in 1776 at the age of 65.

It is difficult to know exactly which objections to the design argument Hume actually endorses because in his *Dialogues* they are all formulated, defended, and criticized in dialogues among fictional characters. In fact it is likely that Hume introduced the objections in this way on purpose. He did not want to criticize arguments for the existence of God openly because to do so would likely have been regarded as blasphemous. Attributing criticisms of the arguments to a fictional character was a convenient way to avoid trouble. To be even more careful, the publisher of the *Dialogues* did not reveal his own or the author's identity.

In what follows we consider objections that are derived from or inspired by Hume's *Dialogues*. For the sake of simplicity, they will be presented as if they are Hume's own objections. However, whether Hume really subscribes to precisely the same objections remains controversial. Also, for the sake of simplicity, the objections are presented as if they have in mind mainly Paley's design argument in *Natural Theology*. It should be noted, however, that Hume's *Dialogues* preceded *Natural Theology*. Hume started writing the *Dialogues* in 1750 but did not finish until 1776, the year he died. They were published posthumously in 1779, which is more than 20 years before Paley's *Natural Theology* was published. *Dialogues*, however, strongly anticipates Paley's argument. Many atheists believe that Hume's objections defeat Paley's as well as many other versions of the design argument.

Objection 1: analogy fails

As we have seen, Paley's argument appeals to an analogy between a watchmaker and the designer of the universe. That is why his argument is sometimes called the 'analogy argument'. The analogy argument has the following generic structure:

1 The universe is similar to a watch.
2 A watch is created by an intelligent designer, in particular, a watchmaker.

Therefore,

3 It is reasonable to conclude that the universe is also created by an intelligent designer.

This argument has the following more general structure:

1 x is similar to y.

2   x has property p (e.g., the property of being created by an intelligent designer).

Therefore,

3   It is reasonable to conclude that y also has property p (e.g., the property of being created by an intelligent designer).

Here is an example of another argument with the same structure:

1   A wolf is similar to a dog.
2   A wolf is a carnivore (i.e., a wolf has the property of being a carnivore).

Therefore,

3   It is reasonable to conclude that a dog is also a carnivore (i.e., a dog also has the property of being a carnivore).

This argument is cogent. However, if an analogy is not appropriate, an argument of the same form could turn out to be uncogent. Consider, for example, the following argument:

1   A bicycle is similar to a tricycle.
2   A bicycle is two-wheeled (i.e., a bicycle has the property of being two-wheeled).

Therefore,

3   It is reasonable to conclude that a tricycle is also two-wheeled (i.e., a tricycle also has the property of being two-wheeled).

Although a bicycle and a tricycle are similar the conclusion does not follow from the two premises. What these examples teach us is that an analogy argument is cogent only if the two items compared are similar *in an appropriate respect*, not merely similar in any arbitrary respect. The above argument about a tricycle is not cogent because a bicycle and a tricycle are not similar with respect to the number of wheels that they have, even though they are similar in other respects, such as the shape of their wheels and seats. So, in order to make an analogy argument sound, the general structure presented above needs to be reformulated as follows:

1   x is similar to y in an appropriate respect.
2   x has property p.

Therefore,

3   It is reasonable to conclude that y also has property p.

For example, the following argument satisfies the above schema:

1   A bicycle is similar to a tricycle with respect to its handlebars.
2   A bicycle has a handlebar with two grips (i.e., a bicycle has the property of having a handlebar with two grips).

Therefore,

3   It is reasonable to conclude that a tricycle also has a handlebar with two grips (i.e., a tricycle also has the property of having a handlebar with two grips).

This argument is cogent. It is not, however, always easy to know in what respect we can appropriately compare two things. Consider Paley's argument again. In what respect should we compare a watch and the universe? It cannot be with respect to the fact that they were both created by an intelligent designer because, if so, Paley has to presuppose that the universe was created by an intelligent designer even before constructing the argument. That would make his argument question-begging.

Hume says that there is no relevant sense of similarity here that allows us to derive the existence of an intelligent designer of the universe. In fact, there are many features of a watch and the universe that are dissimilar. For example, a watch is purely mechanical insofar as it contains no living tissue or parts but the universe, which contains organic matter, is not purely mechanical. To take another example, while the creation of a watch requires pre-existing material, such as gears, hands, glass, and so on, the creation of the universe does not. Many theists think that God created the universe *ex nihilo*, that is, out of nothing. In the case of watch-making, design comes after the creation of the parts, but in the case of the universe, design and the creation of the parts seem to come simultaneously.

Hume also claims that the universe and a watch are dissimilar because, while the creation of the universe is a unique event, which has happened only once, the creation of ordinary objects, such as a watch and a house, has happened many times. When we see a watch we can infer that some watchmaker made it because we have seen many other watches and we know that all of them were built by watchmakers. That is, we make an inference of the following form:

1   We know that Watch 1 was created by a watchmaker.
2   We know that Watch 2 was created by a watchmaker.
3   We know that Watch 3 was created by a watchmaker.

Therefore,

4   It is reasonable to conclude that every watch is created by a watchmaker.

Therefore,

5   It is reasonable to conclude that the watch I have found on the ground was also created by a watchmaker.

The inference from premises (1), (2), and (3) to conclusion (4) is an instance of inductive reasoning; it derives a conclusion about watches in general from premises about particular watches. The inference from conclusion (4) to conclusion (5) is an instance of deductive reasoning because it derives a conclusion about a particular watch from a premise about watches in general.

What is unique about inductive reasoning is that the more observations you have, the more robust your inductive reasoning becomes. Thus the above inductive reasoning about watches becomes more robust as we observe more watches and confirm that they are also created by watchmakers. Hume points out that we cannot construct an instance of strong inductive reasoning to derive the existence of an intelligent designer of the universe because we have never seen other universes that were created by intelligent designers. Paley's inference would be robust if he could form the following inference:

1   We know that Universe 1 was created by an intelligent designer.
2   We know that Universe 2 was created by an intelligent designer.
3   We know that Universe 3 was created by an intelligent designer.

Therefore,

4   It is reasonable to conclude that every universe is created by an intel-
     ligent designer.

Therefore,

5   It is reasonable to conclude that the universe in which we live was also
     created by an intelligent designer.

It is not possible, of course, to form such an inference because our universe
is the only universe that we know.

Is contemporary intelligent design also vulnerable to these criticisms? It
seems not. First, unlike Paley's design argument, the intelligent design argument does not rely on analogy, which could be subjective, in order to detect
design. Instead it relies on properties that can arguably be detected objectively, such as irreducible complexity and specified complexity. Second,
unlike Paley's argument, the intelligent design argument does not focus on
the whole universe. It focuses rather on a very specific biological system,
such as the bacterial flagellum. Therefore, while the objection in question
might refute Paley's design argument it does not refute the contemporary
intelligent design argument.

Objection 2: the argument doesn't prove the existence of God

Hume also contends that *even* if the design argument is successful in deriving
the existence of an intelligent creator, it does not prove the existence of
what Christians believe in, namely a loving God. As we saw above, Paley
says that the argument shows that '[w]e have no reason to fear ... our being
forgotten, or overlooked, or neglected'.[56] Hume maintains, however, that
the argument fails to entail such a claim.

First, Hume contends, the universe cannot be the creation of a loving
God because there are a lot of awful things in the actual world. For example,
many innocent people are killed every year by natural disasters such as earthquakes, floods, and hurricanes. If a loving God were to create a universe He

would create one that is free from these horrible events. Conversely, given that there certainly are horrible events in the actual world a loving God cannot be the creator of the universe. Therefore, Paley's argument proves at most the existence of a designer that is clearly not a loving God.

Second, Hume says, even if we accept Paley's watchmaker analogy, depending on how seriously we take it, we end up deriving a very different conclusion from that of his argument. Usually such complex objects as watches are designed and created by more than one person as a collaborative project and each person in the project is neither all-loving nor all-knowing; after all, they are ordinary humans. They also tend to make many prototypes with defects before producing a perfectly functioning model. If Paley's watchmaker analogy is successful, then perhaps we need to say that a group of multiple intelligent beings, that are neither all-loving nor all-knowing, created many defective prototypes before finally managing to make our properly functioning universe. If that is the case, however, what Paley's argument demonstrates is the existence of something very different from a loving God. Put differently: if we should not ascribe many watchmaker attributes, such as forming a group, creating several defective prototypes, and not being all-loving, to an intelligent designer of the universe, then it is not clear why we should ascribe other specific attributes to it. Paley's use of the watchmaker analogy seems to be very arbitrary.

How could proponents of the design argument respond to Hume? The weakness of his objection is that it is not a criticism of the design argument *per se*. Consider his first point, which says that the intelligent creator, the existence of whom the design argument tries to prove, cannot be a loving God because there are many evil events in this universe. This is actually what philosophers call the problem of evil, according to which, given the existence of evil in this universe, an omniscient, omnipotent, and all-loving God cannot be its creator. Since Paley ascribes omniscience, omnipotence, and all-lovingness to God, he needs to solve the problem of evil in order to defend his theism. However, the problem of evil is distinct from the design argument.

George Berkeley, an eighteenth-century Irish philosopher, encountered and addressed a similar problem in a different context.[57] Some of Berkeley's contemporaries argued that his metaphysical system is untenable because it does not solve the problem of evil. In response to such a criticism, Berkeley did not provide a solution to the problem itself. Instead he pointed out that the problem of evil is something that everyone (or at least every theist) faces and that everyone's problem is no one's problem. That is, the mere fact that Berkeley cannot give an answer to the problem of evil does not undermine his metaphysical system because no one else can answer the problem, either. Paley can respond to Hume's first point in a similar manner here. Hume is right in saying that Paley's design argument cannot be sound unless there is a good solution to the problem of evil. However, that is not an objection to the design argument *per se*. If Hume's point is legitimate, then it can be directed to every single argument for the existence of God as a loving creator. However, it is wrong to characterize the problem of evil as an objection to these specific arguments.

Consider the second point that Hume makes in the above objection, namely that, contrary to what Paley thinks, the design argument does not entail the existence of an all-loving being; it could even entail the existence of a group of intelligent beings rather than that of a single being. This seems to be a good point to make. Paley was too optimistic when he formulated his argument. The argument is not powerful enough to prove the existence of a monotheistic God. If it is successful at all, it proves only the existence of at least one intelligent designer but it does not say exactly how many there are. Moreover, although we can guess that an intelligent designer of the universe is very intelligent and very powerful, we cannot confidently conclude without further argument that it is also all-loving.

Aquinas seems to be more careful in this respect when he defends his version of the design argument. He writes:

> For there is a certain general and confused knowledge of God, which is in almost all men, whether from the fact that, as some think, the existence of God, like other principles of demonstration, is self-evident, as we have stated in the First Book, or, as seems nearer to the truth, because by his natural reason man is able at once to arrive at some knowledge of God. For seeing that natural things run their course according to a fixed order, and since there cannot be order without a cause of order, men, for the most part, perceive that there is one who orders the things that we see. But who or of what kind this cause of order may be, or whether there be but one, cannot be gathered from this general consideration; just as, when we see a man in motion, and performing other works, we perceive that in him there is some cause of these operations which is not in other things, and we give this cause the name of *soul*, but without knowing yet what the soul is, whether it be a body, or how it brings about operations in question.[58]

Here Aquinas seems to agree with Hume's point. From the existence of the ordered universe we can legitimately infer the existence of its cause. However, we cannot know from that fact alone exactly what or who the cause is or exactly how it caused the ordered universe. To discover this we need to undertake additional philosophical or empirical investigations.

Proponents of the contemporary intelligent design argument agree with Aquinas and say that Hume's objection to Paley's argument actually highlights the soundness of their own argument. They argue that even though many, if not most, proponents of the contemporary intelligent design argument believe that the designer in question is God, the argument itself does not say much about the nature of the designer. In particular, as Behe says, it does not say whether the designer is (as we have seen) 'an angel – fallen or not; Plato's demiurge; some mystical new-age force; space aliens from Alpha Centauri; time travelers; or some utterly unknown intelligent being'.[59]

It is interesting to note that our discussion so far reveals an apparent inconsistency in the typical critic's approach to the contemporary intelligent design argument. On the one hand, they often say, as Hume does, that the argument does not prove the existence of *God*; it proves, if anything, merely the existence of an intelligent designer. On the other hand, they also tend to say that the argument should not be taught in schools because it is a theistic argument, i.e., an argument for the existence of God as an object of religious worship.

Objection 3: who created the intelligent designer?

Hume also contends that the design argument is not very helpful because it involves infinite regress. If the universe was created by an intelligent designer, who created the intelligent designer, and who created the creator of the intelligent designer? Suppose that Paley is right in saying that the universe is similar to a watch in an appropriate respect, and that it is reasonable to infer that the universe was created by an intelligent designer, just as a watch was created by a watchmaker. A watchmaker has a functioning body with a complex structure, which makes him intelligent and physically powerful enough to make a watch. This seems to suggest that such a watchmaker was himself created by an intelligent designer. Analogously, the intelligent designer of the universe and its inhabitants must have a functioning body with a complex structure, which makes it intelligent and physically powerful enough to create the universe. This also seems to suggest that the intelligent designer was itself created by an intelligent designer. Thus the claim that the universe was created by an intelligent designer neither proves the existence of God nor solves the origin of everything there is. It only entails an endless chain of designers.

As with the previous objection, this is not an objection to the design argument *per se*, because a similar point can be made against most arguments that conclude that God is the creator of the universe. Consider, for example, the cosmological argument. In his autobiography, the twentieth-century philosopher Bertrand Russell explains that he gave up the First Cause argument, a version of the cosmological argument, on the basis of similar reasoning:

> I may say that when I was a young man and was debating these questions very seriously in my mind, I for a long time accepted the argument of the First Cause, until one day, at the age of eighteen, I read John Stuart Mill's Autobiography, and I there found this sentence: 'My father taught me that the question "Who made me?" cannot be answered, since it immediately suggests the further question "Who made god?"' That very simple sentence showed me, as I still think, the fallacy in the argument of the First Cause. If everything must have a cause, then God must have a cause. If there can be anything without a cause, it may just as well be the world as God, so that there cannot be any validity in that argument. It is exactly of the same nature as the Hindu's view, that the world rested upon an elephant and the elephant rested upon a tortoise; and when they said, 'How about the tortoise?' the Indian said, 'Suppose we change the subject.' The argument is really no better than that. There is no reason why the world could not have come into being without a cause; nor, on the other hand, is there any reason why it should not have always existed. There is no reason to suppose that the world had a beginning at all. The idea that things must have a beginning is really due to the poverty of our imagination. Therefore, perhaps, I need not waste any more time upon the argument about the First Cause.[60]

In order to block this sort of objection proponents of the design argument have to introduce a mechanism to stop the infinite regress. And it is not obvious why they cannot. One possible suggestion is to give a special ontological status to an intelligent designer. So, for example, theists could say that the designer of the universe does not need to be created by someone else because, unlike the universe and its inhabitants, the intelligent designer is not a contingent being but a necessary or self-existing being. While contingent beings like cars, books, planets, human beings, and the universe exist only contingently or accidentally, perhaps the creator of the universe, as a self-existent being, exists necessarily without depending on anything else ontologically. Some claim that the stipulation that the designer exists necessarily is an *ad hoc* response to the objection, but whether there could be necessary beings and whether the designer of the universe can exist necessarily are further questions.

How do contemporary proponents of intelligent design respond to the objection in question? They say they are not concerned with the infinite regress because the sole goal of the argument is merely to show that some intelligent being created the universe. Unlike Paley's argument the contemporary intelligent design argument does not say that the intelligent designer, whose existence the argument entails, must be an ultimate cause. The argument is open to the possibility that the designer is also designed by another intelligent designer, which could be a contingent or necessary being. In other words, the objection in question does not undermine the contemporary intelligent design argument because the conclusion of the argument is more modest than that of Paley's argument.

We have seen that while some of Hume's objections might succeed in refuting Paley's design argument, which tries to prove the existence of God, they do not succeed in refuting the contemporary intelligent design argument, which tries to prove only the existence of an intelligent designer. Another important fact about Hume's objections that we have seen so far is that they are all entirely negative. That is, their goal is merely to locate flaws in the design argument. Thus even if these objections succeed the central mystery remains: what is the cause of the apparent design in nature? Unless Hume provides a plausible account, proponents of the design argument need not give up the notion of an intelligent designer.

In fact, Hume considers a number of naturalistic accounts of the cause of the apparent design in nature. The most plausible one appeals to laws of nature. Newton's three laws, for example, explain relationships between force, mass, inertia, motion, and acceleration, providing the foundations of classical mechanics. Given these simple laws, we can explain, for instance, the formation of the solar system and other galaxies without appealing to the existence of an intelligent designer. In fact, the introduction of an intelligent designer would be redundant given these laws. While the solar system and galaxies apparently exhibit design, no one, even theists, would think that an intelligent designer created them directly. There certainly are natural mechanisms sufficient to produce these complex systems. Similarly, Hume says, the order found in animals and plants should be explained by referring to what he calls 'generation and vegetation', which Hume believes allows us to construct a biological theory that is comparable to Newton's laws in physics. Hume's account of animals and plants is, however, very general and ambiguous. It does not explain, for example, exactly how eyes and wings could be formed through natural processes without an intelligent designer. He tries to find a key in the fact that individual organisms grow and reproduce in their environments, but his account of generation and vegetation does not explain these biological features as clearly and precisely as Newtonian physics explains the motions of planets.

Hume therefore failed to convince proponents of the design argument to give up the existence of an intelligent designer. Critics of the design argument had to wait several decades until Darwin introduced the theory of evolution, which is a convincing alternative to Paley's account of the origin of the biological features of the universe.

6 The theory of evolution

Darwin introduced the theory of evolution in 1859 in his seminal work *On the Origin of Species*. The idea of evolution can be traced back in history much further, however, as far back as Ancient Greece. Anaximander introduced, in the sixth century BCE, the idea that humans evolved from different kinds of animals. An ancient testimony describes Anaximander's theory as follows:

> [Anaximander] declares that in the beginning humans were born from other kinds of animals, since other animals quickly manage on their own, and humans alone require lengthy nursing. For this reason, in the beginning they would not have been preserved if they had been like this.[61]

So Anaximander cites the much longer infancy of human babies, compared with that of other animals he had observed, as evidence that humans had existed in a different state in the past. The following testimonies further explain Anaximander's theory:

> Anaximander says that the first animals were produced in moisture, enclosed in thorny barks. When their age increased they came out onto the drier part, their bark broke off, and they lived a different mode of life for a short time.[62]

> Anaximander ... believed that there arose from heated water and earth either fish or animals very like fish. In these humans grew and were kept inside as embryos up to puberty. Then finally they burst and men and women came forth already able to nourish themselves.[63]

It is remarkable that Anaximander anticipated, however crudely, Darwin's ideas that species evolve and that simple forms precede complex forms.

In *On the Origin of Species* Darwin produced a familiar evolutionary tree, which is also called a 'phylogenetic tree'. The tree is a way of illustrating evolutionary relationships among distinct species in a way that identifies their common ancestors. We can, for example, see on such a tree the evolutionary relationships and common ancestors of birds and mice. Some point out that this way of positioning species in a hierarchical order has its roots in the medieval concept of the 'great chain of being'.[64]

The great chain of being is a pictorial illustration of the relationships that connect all beings, including inorganic substance, plants, animals, human beings, angels, and God. All beings on the chain are ranked in accordance with their attributes. God sits atop the chain because He exemplifies the highest or best possible instance of every attribute. In the chain God is followed by angels, human beings, other animals, plants, and inorganic substance. Just like the phylogenetic tree, the great chain of being displays relationships among distinct beings. Such a hierarchical ordering of individual beings or species was common in religious, philosophical, and political discourse in the medieval period.

As we have seen, the activity of finding connections between beings and presenting their relationships pictorially is nearly as old as human history. In this sense, the basic ideas behind evolution were conceived long ago. Yet these ideas had not been discussed seriously by biologists until the eighteenth century. In the eighteenth century several scientists, including Erasmus Darwin, Charles Darwin's grandfather, tried to develop a proper scientific theory from the idea of evolution. In *Zoonomia* Erasmus Darwin writes as follows:

> From thus meditating on the great similarity of the structure of the warm-blooded animals, and at the same time of the great changes they undergo both before and after their nativity; and by considering in how minute a portion of time many of the changes of animals above described have been produced; would it be too bold to imagine, that in

the great length of time, since the earth began to exist, perhaps millions of ages before the commencement of the history of mankind, would it be too bold to imagine, that all warm-blooded animals have arisen from one living filament, which THE GREAT FIRST CAUSE endued with animality, with the power of acquiring new parts attended with new propensities, directed by irritations, sensations, volitions, and associations; and thus possessing the faculty of continuing to improve by its own inherent activity, and of delivering down those improvements by generation to its posterity, world without end?[65]

Erasmus Darwin focuses here only on warm-blooded animals rather than on all living organisms, but the claim that they might have come from the same ancestor strongly anticipates Charles Darwin's theory of evolution. Erasmus Darwin does not, however, precisely identify a mechanism for evolution. He talks about 'irritations, sensations, volitions and associations' as key factors in evolution but he fails to explain exactly how these phenomena might contribute to the evolution of animals.

Coming up with the basic idea of evolution *per se* is not so difficult. Observations of similarities and dissimilarities between species and individuals across generations give us the intuitive idea that they have evolved into their current forms from common ancestors. However, in order to establish evolution as a proper scientific theory, we must answer the following question: what mechanism preserves specific features of animals and plants while producing changes in their other features?

In 1809, seven years after the publication of Paley's Natural Theology, a French biologist, Jean-Baptiste Lamarck, attempted to answer this question. The core idea of Lamarck's theory, which he introduced in his book Philosophie zoologique, is the 'inheritance of acquired characters'. According to this idea, individual animals and plants develop physiological characters as a result of disease, use/disuse, and accidents and this could eventually contribute to the transformation of their own species. Consider, for example, giraffes' necks. According to Lamarck, their necks are long because their ancestors had stretched their necks so that they could reach leaves of tall trees. Their attempt to stretch their necks throughout generations gradually extended their necks over time and resulted in the long necks that we see today.

Paley mentions, in his Natural Theology, a view that is similar to Lamarck's:

Another system, which has lately been brought forward, and with much ingenuity, is that of *appetencies*. The principle, and the short account, of the theory, is this: Pieces of soft, ductile matter, being endued with propensities or appetencies for particular actions, would, by continual endeavours, carried on through a long series of generations, work themselves gradually into suitable forms: and, at length, acquire, though perhaps by obscure and almost imperceptible improvements, an organization fitted to the action which their respective propensities led them to exert. A piece of animated matter, for example, that was endued with a propensity to *fly*, though ever so shapeless, though no other we will suppose than a round ball, to begin with, would, in a course of ages, if not in a million of years, perhaps in a hundred millions of years (for our theorists, having eternity to dispose of, are never sparing in time), acquire *wings*. The same tendency to locomotion in an aquatic animal, or rather in an animated lump which might happen to be surrounded by water, would end in the production of *fins*: in a living substance, confined to the solid earth, would put out *legs* and *feet*; or, if it took a different turn, would break the body into ringlets, and conclude by *crawling* upon the ground.[66]

Paley rejects the above theory saying, 'The scheme under consideration is open to the same objection with other conjectures of a similar tendency, viz. a total defect of evidence. No changes, like those which the theory requires, have ever been observed.'[67] Yet Lamarck's theory of the inheritance of acquired characters is intuitively plausible and was widely accepted in his time. Even today laypeople often misconstrue Darwin's theory of evolution as advocating something akin to Lamarck's theory. The theory was eventually rejected by biologists, however, because it does not explain how individuals can convey their physiological characters, which are caused by disease, use/disuse, and accidents, to their descendants and ultimately transform their species over time. Darwin's achievement is significant because he finally managed to provide a truly satisfactory solution to this problem by introducing a very simple theory that any intelligent person can understand. It explains, for example, exactly how giraffes' necks could extend little by little over generations.

Charles Darwin was born in 1809 into a wealthy family in Shrewsbury, Shropshire, in England. His father, Robert, and his paternal grandfather, Erasmus (whom we have already encountered), were both physicians. His maternal grandfather, Josiah Wedgwood, was the founder of the renowned Wedgwood pottery firm. Following his father, Darwin studied medicine at the University of Edinburgh, but he found the subject uninteresting. He then switched to study divinity at Christ's College at the University of Cambridge, hoping (somewhat ironically in retrospect) to be trained for the ministry. At Cambridge he deepened his knowledge of zoology and geography. He was then invited in 1831 to join a two-year scientific expedition on HMS *Beagle*. Robert Darwin was unhappy at the prospect of his son's long absence, but Charles Darwin's uncle, Josiah Wedgwood II, persuaded the father to let him go on the trip. Later that year the *Beagle* sailed from Devonport, England. During his trip Darwin was amazed by the rich geographical and biological diversity in nature. He was particularly fascinated by observing distinct forms of finches on the various Galápagos Islands. Darwin noticed that they exhibit variously sized and shaped beaks and that each type is highly adapted to its own environment. This observation inspired him to construct the theory of evolution. Darwin returned to England in 1836 — five rather than two years after his departure.

The British political economist Thomas Malthus maintained in his book *An Essay on the Principle of Population* (first published in 1798) that with unlimited environmental resources the human population would grow exponentially and the world would soon become overpopulated. However, he continued, the propensity of populations to produce more offspring than can possibly survive with the limited resources available to them causes war, famine, and disease, which effectively reduce the size of populations. In other words, war, famine, and disease constitute a 'survival game', which helps in preventing overpopulation.

Darwin read Malthus's book only for amusement. He soon realized, however, that it was relevant to his work because Malthus's theory was also helpful in explaining the diversity of animals and plants. It struck him that given that animals and plants are also involved in similar survival games with limited resources, minute differences among them could be of life-and-death importance. For example, a certain finch might win its survival game because it has a beak of a slightly more advantageous shape than those of others.

Darwin spent more than 20 years developing his ideas and finally announced the theory of evolution in 1858 with Alfred Russel Wallace. Wallace was another biologist, and he arrived at the theory of evolution independently through his fieldwork in the Malay archipelago. In science we occasionally see two or more people reach the same idea at the same time independently. Darwin's and Wallace's paths to evolution represent a particularly remarkable example of this phenomenon. While there are some differences in Darwin's and Wallace's theories, they agreed that their core theses were essentially the same.

Darwin's theory of evolution is based on the idea that all life has descended from a common ancestor. Thus, despite radical differences in appearances, humans, mice, insects, fish, plants, and so on share the same ancestor. Organisms can acquire new traits from mutations in genes or from the transfer of such genes from one population or species to another. Among species that reproduce sexually, organisms can also acquire new traits through genetic recombination. Darwin called the process of preserving beneficial mutations and passing them on to succeeding generations 'natural selection'. (Darwin did not, of course, formulate his theory in terms of genes because On the Origin of Species was published before the birth of genetics.)

Natural selection allows organisms to preserve and accumulate minor genetic mutations that are advantageous for survival. Consider giraffes' necks again. The distant ancestors of modern giraffes had quite short necks. However, by chance some individuals had relatively longer necks. Giraffes with longer necks tended to survive and produce new generations more successfully than shorter-necked giraffes because it was easier for them to reach abundant food in treetops. With each new generation, those surviving offspring with relatively longer necks tended to increase the proportion of long-necked giraffes in the population. Through this gradual process, over time, giraffes acquired very long necks. (The evolutionary process that elongated giraffes' necks is not actually as simple as the description here suggests. For instance, it is not the case that giraffes always eat from treetops. In the dry season they eat from low bushes. In addition, there are biologists who defend alternative variant evolutionary accounts of giraffes' necks. For example, some contend that giraffes developed long necks because it increases the surface areas of their bodies, which is a useful trait in tropical climates. To take another example, some others claim that long necks evolved for fighting because male giraffes use them to club one other. Nevertheless, Darwin's account of the long necks is useful in illustrating the idea of natural selection and, in any case, almost all biologists agree that there is some evolutionary reason that giraffes' necks are so long.)

The theory of evolution explains the magnificent diversity of the natural world with such a simple and elegant idea. When the biologist Thomas Henry Huxley learned the theory of evolution from Darwin, he exclaimed, 'How extremely stupid not to have thought of that!' He also remarked, 'I suppose that Columbus' companions said much the same when he made the egg stand on end.'[68] Julian Huxley, a biologist at Oxford and a grandson of Thomas Henry Huxley, says that Darwin's theory 'is the most powerful and most comprehensive idea that has ever arisen on earth'.[69]

The very last sentence in the first edition of On the Origin of Species read as follows:

> There is grandeur in this view of life, with its several powers, having been originally breathed into a few forms or into one; and that, whilst this planet has gone cycling on according to the fixed law of gravity, from so simple a beginning endless forms most beautiful and most wonderful have been, and are being, evolved.

Curiously enough, Darwin inserted a new phrase in this passage in the second edition, which was published one year later:

> There is grandeur in this view of life, with its several powers, having been originally breathed *by the Creator* into a few forms or into one; and that, whilst this planet has gone cycling on according to the fixed law of gravity, from so simple a beginning endless forms most beautiful and most wonderful have been, and are being, evolved. (Emphasis added.)

Some believe that this insertion shows how much Darwin was pressed by religious believers in response to his theory of evolution. In fact, he once said in a letter that proposing the theory of evolution 'is like confessing a murder'.[70] However, it is not obvious that the above insertion proves that Darwin harbored such a fear. The insertion might merely represent the widely known fact that Darwin himself was always undecided about the existence of God. In a letter of 1879 he wrote as follows:

> It seems to me absurd to doubt that a man may be an ardent Theist & an evolutionist ... But as you ask, I may state that my judgment often fluctuates. Moreover whether a man deserves to be called a theist depends on the definition of the term: which is much too large a subject for a note. In my most extreme fluctuations I have never been an atheist in the sense of denying the existence of a God. – I think that generally (& more and more so as I grow older) but not always, that an agnostic would be the most correct description of my state of mind.[71]

Although, as we have noted, Darwin studied to be an Anglican parson in his youth, he did not seem to be convinced by Christianity. In 1880 he wrote in a letter that, 'I am sorry to have to inform you that I do not believe in the Bible as a divine revelation, & therefore not in Jesus Christ as the Son of God.'[72] It is probably reasonable to assume that Darwin was an agnostic who was sometimes attracted to a non-religious form of theism, such as deism or pantheism.

Darwin suffered from endless pain and illness throughout his life. His health was generally poor and he often had to stay in bed for many months without being able to work. No one knows what caused his illness. Some believe that it had a psychological cause because Darwin himself observed that his condition often worsened following a stimulating event such as a meeting with other people. Others believe that Darwin caught a tropical disease during the *Beagle* expedition. Darwin recalls that he was indeed bitten by insects several times. He tried all sorts of remedies and consulted over 20 doctors but none of them was helpful. He suffered a heart attack and died in 1882 at the age of 73. His last words, spoken to his wife and cousin Emma, were, 'I am not in the least afraid to die.'

As noted above, although Hume provided a number of powerful reasons for rejecting the design argument he failed to provide a compelling positive naturalistic account of the origin of biological organisms. That is why until the mid-nineteenth century most thinkers had not abandoned Paley's theistic account. Paley's account was *prima facie* plausible and also compatible with known scientific facts. Thus even Richard Dawkins, one of the fiercest contemporary critics of the design argument, remarks, 'Paley's argument is made with passionate sincerity and is informed by the best biological scholarship of his day.'[73] It was reasonable for people at the time to accept Paley's account as the best available hypothesis concerning the origin of biological organisms.

However, with the publication of *On the Origin of Species* Paley's theory was no longer tenable, because Darwin finally succeeded in establishing a viable non-theistic account of the origin of biological organisms. Darwin declares his triumph by saying, 'The old argument from design in Nature, as given by Paley, which formerly seemed to be so conclusive, fails, now that the law of natural selection has been discovered.' He continues:

> We can no longer argue that, for instance, the beautiful hinge of a
> bivalve shell must have been made by an intelligent being, like the

hinge of a door by man. There seems to be no more design in the variability of organic beings, and in the action of natural selection, than in the course which the wind blows.[74]

On the Origin of Species marked its 150-year anniversary in 2009. The theory of evolution has been tested constantly by scientists around the world but, according to the vast majority, no piece of empirical evidence has ever contradicted the core of the theory. That is why most scientists regard the teaching of intelligent design with its attempt to identify 'gaps' in the theory of evolution as a major retrogression in scientific education.

7 Judge Jones's verdict on intelligent design

In December 2005 US District Judge John E. Jones III ruled against the teaching of intelligent design in Dover, Pennsylvania. He concluded that the introduction of intelligent design in biology classes violates the Establishment Clause. The Establishment Clause is widely interpreted as prohibiting the teaching of religion in public schools. This was a great victory for the plaintiffs, that is, a group of parents of students enrolled in the Dover Area School district. Because of this historic decision, Judge Jones was named by Time magazine as one of the 100 most influential people of the year.

It was not very surprising that the defendants lost at trial, given that earlier attempts to introduce creationism into biology classes had been consistently unsuccessful. Even worse, they were unable even to mount an impressive case. They had initially designated eight expert witnesses, including some from the Discovery Institute, such as William Dembski, Stephen Meyer, and John Angus Campbell, but only three of the eight ended up testifying. It is not clear why the other five did not testify, but the Discovery Institute mentioned that they were not satisfied with the Dover policy. In particular, they claimed that they never demanded that intelligent design itself should be taught in schools; they only wanted schools to teach that there are gaps in the theory of evolution.

In the 139-page findings of fact and decision, Judge Jones says:

> To conclude and reiterate, we express no opinion on the ultimate veracity of ID [intelligent design] as a supernatural explanation. However, we commend to the attention of those who are inclined to superficially consider ID to be a true 'scientific' alternative to evolution without a

true understanding of the concept the foregoing detailed analysis. It is our view that a reasonable, objective observer would, after reviewing both the voluminous record in this case, and our narrative, reach the inescapable conclusion that ID is an interesting theological argument, but that it is not science.[75]

Judge Jones makes three important points in the above quote: (i) intelligent design is a theological argument; (ii) intelligent design is not science; (iii) the court does not express any opinion about the veracity of intelligent design (as a theological argument).

While the decision prohibiting the teaching of intelligent design in public schools seems reasonable enough, the judge's own arguments for the three points noted above seem surprisingly weak.

(i) *Intelligent design is a theological argument.* Jones says that intelligent design is theological rather than scientific. Many supporters of intelligent design are conservative Christians who want to promote intelligent design because of its consistency with their religious commitments. Recall the Wedge, the top-secret document leaked from the Discovery Institute. The document explicitly says, 'Design theory promises to reverse the stifling dominance of the materialist worldview, and to replace it with a science consonant with Christian and theistic convictions.' It seems practically difficult to present intelligent design as a completely religiously neutral doctrine. This is also manifest in the production of the pro-intelligent design textbook *Of Pandas and People*, which the school board encouraged students to read. A philosopher, Barbara Forrest, went through four different versions of drafts of the book over many years. She discovered in one of them a curious typographical error: 'cdesign proponentsists'.[76] Interestingly enough, this version was written in 1987, almost immediately after the Louisiana case in which the Supreme Court ruled that teaching creationism in public schools violates the Establishment Clause. Forrest cited this instance as evidence that the authors of the book mechanically replaced every instance of the word 'creator' and its cognates with corresponding variations on 'intelligent designer'. In this case the typographical error is the result of unsuccessfully replacing 'creationists' with 'design proponents'. Forrest claims that this typographical error uncovers the link between intelligent design and creationism, the latter of which is clearly religious, even according to many proponents of intelligent design. She maintains that the error proves conclusively that proponents of intelligent design are not being honest when they claim that intelligent design is distinct from creationism.

At one point Judge Jones states, 'ID cannot uncouple itself from its creationist, and thus religious, antecedents', and at another point he states, 'ID is [a] ... theological argument'. These two statements are distinct. All the evidence above motivates the first statement but not the second. Since there is a very close connection between the promotion of intelligent design and the promotion of a particular religious view it is practically (but not necessarily conceptually) impossible to separate intelligent design from religion. That might be a good reason to ban the teaching of intelligent design. However, contrary to Judge Jones's claim, it does not entail that intelligent design itself is a theological argument.

Consider the following historical example. In 1927 a Belgian Roman Catholic priest and astronomer, Georges Lemaître, introduced a precursor of the big bang theory, which he derived from Albert Einstein's general theory of relativity (see the next part of this book for details). Many scientists responded to Lemaître that his theory is religious rather than scientific because he hid a religious motivation to defend it. According to them, he tried to refute the then widely accepted idea that the universe is infinitely old and replace it with the apparently religious idea that the universe was created by some supernatural force some finite amount of time in the past. While Lemaître denied that he had such a religious motivation, whether or not he had it does not determine whether or not his theory itself is religious. After all, no one today thinks that the big bang theory is religious. Similarly, whether or not its proponents have a religious motivation does not determine whether or not intelligent design itself is religious. At least it is formulated in such a way that it does not invoke theistic notions. Thus Judge Jones is not right in calling it a 'theological argument' even though the promotion of intelligent design is *practically* inseparable from a specific religious position.

(ii) *Intelligent design is not science.* The second point that Judge Jones makes is that intelligent design is not science. He writes:

> After a searching review of the record and applicable case law, we find that while ID arguments may be true, a proposition on which the court takes no position, ID is not science. We find that ID fails on three different levels, any one of which is sufficient to preclude a determination that ID is science. They are: (1) ID violates the centuries-old ground rules of science by invoking and permitting supernatural causation; (2) the argument of irreducible complexity, central to ID, employs the same flawed and illogical contrived dualism that doomed creation

science in the 1980's; and (3) ID's negative attacks on evolution have been refuted by the scientific community.[77]

Judge Jones's reasoning seems to be confused. Statement (1) says that intelligent design is not science because it invokes and permits supernatural causation. First, it is false that intelligent design *invokes* supernatural causation, if by that term Judge Jones means entailment or presupposition. While it might be a cheap trick, the theory of intelligent design is formulated purposefully in such a way that it does not require supernatural causation, such as an act of God. Second, while it is true that intelligent design *permits* supernatural causation, the mere permission of supernatural causation does not make a theory unscientific, or so theists such as Judge Jones himself should think. As a Christian, Judge Jones believes in the existence of God as a creator. Thus he has to say that all true theories permit supernatural causation. However, if he says that the mere permission of supernatural causation makes a theory unscientific, he has to accept the disastrous claim that no true theory, not even the theory of evolution, is scientific!

Statement (2) says that intelligent design is not science because it employs a 'flawed and illogical contrived dualism'. Judge Jones does not define what the dualism is, but he refers to the dualism according to which 'one must either accept the literal interpretation of Genesis or else believe in the godless system of evolution'. This view was mentioned in the Arkansas case that we saw earlier. This dualism is, however, irrelevant because intelligent design does not talk about the literal interpretation of Genesis. In fact, many active supporters of intelligent design, such as Michael Behe and William Dembski, reject the literal interpretation. Perhaps it is more charitable to think that what Judge Jones has in mind here is the weaker view that one must either accept theism or else believe in the godless system of evolution. In fact, he contends as follows:

> Both Defendants and many of the leading proponents of ID make a bedrock assumption which is utterly false. Their presupposition is that evolutionary theory is antithetical to a belief in the existence of a supreme being and to religion in general. Repeatedly in this trial, Plaintiffs' scientific experts testified that the theory of evolution represents good science, is overwhelmingly accepted by the scientific community, and that it in no way conflicts with, nor does it deny, the existence of a divine creator.[78]

But it seems far too strong to say that the view that theism and evolution are incompatible is 'flawed and illogical' and 'utterly false'. The compatibility of evolution and theism has long been discussed among philosophers and scientists, and there are many who believe, contrary to what Judge Jones thinks, that they are indeed incompatible. For example, some atheists claim that they are incompatible because the process of natural selection constitutes a strong form of the problem of evil which undermines the existence of God.[79] To take another example, such critics of intelligent design and creationism as Richard Dawkins reject theism precisely because they think that evolution constitutes an empirical refutation of the traditional theistic worldview.

Another related point that tends to be overlooked is that the Dover trial was not the battle between anti-religious scientists and devoted religious believers it is often portrayed as. The defendants are, of course, promoters of intelligent design who are all religious believers. However, the plaintiffs, the parents of students enrolled in the Dover Area School district, and, as mentioned above, Judge Jones himself are also religious believers. Even the biologist Kenneth R. Miller, who, as mentioned below, testified against Behe's claim about irreducible complexity most forcefully, is a Christian theist. He explicitly states, in his testimony, 'I believe that God is the author of all things seen and unseen.' Thus it would be more accurate to describe the Dover trial as a battle between religious believers who support evolution and other religious believers who are critical of evolution.

Finally, Statement (3) says that intelligent design is not science because its negative attacks on evolution have been refuted by the scientific community. This claim seems to be more plausible than (1) and (2), even though the mere fact that intelligent design has been refuted does not entail that intelligent design is not science. This is because whether a theory is true is distinct from whether it is scientific. There are scientific theories that have been refuted; the fact that they have been refuted makes them false but not unscientific. (Similarly, there are true theories that are not scientific; the fact that they are not scientific does not make them false.)

Providing objective criteria on the basis of which to distinguish science from non-science or pseudo-science is a difficult task. This is known as the 'demarcation problem', which philosophers of science have disputed for a long time without reaching a consensus. It seems unlikely that Judge Jones's attempt to provide universal criteria for science and show that intelligent design is indeed not science will settle the dispute among philosophers of science. As we have seen, it was unnecessary to show that intelligent design is not science in order to exclude it from public schools.

(iii) *The court does not express any opinion about the veracity of intelligent design (as a theological argument)*. Judge Jones says that while the court concludes that intelligent design is not science it does not decide whether it is cogent. This is because not being science is a sufficient reason to ban the teaching of intelligent design in public schools. This seems to be a strategic mistake, however, because it is much more difficult to show that intelligent design is not science than to show that it has not been established as a powerful hypothesis. As mentioned above, there is no consensus about how to demarcate science from non-science in spite of a long history of philosophical dispute. On the other hand, there is a wide consensus among the majority of scientists that, whether or not it is science, intelligent design has not been established as a viable alternative to evolution.

As we saw earlier, one of the central notions in intelligent design is irreducible complexity, which was introduced by Behe. He tries to establish intelligent design by showing that some organisms are irreducibly complex. His prominent example is the bacterial flagellum. He maintains that the theory of evolution is not correct because there cannot be a step-by-step account of the evolution of the bacterial flagellum. In particular, given that the bacterial flagellum is irreducibly complex, it cannot have any functional precursors that are missing one or more of its parts. If we remove one part of the flagellum it loses its function completely.

One of the witnesses for the plaintiffs was Kenneth R. Miller from Brown University. As a biologist, his main job at the trial was to refute Behe's argument. Miller maintained that, contrary to what Behe says, scientists have indeed found a functional precursor to the flagellum: the type III secretory system (TTSS). The TTSS consists of a smaller subset of the full complement of proteins in the flagellum. The system, which has a syringe mechanism, injects protein toxins into cells; this could cause serious harm to the human body. The syringe of the TTSS corresponds to the pump of the flagellum that powers the motor that runs the flagellum. Behe might be right in saying that the bacterial flagellum is irreducibly complex if we focus only on the motor function of the flagellum. However, that is not the right way of looking at the flagellum. There is a functional precursor of the flagellum, namely, the TTSS, that uses the same parts for a different function: syringing. Scientists are still discussing whether the TTSS is really a precursor to the bacterial flagellum but it is much more plausible to think that it (or something that is sufficiently similar to it) is a precursor, than that an intelligent designer created the flagellum. In order to illustrate his point, Miller draws an analogy. Perhaps, as Behe says, a mousetrap is an irreducibly complex system if we focus only on the parts of the mechanism in virtue of which it is able to trap a mouse and define that as its function. However, we can imagine a precursor of a mousetrap consisting of a subset of its parts but with an entirely different function. At trial Miller demonstrated this by showing everyone a bulky tie clip that he was wearing, which was essentially a mousetrap with some missing parts! What Miller showed is not that intelligent design is not science but that it has not been established as a viable alternative to evolution.

Our discussion seems to entail the following: (a) it is *practically* impossible to separate intelligent design from associated religious activities, even though there is no immediate conceptual connection between intelligent design and religion; (b) intelligent design has not been established in the scientific community as a serious alternative to evolution.

These two conclusions seem to be sufficient to exclude intelligent design from biology classes in public schools. That is, it was unnecessary for Judge Jones to risk provoking additional controversies by claiming that intelligent design is a theological argument or that it is 'utterly false' that evolution and theism are incompatible. He could have said instead that, whether or not it is science, intelligent design has not been established as a viable alternative to evolution. In order to establish intelligent design as a rigorous scientific theory its proponents need to do much more empirical research and publish a substantial number of papers in mainstream peer-reviewed journals in relevant fields. If they accomplish that much, it might finally be reasonable to separate intelligent design from associated religious activities and consider it for inclusion in public school science curricula. Until then, we do not need to introduce it in biology classes, just as we do not need to introduce many other speculative hypotheses that have not been established.

Antony Flew said that he converted from atheism to theism because he followed Socrates' principle, 'follow the evidence wherever it leads'. He believed that the best available biological evidence led him to intelligent design, which he thought entailed theism and, in particular, deism. Flew, however, seemed to have lost his way at the end of his life. First, as proponents of intelligent design keep emphasizing, intelligent design itself does not entail theism; thus he did not need to give up atheism, which he had defended for a long time. Second, if Flew had followed the best available biological evidence he would have reached evolution rather than intelligent design.

PART III

THE BIG BANG, INFINITY, AND THE MEANING OF LIFE

That anything exists at all does seem to me a matter for the deepest awe.

J. J. C. Smart

I should say that the universe is just there, and that's all.

Bertrand Russell

1 The big bang

In the autumn of 1849 Edgar Alan Poe, one of the best-known American mystery writers, was involved in an event as mysterious as any in his novels. He suddenly disappeared for three days. People had seen him behaving drunkenly at a birthday party but no one knew where he went afterwards. A few days later he was found semi-conscious on a street in Baltimore. Strangely enough, he was wearing clothes that did not seem to belong to him. It was unclear what had happened to him because he was not coherent enough to explain anything about his condition or his recent whereabouts. He was taken to the Washington College Hospital but died four days later. Some claim that he was murdered; some claim that he was overly drunk; some claim that he was ill.

One year before his death, Poe wrote a piece of non-fiction entitled *Eureka*, with two subtitles: *A Prose Poem* and *An Essay on the Material and Spiritual Universe*.[1]

In this work, based on a lecture he gave in the same year, Poe speaks of 'the Physical, Metaphysical and Mathematical – of the Material and Spiritual Universe; of its Essence, its Origin, its Creation, its Present Condition and its Destiny'.

Many readers thought that Poe was not very serious about this work. For example, one of the philosophers mentioned in it is a Turkish man called 'Aries Tottle', who can 'expel superfluous ideas through the nose'. Although *Eureka* was not well received, Poe regarded it as the best work of his entire career. A long time passed before people realized that *Eureka* was indeed an impressive work containing a number of insightful ideas. The most important idea in the work is a cosmological theory according to which there was only 'Oneness' or a 'primordial particle' at the birth of the universe. This particle's existence is, Poe says, 'sufficient to account for the constitution, the existing phaenomena and the plainly inevitable annihilation of at least the material Universe'. The current state of the universe can be explained, according to Poe, by reference to a force that makes the primordial particle into 'the abnormal condition of Many'. Almost 80 years after Poe died, a similar theory was introduced by scientists. This theory is known today as the 'big bang theory'.

In 1927 a Belgian Roman Catholic priest and astronomer, Georges Lemaître, introduced the 'hypothesis of the primeval atom', which he derived from Albert Einstein's general theory of relativity. According to this hypothesis, the universe has been expanding since its birth. This means that, moving the clock backwards, the universe used to be a highly compressed 'cosmic egg', which expanded at the moment of creation. Einstein was skeptical about this hypothesis because he believed, as did most cosmologists at the time, that the universe as a whole was always in an unchanging, steady state. However, the big bang theory, which is based on Lemaître's original hypothesis, is now *the* most widely accepted theory concerning the earliest stage of the universe.

The big bang theory says that approximately 15 billion years ago the universe existed as a state of infinitesimal density and temperature called a 'singularity'. The entire universe itself was extremely hot and compressed to a size smaller than a pinhead. Over time, according to the theory, it has expanded into the vast and cooler universe that we inhabit now. The fact that the universe is expanding also entails that the universe is not infinitely large. On the contrary, it is spatially and temporarily limited.

There is considerable theoretical and empirical evidence for the big bang theory, but the following three phenomena represent the strongest lines of evidence:

1   *Hubble's discovery.* If we observe through a spectroscope an object that is moving away from us, the wavelength of the object shifts toward the red end of the spectrum. (On the other hand, if we observe an object that is moving toward us, the wavelength of the object shifts toward the blue end.) This is the Doppler effect, the basis of the design of radar guns used by police to measure the speed of cars. In the 1920s Edwin Hubble observed that the colors emitted by distant galaxies are shifted consistently toward the red end of the spectrum. This observation supports the hypothesis that the universe is expanding. Hubble's law states that the observed velocities of galaxies are proportional to the distances from the galaxies to us. That is, the further away the galaxies are, the faster they move away from us.

2   *The abundance of helium.* On the one hand, the universe is uniformly abundant with helium. At the same time, however, stars could not very easily have produced so much helium in 15 billion years. The big bang theory provides a promising answer to this problem. According to the theory, the high density and temperature at the very early stages of the universe, a time that is sometimes referred to as the 'first three minutes', were ideal for making helium from hydrogen, and thus a large proportion of the helium we now observe could have been produced then. Spectroscopic observations of stars and galaxies show that the universe consists of about 75 percent hydrogen and 24 percent helium. This is consistent with what the big bang theory predicts.[2]

3   *Cosmic microwave background radiation.* If the big bang really occurred, the universe must have been extremely hot at the beginning. The existence of the cosmic microwave background radiation indeed confirms the high temperature of the universe at its birth. In 1964 Arno Penzias and Robert Wilson at Bell Telephone Laboratories used an antenna to study radio emissions from the Milky Way. Their antenna received strange random signals. When they found droppings from pigeons in the horn of the antenna, they thought they had identified the source of the signals. However, even after shooing the pigeons away the signals remained. They discovered later that the signals were actually caused by 2.725° K cosmic microwave background radiation, which represents

the enduring echoes of the big bang. In 1978 Penzias and Wilson were awarded the Nobel Prize in Physics for this discovery.

The big bang theory is also indirectly supported by our everyday, or, more precisely, every-night, observations. Most of us take it for granted that the sky is dark at night. But why is it so? One might think that it is because there is no sunlight at night, but this is not a satisfactory answer. Suppose for a moment that the distribution of stars is more or less the same throughout the universe and that the universe is infinitely old and infinitely large. Imagine now a spherical shell containing the earth at its centre and many other stars elsewhere. If we double the radius of the shell, then, according to Isaac Newton's inverse-square law, stars in the enlarged shell will be only one quarter as bright as they were in the original shell. At the same time, however, there will be four times more stars in the larger shell than in the original shell. This means that the overall contribution of stars to the brightness of the night sky remains the same. As we continue expanding the shell in this manner the brightness of the night sky must increase indefinitely. However, the sky is mostly dark at night. This puzzle is called 'Olbers' paradox', named after a German astronomer.

In *Eureka*, Poe anticipated a satisfactory solution to Olbers' paradox. He writes:

No astronomical fallacy is more untenable, and none has been more pertinaciously adhered to, than that of the absolute *illimitation* of the Universe of Stars. The reasons for limitation, as I have already assigned them, *a priori*, seem to me unanswerable; but, not to speak of these, *observation* assures us that there is, in numerous directions around us, certainly, if not in all, a positive limit – or, at the very least, affords us no basis whatever for thinking otherwise. Were the succession of stars endless, then the background of the sky would present us an uniform luminosity, like that displayed by the Galaxy – *since there could be absolutely no point, in all that background, at which would not exist a star*. The only mode, therefore, in which, under such a state of affairs, we could comprehend the *voids* which our telescopes find in innumerable directions, would be by supposing the distance of the invisible background so immense that no ray from it has yet been able to reach us at all. That this *may* be so, who shall venture to deny? I maintain, simply, that we have not even the shadow of a reason for believing that it *is* so.

Poe's answer to Olbers' paradox is that the night sky is mostly dark because the universe has a positive limit. Since the universe is only finitely old and finitely large there cannot be infinitely many stars. Thus it is not the case that if we draw a line towards the sky, no matter the direction, we hit a shining star eventually. There are many lines that do not hit a shining star before reaching the end of the universe. The darkness of the sky indirectly supports the big bang theory, according to which the universe is spatio-temporarily finite.

Scientists who are skeptical about the big bang theory have introduced alternatives. One of the most prominent of these theories is the steady state theory introduced by Fred Hoyle, Thomas Gold, and Hermann Bondi, which will be discussed in detail below. In 1949, when Hoyle was on a BBC radio program, he referred rather cynically to the theory that he was criticizing as 'the big bang idea'. Since then the term 'the big bang' has been used universally. This term is misleading, however, because it gives the impression that there was an enormous explosion at the beginning of the universe. When matter explodes it blasts out from a central location and quickly fills up any empty space around it. The big bang is therefore not an instance of an explosion, because it does not fill up empty space that is already there; the big bang is an *expansion* of space and time. Some people have thought, therefore, that the name 'the big bang' should be replaced with something more appropriate. In 1993 *Sky and Telescope* magazine organized a contest to choose a new name. Readers from 41 countries submitted over 13,000 entries, which include 'Hubble Bubble', 'The Bottom Turtle', 'Super Seed', 'Planck Point', and 'You're Never Going to Get It All Back in There Again'. The judges, Carl Sagan, Hugh Downs, and Timothy Ferris, struggled to choose the best one. At the end they decided that the winner was not among those who submitted the entries but someone who did not even participate in the contest – namely, Fred Hoyle! They concluded that 'big bang' was after all the best name.[3] (Hoyle was an interesting figure in the context of our discussion; he was critical not only of the big bang theory but also the theory of evolution. He believed that life began in space under the direction of an intelligent designer. See the quotation from him at the beginning of Part II of this book.)

Many scientists, including Hoyle, found the big bang theory unbelievable because they had thought that the universe was eternal and homogeneous – that is, that the universe had always existed and that its overall state always remained the same without any beginning or end. On the other hand, many theists were pleased with the big bang theory because it seemed to be compatible with what they had believed: the universe was created by God in the finite past. When Lemaître introduced a prototype of the big bang theory many critics alleged that his theory was religious rather than scientific. That is, they claimed that Lemaître, as a Roman Catholic priest, defended the theory on the basis of his religious commitment, rather than genuine scientific interest. Lemaître denied this allegation: 'As far as I can see, such a theory remains entirely outside any metaphysical or religious question. It leaves the materialist free to deny any transcendental Being.'[4]

Pope Pius XII, however, was excited about the idea of the big bang and explicitly claimed that it supports arguments for the existence of God. He remarked, 'true science discovers God in an ever increasing degree – as though God were waiting behind every door'.[5] He told the Pontifical Academy of Sciences that Thomas Aquinas's 'proofs' of God as an unmoved mover were now reinforced by the new scientific discoveries. In response to the question 'what preceded time?', the pope said:

> [A] creative omnipotence whose power ... called to existence, through an act of love, matter and exuberant energy. Modern science bears witness to that primordial order of 'Let there be light' when nuclear particles broke forth from inert matter and ... radiated forth, reuniting into galaxies.

He continued:

> What, then, is the importance of modern science for the argument for the existence of God based on the mutability of the cosmos? By means of exact and detailed research ... it has considerably broadened and deepened the empirical foundation on which this rests ... It has, besides, followed the course and the direction of cosmic developments and ... pointed to their beginning in time some five billion years ago. Thus, with that concreteness which is characteristic of physical proofs, it has confirmed the contingency of the universe and also the well-founded deduction as to the epoch when the cosmos came forth from the hands of the Creator.[6]

The pope concluded, 'Hence, creation took place in time. Therefore, there is a creator, therefore, God exists.'

The pope's reasoning seems too facile. Since, as Lemaître correctly says, the big bang theory itself is distinct from theism, accepting the theory does not in itself commit one to affirm the existence of God. Nevertheless, the scientific discovery of the spatio-temporal limit of the universe does seem to have implications for the argument for the existence of God that the pope has in mind, namely, the cosmological argument.

Over the last few decades the philosopher William Lane Craig has argued that the big bang theory is particularly useful in strengthening a unique version of the cosmological argument called the 'Kalām cosmological argument'. This argument was originally introduced by medieval Islamic theologians, most notably Abū Ḥāmed Muḥammad ibn Muḥammad al-Ghazālī, but Craig revived and reinforced it in the 1970s. The big bang theory is one of two great scientific developments that Craig utilizes in order to strengthen the Kalām cosmological argument. The other development that he utilizes is the mathematics of infinity.

2 Infinity

The concept of infinity was already a subject of intellectual discussion in Ancient Greece. Anaximander of Miletus said that the fundamental principle of the world is the *apeiron*, or the infinitude. Anaximander regarded the *apeiron* as something that exists eternally without decaying and generates materials perpetually. For Anaximander the *apeiron* was the principle underlying an endless series of cycles in nature and human existence.

Zeno of Elea is another ancient Greek philosopher who was fascinated by the concept of infinity. He introduced a series of paradoxes that illustrate the perplexity of infinity. One of the best known is called the 'paradox of dichotomy'. Aristotle describes the paradox as 'the argument which says that there is no motion because that which is moving must reach the midpoint before the end'.[7] Suppose you are running. In order to reach your destination, you need to reach the halfway point between your starting point and the destination. But in order to reach the halfway point, you need to reach the halfway point to the halfway point. However, in order to reach the halfway point to the halfway point, you need to reach the halfway point to the halfway point to the halfway point, and so on *ad infinitum*. This means that in order to travel a finite distance one has to travel an infinite number of finite distances, which seems impossible.

While the puzzling nature of infinity had been discussed by philosophers – including Aristotle, Aquinas, and Kant – throughout history, it was not very seriously discussed among mathematicians until relatively recently.

Georg Cantor is the mathematician who developed a rigorous and systematic foundation for the mathematical study of infinity. His system answers a number of perennial questions about infinity.

Cantor was born in St. Petersburg, Russia, in 1845. His father, born a Jew, was a Danish merchant who converted to Protestantism; his mother was a Roman Catholic who converted to Protestantism upon marriage. The family moved to Germany when Cantor was a young boy and he stayed there for most of the rest of his life. In 1862 he entered the University of Zurich but transferred to the University of Berlin to study mathematics, physics, and philosophy. He was awarded a doctorate in 1867 but he encountered difficulty in securing an academic position. He was employed as an unpaid lecturer, and later as an assistant professor, at the University of Halle. He was unhappy with his job at Halle; he thought that he deserved a better position at a more prestigious university. Nevertheless he made a number of important discoveries at Halle. For example, he discovered there that the set of natural numbers (i.e., {1, 2, 3, 4, 5, ...}) had the same number of members as the set of even numbers greater than zero (i.e., {2, 4, 6, 8, 10, ...}) He also discovered that there is a one-to-one correspondence of points on a line segment and points in a square, or points in any n-dimensional space. He could discover these facts because he invented a mathematical method that could be used to measure and compare infinitely large sets of different kinds. Cantor was very surprised by some of his own discoveries. In a letter to the mathematician Richard Dedekind, Cantor wrote famously, 'I see it, but I don't believe it!'

Most mathematicians at the time, however, did not take the concept of infinity seriously; talking about infinity was almost taboo in mathematics. Carl Friedrich Gauss, one of the most influential mathematicians of the nineteenth century, remarked:

> I protest against the use of infinite magnitude as something completed, which in mathematics is never permissible. Infinity is merely a *façon de parler*, the real meaning being a limit which certain ratios approach indefinitely near, while others are permitted to increase without restriction.[8]

Gauss's remark assumes the distinction between actual infinity and potential infinity that we will address below. It is alleged that Henri Poincaré had a similar opinion about infinity and expressly criticized Cantor's set theory, saying that later generations would regard it as 'a disease from which one has recovered'.[9] Despite all the criticisms, Cantor was very confident in his work on infinity. He wrote:

> My theory stands as firm as a rock; every arrow directed against it will return quickly to its archer. How do I know this? Because I have studied it from all sides for many years; because I have examined all objections which have ever been made against the infinite numbers; and above all because I have followed its roots, so to speak, to the first infallible cause of all created things.[10]

In the second half of his life Cantor suffered from severe depression. Some claim that it was triggered by the ill-treatment at the hands of other mathematicians that he had experienced. Leopold Kronecker, Cantor's former teacher and an influential mathematician at the University of Berlin, was particularly harsh on Cantor, criticizing him publicly. He attacked Cantor by calling him a 'scientific charlatan', a 'renegade', and a 'corrupter of youth'.[11] Cantor always wanted to escape from Halle and secure a more prestigious academic position, but Kronecker's attack made such a move impossible. Others claim that Cantor's depression was caused by the difficulties of his mathematical work. He was particularly tormented by the 'continuum hypothesis' that he himself introduced in 1877. This hypothesis is concerned with the ordering of infinite sets of unequal sizes. The hypothesis says, roughly speaking, that there is no set whose size (cardinality) is greater than the size of the set of natural numbers but smaller than the size of the set of real numbers. (Real numbers are numbers that can be written in decimal notation, including ones that need infinite decimal expansion (e.g., 0.455342709932 ...).) At one time Cantor thought that he had succeeded in proving the hypothesis, but he then found a mistake in his proof. At another time he thought that he had succeeded in disproving the hypothesis but, again, he found a mistake in his disproof. It is not surprising that Cantor could neither prove nor disprove the hypothesis. Indeed, the very fact that he could not determine the truth or falsity of the hypothesis shows that he was on the right track. Nearly a half century after Cantor's death it was shown through work done by Kurt Gödel and Paul Cohen that the hypothesis can be neither proved nor disproved using standard Zermelo–Fraenkel set theory. Tiring of incurring the hostility of fellow mathematicians, Cantor shifted his interests to two other domains. The first was literature. He tried to prove that Francis Bacon was the real author of Shakespeare's works. In 1896 and 1897 he published pamphlets defending his Bacon–Shakespeare theory. (The philosopher Friedrich Nietzsche was another prominent defender of that theory.) Cantor's second interest, one that absorbed him utterly, involved tracing out the religious implications of his work on infinity. He enjoyed discussing them with theologians and philosophers and even sent a letter and pamphlets about the issue to Pope Leo XIII. Cantor held that his mathematical work on infinity did not undermine God's infinity because God's infinity is the 'absolute infinite', which transcends other forms of infinity. Cantor even believed that he had succeeded in establishing his set theory thanks to God's help. He wrote, 'I entertain no doubts as to the truth of the transfinites, which I have recognized with God's help and which, in their diversity, I have studied for more than 20 years; every year, and almost every day brings me further in this science.'[12] Cantor recognized himself as a servant and messenger of God. He believed that he had been unable to secure a prestigious academic position, which would have allowed him to concentrate on research in pure mathematics, because God wanted him to work on theological issues instead. He remarked:

> Now I only thank God, the all-wise and all-good, that He always denied me the fulfillment of this wish [for a university position at either Göttingen or Berlin], for He thereby constrained me, through a deeper penetration into theology, to serve Him and His Holy Roman Catholic Church better than I would have been able to with my probably weak mathematical powers through an exclusive occupation with mathematics.[13]

Cantor was hospitalized many times before his death. His mathematical work finally attracted the attention it deserved towards the end of his life, but it was too late to redeem his broken life. He became ill and the deprivations of the First World War prevented him from taking in enough nutrition. Cantor did not manage to get out of Halle and died of a heart attack in a psychiatric institution in 1918.

Contrary to Poincaré's prediction, people today do not regard Cantor's work as 'a disease from which one has recovered'. On the contrary, they regard it as among the most original and important contributions ever made to the foundation of mathematics.

Consider the set of natural numbers {1, 2, 3, 4, 5, ...} and the set of even numbers greater than zero {2, 4, 6, 8, 10, ...}. Which is larger? One might think that the set of natural numbers is twice as large as the set of even numbers greater than zero because that is true in the case of finite sets. For example, the set of natural numbers up to 10, {1, 2, 3, 4, 5, 6, 7, 8, 9, 10}, has twice as many members as the set of even numbers greater than zero up to 10, {2, 4, 6, 8, 10}. According to Cantor, however, when it comes to infinity, the set of natural numbers is only as large as the set of even numbers greater than zero because there is a one-to-one correspondence between these two sets (Table III.1).

There is always an even number greater than zero to pair up with a natural number and we never exhaust them. This means that there are as many even numbers greater than zero as there are natural numbers. A set that has as many members as that of the set of natural numbers or its subset is called a 'countable set'. So, the set of natural numbers and the set of even numbers greater than zero are both, of course, countable sets. Does this mean that all infinite sets are countable sets? In other words, are all infinite sets of the same size with the same number of elements? Surprisingly enough, Cantor's answers to these questions are negative. He says that there are sets that are larger than countable sets. To take one example, the set of real numbers is larger than countable sets, despite the fact that they both contain infinitely many members.

Consider, for the sake of simplicity, the set consisting only of real numbers between the interval of 0 and 1. If we think that there is a one-to-one correspondence between natural numbers and real numbers between 0 and 1 we might construct a table as shown in Table III.2.

Cantor says, however, that there cannot be a one-to-one correspondence between these two sets because there is always a real number that does not have a corresponding member in the set of natural numbers. In order to specify what such a real number looks like, Cantor uses a technique called 'diagonalization' (Table III.3).

Table III.1   There is a one-to-one correspondence between the set of natural numbers and the set of even numbers greater than zero

Natural numbers		Even numbers greater than zero
1	↔	2
2	↔	4
3	↔	6
4	↔	8
5	↔	10

Table III.2   Is there a one-to-one correspondence between the set of natural numbers and the set of real numbers?

Natural numbers		Real numbers
1	↔	0.5072900061 …
2	↔	0.3842400493 …
3	↔	0.3123218343 …
4	↔	0.9727118554 …
5	↔	0.8824634206 …
6	↔	0.7123219138 …

Write '0.' on a piece of paper. Now focus on the diagonal numbers that are shown in bold in Table III.3. The first number is 5, which is in the first decimal place of the first real number; the second number is 8, which is in the second decimal place of the second real number; the third is 2, which is in the third decimal place of the third real number; and so on. Adding 1 to each of these numbers, we obtain 6, 9, 3, and so on. If we write these numbers after '0.' we obtain '0.693872 …'. This number with infinitely many digits never appears in Table III.3, no matter how complete it is. This is because we constructed the number in such a way that any number that could appear in the table would be different from it with respect to at least one of its digits. However, if the set of real numbers between 0 and 1 was only as large as the set of natural numbers, the situation would not be like this because in such a case there should be a one-to-one correspondence between these numbers. The set of real numbers between 0 and 1 and, consequently, the set of real numbers are, therefore, larger than the set of natural numbers. That is, the set of real numbers is not a countable set. This is a remarkable discovery because it shows that there are different sizes of infinity.

Table III.3   Cantor uses the diagonalization method to prove that there cannot be a one-to-one correspondence between the set of natural numbers and the set of real numbers

Natural numbers		Real numbers
1	↔	0.**5**072900061 …
2	↔	0.3**8**42400493 …
3	↔	0.31**2**3218343 …
4	↔	0.972**7**118554 …
5	↔	0.8824**6**34206 …
6	↔	0.71232**1**9138 …

By definition, infinity is indefinitely large. So it sounds absurd to say, 'Which one is larger between Set 1 with infinitely many members and Set 2 also with infinitely many members?' Yet Cantor has shown in a mathematically rigorous manner that such a question is legitimate in certain cases and that Set 1 could be larger than Set 2 or vice versa.

Given Cantor's theories of infinity it is possible to perform arithmetical operations on the sizes of infinite sets. Symbolize the size of an infinitely large countable set, such as the set of natural numbers, as '$\aleph_0$' (reads 'aleph null' or 'aleph zero'). Then, for instance, the following are true:

(1) $\aleph_0 + n = \aleph_0$.
(2) $\aleph_0 + \aleph_0 = \aleph_0$.

Equation (1) means, roughly speaking, that a countable infinity plus a finitude is a countable infinity. So, even if you add, say, five members to the set of natural numbers the size of the set does not change. People often find this counterintuitive because the same calculation does not apply to finite sets. For example, if we add five members to a set of 10 members, then the size of the set will increase to 15. Equation (2) means, roughly speaking, that a countable infinity plus a countable infinity is a countable infinity. So, even if you double the size of the set of natural numbers, the size of the set does not change at all. People find this also counterintuitive because, again, the same calculation does not apply to finite sets. For example, if we double the size of a set of five members, the size will increase to 10. Equation (2) implies the following:

(3) $\aleph_0 + \aleph_0 + \aleph_0 = \aleph_0$.

Equation (2) is equivalent to the following:

(4) $\aleph_0 \times 2 = \aleph_0$.

And 3 is equivalent to the following:

(5) $\aleph_0 \times 3 = \aleph_0$.

From this we can guess:

(6) $\aleph_0 \times n = \aleph_0$.

And (6) is indeed true, where n is any natural number. Any number multiplied by zero is zero, so the following is true:

(7) $\aleph_0 \times 0 = 0$.

How about the operations of subtraction and division? They are prohibited conventionally because they do not produce consistent results. Consider, for example, the following:

(8) $\aleph_0 - \aleph_0$.

Equation (8) gives different results depending on what sort of sets we have in mind. For example, if we subtract the size of the set of natural numbers, $\{1, 2, 3, \ldots\}$, from the size of the set of natural numbers, $\{1, 2, 3, \ldots\}$, then we obtain 0, so $\aleph_0$ minus $\aleph_0$ is 0. However, if we subtract the size of the set of natural numbers that are greater than 2, $\{3, 4, 5, \ldots\}$, from the size of the set of natural numbers, $\{1, 2, 3, \ldots\}$, then we obtain $\{1, 2\}$, so $\aleph_0$ minus $\aleph_0$ is 2. If we subtract the size of the set of even numbers greater than zero, $\{2, 4, 6, \ldots\}$, from the size of the set of natural numbers, $\{1, 2, 3, \ldots\}$, then we obtain the size of the set of odd numbers $\{1, 3, 5, \ldots\}$, so $\aleph_0$ minus $\aleph_0$ is $\aleph_0$. Thus we cannot obtain consistent results for subtraction.

Equation (6) says '$\aleph_0 \times n = \aleph_0$'. This means, for example, that the following are true:

(9) $\aleph_0 \times 5 = \aleph_0$
(10) $\aleph_0 \times 6 = \aleph_0$.

From (9) and (10) we might think we can derive the following, respectively:

(11) $\aleph_0 / \aleph_0 = 5$
(12) $\aleph_0 / \aleph_0 = 6$.

Thus we do not obtain consistent results for division, either.

As mentioned earlier, the big bang theory and the mathematics of infinity represent two main developments in science to which contemporary proponents of the *Kalām* cosmological argument appeal. Before introducing the *Kalām* cosmological argument itself, however, we need to review the history of the cosmological argument in all its forms.

3 History of the cosmological argument

The cosmological argument is as old as any of the other major arguments for the existence of God. One of the earliest formulations of the argument can be found in the work of Plato.

Plato was born in 427 or 438 BCE in Athens to a wealthy, aristocratic family. 'Plato' was not his real name. His real name was 'Aristocles', after his grandfather. According to one story, his wrestling coach, Ariston of Argos, gave him the name 'Plato', meaning 'broad', on account of his robust body. Plato was obviously very athletic; some even believe that he was a champion wrestler.[14] The son of a politically powerful family, Plato, as a young man, turned naturally to politics as well as writing poetry and tragedies. His life was shaped more profoundly, however, by his acquaintance with Socrates. Plato would eventually witness Socrates' death, as a result of which he would devote himself to writing philosophical dialogues which record Socrates' teaching. Through the dialogues Plato succeeded in reviving Socrates and his philosophy. The public welcomed Plato's work and presumably demanded that he write more. Socrates continued appearing in Plato's later dialogues but scholars agree that in the later dialogues Plato voiced his own ideas and theories through the character of Socrates. Socrates the dialogic character therefore represents two different philosophers – Socrates himself and his student Plato – throughout a series of dialogues. Plato's dialogues are the oldest philosophical works that have survived intact. Although Plato is an early figure in the history of philosophy, his work is far from immature. The twentieth-century philosopher Alfred North Whitehead once remarked, 'The safest general characterization of the European philosophical tradition is that it consists of a series of footnotes to Plato.'[15] Plato is also regarded as one of the founders of the Western education system. In 387 BCE he established the Academy in Athens, where students and teachers devoted themselves to research and teaching in science and philosophy. It is alleged that Plato wrote the later dialogues in his final years at the Academy. He died in 347 BCE at around the age of 80, leaving the Academy to his nephew Speusippus. The Academy existed for over 900 years until the sixth century, when it was closed down by the Christian Emperor Justinian.

The *Laws* is Plato's longest and last dialogue. In this work an 'Athenian stranger', who reminds us of Socrates, and Cleinias discuss, among many other subjects, the existence of gods. Cleinias attempts to prove the existence of gods as follows:

> Well, just look at the earth and the sun and the stars and the universe in general; look at the wonderful procession of the seasons and its articulation into years and months! Anyway, you know that all Greeks and all foreigners are unanimous in recognizing the existence of gods.[16]

As scholars point out, this passage seems to combine two arguments for the existence of gods.[17] The first is a version of the design argument, according to which the beauty and the ordered structure of nature prove the existence of gods. The second is the argument from consensus, according to which the fact that everyone, even foreigners with different cultural backgrounds and ways of thinking, recognize the existence of gods. The Athenian stranger, however, rejects these arguments:

> When you and I present our proofs for the existence of gods and adduce what you adduced – sun, moon, stars and earth – and argue they are gods and divine beings, the proselytes of these clever fellows will say that these things are just earth and stones, and are incapable of caring for human affairs, however much our plausible rhetoric has managed to dress them up.[18]

The Athenian does not deny that the beauty and the structured order of nature indicate the existence of gods, but he thinks that the above-mentioned arguments would not convince people who are already committed to atheism. They would simply say that nature consists of material objects like earth and stones, in which there is no sign of the intelligence or care of gods. An argument for the existence of gods has to be powerful enough to convince atheists who find nothing religiously significant in earth and stones. The Athenian then endeavors to replace these unconvincing arguments with a version of the cosmological argument, which he finds much more powerful than Cleinias' arguments.

The Athenian tries to derive the existence of the gods by focusing on the fact that some things in the universe are in motion. The Athenian introduces two kinds of motion: (i) communicated motion, which imparts motion to something else and is itself changed by another thing; and (ii) self-generated motion, which moves both itself and other things. The Athenian argues that the ultimate source of all motion must be self-motion:

> [W]hen we find one thing producing a change in another, and that in turn affecting something else, and so forth, will there ever be, in such

a sequence, an original cause of change? How could anything whose motion is transmitted to it from something else be the *first* thing to effect an alteration? It's impossible. In reality, when something which has set itself moving effects an alteration in something, and that in turn effects something else, so that motion is transmitted to thousands upon thousands of things one after another, the entire sequence of their movements must surely spring from some initial principle, which can hardly be anything except the change affected by self-generated motion.

What then is the self-generated motion? The Athenian identifies it with a soul, because anything self-moving must be alive. Moreover, he says, such a soul must be a special kind of soul:

[T]he whole course and movement of the heavens and all that is in them reflect the motion and revolution and calculation of reason, and operate in a corresponding fashion, then clearly we have to admit that it is the best kind of soul that cares for the entire universe and directs it along the best path.[19]

The Athenian concludes that his argument, unlike Cleinias', shows that there are intelligent, caring gods. This is what is known as Plato's cosmological argument.

As we saw in Part I of this book, the ontological argument is an *a priori* argument. That is, it derives the existence of God without relying on any empirical findings. The cosmological argument is an *a posteriori* argument because, unlike the ontological argument, but like the design argument, it does appeal to empirical findings, namely the existence of the universe and the motion of objects in it. Any argument with at least one *a posteriori* premise is an *a posteriori* argument (although having at least one *a priori* premise does not make an argument *a priori* — an *a priori* argument can have only *a priori* premises).

The core of Plato's cosmological argument was revived by Thomas Aquinas as the first of his 'Five Ways' to prove the existence of God. Therefore, as we see later, most objections to the First Way are equally applicable to Plato's version of the argument.

Thomas Aquinas was born in 1225. He is commonly referred to as 'Aquinas' but that represents his residence rather than his surname. Aquinas's father was count of Aquino and his mother was countess of Teano. After being trained by the Benedictine monks in Monte Cassino, Aquinas was sent to the University of Naples in 1236. There he met John of St. Julian, a Dominican preacher.

In the early 1240s Aquinas received the habit of the order of St. Dominic, which did not make Aquinas's family happy. Fearing that Aquinas's mother might try to change his mind, the Dominicans sent Aquinas to Rome and then to Paris or Cologne. While Aquinas was drinking from a spring near the town of Aquapendente his brother captured him and took him back to Monte San Giovanni, where his parents lived. Aquinas's family detained him for two years and tried hard to persuade him not to join the Dominicans. His brother even hired a beautiful prostitute to seduce him. Aquinas managed to drive the prostitute from his room with an iron from the fire. Immediately after this incident Aquinas prayed to God. He fell into a gentle sleep and two angels appeared. They told him that his prayer had been heard. The angels placed around his waist a white band and said 'We gird thee with the girdle of perpetual virginity.' After that Aquinas never experienced any temptation of the flesh. Aquinas's mother concluded that her family's efforts had failed and she let Aquinas escape.

In 1245 Aquinas was enrolled at the University of Paris, where he met Albertus Magnus, a Dominican scholar. Magnus had profound knowledge of not only theology and philosophy but also chemistry, astronomy, and biology. He was a well-known advocate of the compatibility of religion and science. It is reported that Magnus made an automaton that spoke like a woman and showed it to Aquinas. Aquinas demolished it, claiming it was satanic. Following Magnus, Aquinas moved to Cologne and taught there as an apprentice professor. In 1256 Aquinas was appointed regent master at Paris, where he began writing the first of his two most important works, Summa contra Gentiles. He completed the work after returning to Naples. In 1265 he moved to Rome to establish a stadium, an institution of higher learning, and began writing the second of his most important works, Summa Theologica, in which he introduced the Five Ways to prove the existence of God. He stayed in Rome until 1268, when he was called back to Paris. In 1272 he established a stadium in Naples and worked there as regent master.

Aquinas continued writing but something strange happened to him towards the end of his life. In 1274 he suddenly stopped working. His companion Reginald of Piperno asked Aquinas why he would leave Summa Theologica unfinished if it was nearly done. Aquinas replied to him, 'I cannot, because all that I have written now seems like straw.' This kind of pessimistic remark was not typical of Aquinas, who was known for his strength and liveliness.

Some attributed Aquinas's depression to a possible nervous breakdown or a stroke. In fact, people thought that he did not look very well physically at the time. It seems, however, that something philosophically or religiously significant had happened to him. Not satisfied with Aquinas's response to his questioning, Reginald begged for further explanation. Aquinas finally responded, 'Everything that I have written seems to me as worthless in comparison with the things I have seen and which have been revealed to me.'[20] With this remark Aquinas was evidently referring to a number of religious experiences that he had had throughout his life. As he grew old he seems to have had them more frequently and often more intensely. Before he stopped working in 1273 he had a particularly long religious experience that made him question his scholarly work. In Part I of this book we discussed Pascal's religious experience. When Pascal had the mystical experience he was confident that what he encountered was not the God of the philosophers but the God of Abraham, Isaac, and Jacob. That is, he thought that what he encountered through the experience was fundamentally distinct from the concept of God that philosophers and theologians discuss in a scholarly manner. Aquinas's religious experience seems to have made him realize much the same thing. Summa Theologica is regarded as one of the most important works of the Middle Ages; it provides a very comprehensive and thorough philosophical and theological treatment of the existence and nature of God and Christian doctrines. Aquinas thought, however, that what he addressed in the work was completely different from the God that he experienced directly and vividly.

After this incident his health worsened. One day when he was riding on a donkey he was hit on the head by a tree branch and fell off the donkey. Staying with his niece at the castle of Maenza, Aquinas was aware that his life was approaching its end. He said, 'If the Lord is coming for me, I had better be found in a religious house than in a castle.'[21] He was thus taken to the Cistercian Fossanova Abbey and died there. He did not complete Summa Theologica.

As mentioned above, Aquinas introduces in Summa Theologica the 'Five Ways' to prove the existence of God, which can be summarized as follows:

- First Way: the argument from motion
- Second Way: the argument from causation
- Third Way: the argument from contingency
- Fourth Way: the argument from perfection
- Fifth Way: the argument from design

Let us briefly consider the Fourth and Fifth Ways first, because they are not directly relevant to the cosmological argument.

The Fourth Way tries to demonstrate the existence of God by referring to the existence of the 'gradation' of properties. We compare properties of objects in everyday life. For example, we say that A is better than B, or that A is more beautiful than B. Aquinas maintains that 'more' and 'less' are predicated of things in accordance with their resemblance to something that is the corresponding maximum. That is, according to Aquinas, when we say that A is more beautiful than B, for example, we mean that A is closer to the most beautiful thing than B is. If this is correct, then there must be something that is maximally good, beautiful, and so on. Such a being is, Aquinas says, God. This is a unique argument for the existence of God, which tends to be neglected.

The Fifth Way tries to prove the existence of God by appealing to the 'governance of the world'. Aquinas says that even natural bodies that lack intelligence act in such a way that they obtain the best result. However, Aquinas says, without intelligence nothing can move towards the end unless it is directed by something with knowledge and intelligence. Therefore, Aquinas concludes, there must be an intelligent being that directs natural bodies to their end, and that being must be God. This is a version of the design argument that we saw in Part II of this book.

Again, our focus here is on the first three ways because they are versions of the cosmological argument. In the First Way, Aquinas refers to motion in the universe. There are many things in the universe that are in motion, such as people, clouds, and planets. Suppose that object A is in motion. This means that A must be put in motion by another object in motion, call it B. Given that B is also in motion, however, B itself must be put in motion by something else, call it C. Given that C is also in motion, however, C itself must be put in motion, and so on. Aquinas claims that the regress cannot continue infinitely because there would then be no first move and, consequently, no movement to start the chain of movements in the first place. This contradicts the obvious fact that there *are* things in motion right now. Therefore, Aquinas concludes, there must be a first mover, which 'everyone understands to be God'.[22] This argument is similar to Plato's cosmological argument.

The Second Way is comparable to the First Way, but it is formulated in terms of causation rather than motion. We see in nature chains of efficient causes, which bring about something or change something, and their effects. In these chains efficient causes are causes of certain effects as well as effects of some other efficient causes. As in the case of motion, a chain of efficient causes cannot be traced back infinitely. Suppose that there is no ultimate cause. Then there is no effect and hence there cannot be any intermediate efficient causes. Therefore, Aquinas concludes, a first efficient cause must exist, 'to which everyone gives the name of God'.[23]

In the Third Way, Aquinas focuses on the distinction between necessity and possibility. Most, if not all, things in the universe exist only contingently, that is, it could have been the case that they do not exist even though, as a matter of contingency, they do. For example, the rose in my garden exists only contingently because it would not have existed had no one planted it there. Nelson Mandela exists only contingently because he would not have existed had his parents never met. Aquinas says that since all these things are contingent they cannot exist all the time. This means, he continues, that there must have been a time when no contingent beings existed. However, if there was a time when no contingent beings existed and if everything is contingent, then it would have been impossible for any contingent being that we see now to have been brought into existence. It would be a pure mystery why contingent beings like the rose in my garden and Mandela exist now. This means, according to Aquinas, that not everything is contingent; there is something that exists necessarily. He claims that such a necessary being exists of its own necessity without relying on any other being. Therefore, Aquinas concludes, what 'all men speak of as God' exists.[24]

The Third Way seems to be the least compelling one among the above three. Let us briefly review several objections to it before focusing on the other two.[25]

First, it is not clear why there has to be a time when nothing exists if everything in the universe is contingent. Even if we grant that the universe is eternal and that everything in the universe is contingent, we can conceive of the eternal history of the universe where there is always at least one contingent being. As Graham Oppy says, even if for each contingent being there was a time it did not exist, it doesn't follow that there was a time when no contingent beings existed.[26] There is nothing incoherent in the notion of an infinite temporal chain of contingent beings. For example, we can conceive of the following situation: contingent being A exists for a certain period of time. At the same time that A ceases to exist another contingent being B comes into existence. (Perhaps the disappearance of A causes the appearance of B.) B remains existent for a certain period of time. At the same time that B ceases to exist another contingent being C comes into existence, and so on. This situation contradicts Aquinas's claim that if everything is contingent there has to be time when nothing exists.

Second, Aquinas's Third Way seems to mix up the notions of contingent existence and non-eternal existence. In particular, the Third Way assumes that no contingent beings can exist eternally, which is far from obvious. Using the terminology we introduced in Part I of this book, contingent beings are those that exist in some but not all possible worlds. Mandela is a contingent being because while he exists in the actual world he does not exist in a world in which, for example, his parents did not meet. (On the other hand, necessary beings are those that exist in all possible worlds. God is, according to many theists, a necessary being insofar as He exists in all possible worlds.) Contingent existence does not entail non-eternal existence, nor does the latter entail the former, because we can conceive of a being such that: (i) it exists in some but not all possible worlds and (ii) it exists eternally. Such a being is an eternal contingent being. Arguably, we can also conceive of a being such that: (i) it exists in all possible worlds and (ii) it does not exist eternally. Such a being is a non-eternal, non-contingent (necessary) being. This means, contrary to the presupposition of the Third Way, that contingent existence and non-eternal existence are distinct notions.

Aquinas's First and Second Ways seem to be more powerful than the Third Way; in fact they number among the most common formulations of the cosmological argument. Both of them try to prove the existence of God by appealing to the impossibility of infinite regress. Let us examine existing objections to them in greater detail. Notice that these objections are equally applicable to Plato's cosmological argument because that argument is similar to Aquinas's First Way.

Objection 1: is Aquinas's conception of causation correct?

Aquinas's Second and Third Ways are based on the ordinary conception of causation, according to which every motion or effect has a cause. One might try to undermine both ways by rejecting such a conception. David Hume, for example, allegedly proposes an alternative notion of causation that would seem to refute Aquinas's conception. Considerable controversy remains about the correct interpretation of Hume's texts, but according to one interpretation, he advances the following idea: our inductive reasoning is based on our observation of events. In particular, it is based on our experience of the 'constant conjunctions' of events. After repeated observations of one billiard ball hitting another billiard ball, for example, we think that the movement of the second billiard ball is caused by the impact with the first billiard ball. Upon reflection, however, we realize that we cannot see the power, force, or whatever it is that causes the second billiard ball to move on impact. All we see is that the second billiard ball moves whenever the first billiard ball hits it. We have developed a concept of causation by observing such sequences of events many times, but in itself our attribution of causation amounts to nothing but the mental act of associating one event with another. If we look at causal events in this way, Aquinas's ordinary conception of causation does not seem to be correct.

Hume is right in thinking that we can conceive of a scenario in which there is an appearance of causation even though relevant causation is completely absent. For example, we can conceive of a scenario in which a billiard ball appears to cause the movement of another billiard ball merely because the two balls are elaborately controlled by magnets hidden under the table. Nonetheless, though this kind of scenario is certainly conceivable and possible, it still appears impossible that there can be an effect or motion without any cause at all.

Hume's notion of causation is controversial because it is a version of skepticism, which flies in the face of our common sense. This, of course, does not mean that Hume's notion is incorrect, but one possible reply is that even if Hume is right in denying that our concept of causation corresponds to something real in the world, his argument does not prove that causation is an illusion. Through his method he can prove only that we cannot know with certainty that causation is real, and this weakens his argument as an objection to the First and Second Ways.

Objection 2: why is infinite regress impossible?

Aquinas says that there must be a first cause because an infinite regress of motions and causes is absurd. But why is it absurd? Some philosophers and scientists believe that the universe is eternally old. If the universe is eternally old, then it does not seem to be absurd to think that the regress of motions and causes traces back down an infinitely long chain.

Aquinas thinks that the absurdity of an infinite regress of motions and causes stems from the idea that such a sequence has no beginning. If there is no beginning, he claims, there cannot be a first motion or cause to start with. If there is no first motion or cause to start with, he continues, there cannot be any motions and effects right now. Critics might respond, however, that this claim makes sense only for a finite regress of motions and causes. It is certainly true that any *finite* chain of motions and causes must have a first motion or cause to initiate the chain. An infinite regress of motions and causes does not have a first motion or cause, however, critics might say, precisely because it is infinite. As we shall see below, the *Kalām* cosmological argument addresses this difficulty by explaining more thoroughly why an infinite regress cannot be realized in the actual world. In order to do that, the argument appeals to the mathematics of infinity.

Objection 3: what caused God?

On the face of it, in defending the First and Second Ways Aquinas assumes that everything has to be caused by something else. He seems to think that there cannot be any motions or effects without causes. However, by saying that God does not need any cause Aquinas seems to be contradicting his own assumption. If *everything* is caused by something else, God has to be caused by something else as well. Thus the introduction of God, or anything else, does not help to eliminate the infinite regress.

Aquinas thinks that this is not a tenable objection because it overlooks the fundamental ontological difference between God and contingent beings. God, unlike contingent beings, exists necessarily. That is why, Aquinas says, only God can be the first cause and the cause of His own existence. He does not need an external cause to bring about His existence, because He Himself is the cause.

It is, however, unclear why only God can have such a special ontological status. Some atheists might claim that if theists are allowed to stipulate that God exists necessarily they are equally allowed to stipulate that the universe exists necessarily. If God is, as Anselm says, that-than-which-no-greater-can-be-thought or, as Descartes says, a supremely perfect being, then perhaps God must exist necessarily. However, that does not rule out that the universe also exists necessarily. As we see below, the *Kalām* cosmological argument is carefully formulated so as to avoid this objection.

If Aquinas is a representative medieval proponent of the cosmological argument, Gottfried Wilhelm Leibniz is a representative early modern proponent.

Leibniz was born in Leipzig in 1646. His father Friedrich Leibniz was a professor of moral philosophy and his mother Catharina Schmuck was a daughter of a prominent lawyer. Leibniz's father died when Leibniz was six years old, and hence he was raised by his mother. Leibniz was deeply influenced by her moral and religious views. His father left a personal library, from which Leibniz benefited intellectually when he was small.

Leibniz entered the University of Leipzig at the age of 12 and earned a bachelor's degree in philosophy in 1662, a master's degree in philosophy in 1664, and a bachelor's degree in law in 1665. He was refused the doctorate in law at Leipzig, so he moved to the University of Altdorf and received a doctorate in law there in 1667. He was promised a chair at Altdorf but declined the offer. His first job, brief though it was, was that of secretary to a society of alchemists at Nuremberg. When he was young Leibniz had a passion for alchemy and even wrote several papers on the subject. Later, however, he abandoned alchemy, claiming that it was nothing but superstition. Leibniz was soon after hired by Baron Johann Christian von Boineburg, a former chief minister of the elector of Mainz. In the following few years Leibniz worked on a number of political and scientific projects. One of his most prominent projects at the time was the development of a calculator. Inspired by a pedometer that he saw in Paris he decided to make a calculator that could perform addition, subtraction, multiplication, and division. He completed the design of his calculator by 1674 and had a craftsman in Paris build a prototype. He called the machine the 'Stepped Reckoner'. Only two units have survived to the present day. One of them was found in 1879 in an attic at the University of Göttingen while a worker was fixing a leak in the roof. This unit is now housed in the State Museum of Hanover. The other one is housed in the Deutsches Museum in Munich. (It is interesting to note that Pascal, another prominent figure in the philosophy of religion, also built a calculator, which he called the 'Pascaline'. Unlike Leibniz's Stepped Reckoner, the Pascaline could perform only addition and subtraction.) Leibniz also invented the modern form of the binary numeral system, which is used in electronic computers today. He did not incorporate his binary arithmetic into his calculator, but had he done so perhaps he could have invented something comparable to modern digital computers. He built a calculator because, he says, 'it is unworthy of excellent men to lose hours like slaves in the labor of calculation which could safely be relegated to anyone else if machines were used'.[27]

Another of Leibniz's great contributions to science was the development of calculus. It is now widely agreed among historians of science that Leibniz and Newton invented the foundations of calculus independently. At the time, Newton believed that Leibniz stole his ideas. Apparently Newton's work preceded Leibniz's, but Leibniz published his work before Newton published his. Today Leibniz's rather than Newton's notation is commonly used in mathematics.

In 1676 Leibniz was appointed librarian to the duke of Brunswick in Hanover and retained the position until his death. In his spare time he read and wrote about many topics and made significant contributions in numerous fields including geology, linguistics, historiography, mathematics, physics, philosophy, theology, etymology, genealogy, history, politics, and economics. Leibniz never married and died in Hanover in 1716 at the age of 70. Few of his writings were published when he was alive and many of them remain unpublished. However, his work was known internationally because he corresponded with many important intellectuals of his time.

The only philosophy book that Leibniz published when he was alive is *Essays on Theodicy, Concerning the Goodness of God, the Freedom of Man, and the Origin of Evil*, in which he addresses the problem of evil. The problem asks why there are evil events in the actual world if an omnipotent and omnibenevolent God is its creator. Many philosophers have tried to respond to this problem by arguing that it is not God's fault that the actual world is not the best possible world but rather it is the fault of free human beings who perform morally wrong actions.[28] Leibniz, however, responds to the problem of evil by insisting that this is the best possible world. He says that given that God is an omnipotent and omnibenevolent creator this *must* be the best possible world. According to Leibniz, evil events are necessary to maximize the goodness of the world. That is, a removal of an instance of evil in the actual world would diminish, rather than increase, the overall greatness of the world. Similarly, the addition of a good event would diminish, rather than increase, the greatness of the actual world.

Leibniz tried to prove the existence of God by advancing yet another form of the cosmological argument. While Leibniz's argument initially appears similar to Aquinas's Third Way, it has its own unique features. The first unique feature is that it is formulated in terms of an *explanation* of the origin of the universe rather than in terms of motions and causes in the universe. The second unique feature, which is more distinctive, is that it relies on the following principle:

> The Principle of Sufficient Reason: No fact can be real or existing and no statement true unless it has a sufficient reason why it should be thus and not otherwise.[29]

According to Leibniz, there are two kinds of truths: truths of reasoning and truths of fact. Truths of reasoning are necessarily true and their denials are impossible. A truth of reasoning can be analyzed 'in resolving it into simpler ideas and into simpler truths until we reach those which are primary'. The simplest ideas, as well as axioms and postulates in mathematics, represent the primary principles that do not require any proof. On the other hand, truths of fact are only contingently true and their denials are possible; these truths require a sufficient reason.

Imagine, Leibniz says, that there is a copy of a geometry book on a desk. The existence of the copy on the desk is a truth of fact because it could have been the case that there is no copy on the desk. If someone asks why there is a copy on the desk it is not satisfactory to answer, 'it just exists there without any reason'. Such an explanation violates the principle of sufficient reason. What if, then, someone explains as follows: 'the copy is made from an older copy of the same book, and the older copy is made from an even older copy of the same book, and so on, *ad infinitum*'. Leibniz says that such an explanation is also unsatisfactory because it does not explain why there could be any copy in the first place, arguing that this example is analogous to the origin of the universe. When Bertrand Russell, a prominent atheist philosopher, had a famous debate on the existence of God with Father Frederick C. Copleston on BBC radio in 1948 he said 'the universe is just there, and that's all'. Leibniz would not accept such a claim because it violates the principle of sufficient reason. According to Leibniz, the existence of the universe comprises truths of fact which demand sufficient reasons outside the universe. Leibniz contends, 'the ultimate reason for things must be a necessary substance, in which the detail of the changes shall be present merely potentially, as the fountain-head, and this substance we call God'.[30] Leibniz thinks that God qualifies as the sufficient reason for the existence of the universe because He is a necessary being that is its own sufficient reason. As we shall see below, Leibniz's insights are applied in the *Kalām* cosmological argument.

4 The *Kalām* cosmological argument

In the late 1970s the American philosopher William Lane Craig wrote a massive doctoral dissertation on the cosmological argument at the University of Birmingham in the United Kingdom under the supervision of John Hick, one of the most influential contemporary philosophers of religion. Craig's dissertation was later published as two books: *The Cosmological Argument from*

Plato to Leibniz and *The Kalām Cosmological Argument*. As the title suggests, Craig defended the *Kalām* cosmological argument in the latter.

As mentioned earlier, the *Kalām* cosmological argument was originally introduced by medieval Islamic theologians. The argument had been neglected for a long time, but Craig sheds light on it by clarifying its structure and improving its strengths significantly. In particular, he tries to strengthen one of the premises of the argument by adapting the two modern scientific developments that we saw above: the big bang theory and the mathematics of infinity. In addition, the argument appeals to a version of the principle of sufficient reason.

The *Kalām* cosmological argument is strikingly simple; it consists of only two premises and a conclusion:[31]

1   Whatever begins to exist has a cause of its existence.
2   The universe began to exist.
3   Therefore, the universe has a cause of its existence.

This argument is formally valid, which means that if the premises, (1) and (2), are true, then it logically follows that the conclusion, (3), is also true. How then can we show that the premises are true?

Premise (1) is a version of the principle of sufficient reason, the principle that Leibniz used to construct his version of the cosmological argument. It seems easy to accept this premise intuitively. Things around us, such as tables, chairs, cars, plants, and animals have not been in existence eternally. They began to exist at some point. We all know that they have causes of their existence; they do not just pop into being. It would be absurd to say, for example, that a giant crocodile could suddenly come into existence in front of us without any cause. Premise (1) is also supported inductively: we have encountered uncountably many things throughout the history of the human race but we have never seen anything that came into existence without any cause.

Recall Leibniz's original formulation of the principle of sufficient reason: 'No fact can be real or existing and no statement true unless it has a sufficient reason why it should be thus and not otherwise.' Premise (1) is slightly different because, unlike Leibniz's formulation, it focuses on things that *begin* to exist and it is formulated in terms of cause rather than reason or explanation.

Arguably, premise (2), that the universe began to exist, is more controversial than premise (1). Some people would reject premise (2) right away because they believe that the universe is infinitely old. Craig tries to convince such people of the truth of premise (2) by providing several sub-arguments for it. Let us examine three of them.

Sub-argument A: argument based on the impossibility of an actual infinity

Craig formulates the first sub-argument for premise (2) as follows:

(2.11)   An actual infinity cannot exist.
(2.12)   An infinite temporal regress of events is an actual infinity.
(2.13)   Therefore, an infinite temporal regress of events cannot exist.
(2.14)   Therefore, the universe began to exist.

In the above argument, Craig relies on the distinction between potential infinity and actual infinity. A potential infinity is a process that comes closer and closer to infinity but never reaches it. Consider a computer monitor that displays a natural number and increments it every second. Starting with '1', it displays '2' after one second, '3' after two seconds, '4' after three seconds, and so on. This is an example of potential infinity. The number displayed on the monitor comes closer and closer to infinity every second, but there will be no time when it actually displays an infinitely large number. An actual infinity is, on the other hand, a completed process that has actually reached infinity. For example, if you can have infinitely many marbles in your bag, then the number of marbles in the bag is an actual infinity. It is not that there are merely many, many marbles in your bag. There are *actually* infinitely many marbles in your bag. Premise (2.11) of the above argument says, however, that an actual infinity, such as a bag of infinitely many marbles, cannot exist. In order to show that, Craig appeals to the so-called Hilbert's Hotel, which was originally introduced by the German mathematician David Hilbert.

According to the 2008 edition of *Guinness World Records*, the largest hotel by number of rooms is the First World Hotel in Malaysia. This hotel in Genting Highlands, known as the 'Las Vegas of Malaysia', has 6,118 rooms. Suppose, for the sake of simplicity, that all 6,118 rooms are guest rooms and that each of them can accommodate only one person. This means that if there are 6,118 people staying in the hotel, then the manager of the hotel cannot check in a new guest until someone checks out and the number of occupants becomes 6,117 or less. Hilbert's Hotel is, however, very different. It is much larger than the First World Hotel; in fact, it is *infinitely* larger than that. It is not that Hilbert's Hotel has 1,000 rooms, 1 million rooms, or 1 trillion rooms. It has infinitely many rooms. Suppose that the hotel is completely full at the moment because infinitely many people are staying there. Now imagine that a new guest arrives and asks for a room (Figure III.1).

What is surprising is that despite the fact that all the rooms are occupied, the manager of the hotel can check in the new guest. All he need do is move a guest from room 1 to room 2, another from room 2 to room 3, another from room 3 to room 4, and so on. As a result, room 1 will be vacant and the manager can accommodate the new guest there (Figure III.2). However counterintuitive this is, it would be a possible scenario if it were possible for an actual infinity to exist because, as we saw earlier, according to Cantor, $\aleph_0 + n = \aleph_0$, that is, roughly speaking, a countable infinity plus a finitude is a countable infinity. The situation could be even stranger. Suppose that the hotel is completely full but an infinite number of new guests arrive and ask for rooms. The manager can still check them in by moving a guest from room 1 to room 2, another from room 2 to room 4, another from room 3

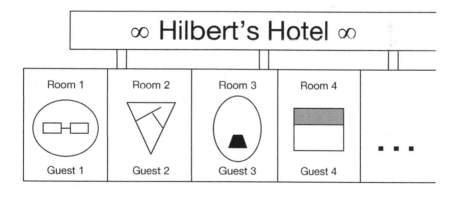

New guest

Figure III.1   A new guest arrives at Hilbert's Hotel, only to find that its rooms are already completely occupied by infinitely many guests.

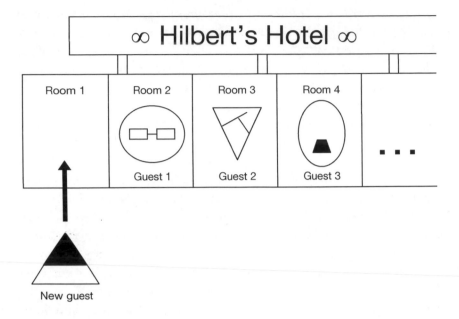

Figure III.2   Even though all the rooms are completely occupied, the manager can check in the new guest by reallocating other guests.

to room 6, and so on. By doing this all the current guests will be accommodated in even-numbered rooms. In this way the manager can accommodate all the infinitely many new guests in odd-numbered rooms. This is possible because, again, as we saw above, $\aleph_0 + \aleph_0 = \aleph_0$, which means, roughly speaking, that a countable infinity plus a countable infinity is a countable infinity. Suppose now that some of the guests check out. Let's assume that 2 million guests are unsatisfied with the service at Hilbert's Hotel and move to another hotel in town. Strangely enough, the hotel remains completely full. This is because $\aleph_0 - n = \aleph_0$, where n is a natural number. This means, roughly speaking, that a countable infinity minus a finitude is a countable infinity.

Craig maintains that the absurdity of Hilbert's Hotel shows that infinity is purely a mathematical concept and that it cannot be realized in the actual world. That is, it is impossible for infinitely many actual objects to exist. This establishes (2.11), that is, an actual infinity cannot exist.

Craig illustrates the same point by introducing another example. The British Library in London is said to be the largest library in the world by number of holdings. It has approximately 150 million items and approximately 388 miles of shelves. (In terms of shelf space the Library of Congress in Washington, DC is the largest. It has approximately 130 million items and approximately 530 miles of shelving.) What we consider here is, however, a library that is much larger than the British Library or the Library of Congress. In fact, it is *infinitely* larger than these libraries. The library in question – call it 'Craig's Library' – has infinitely many items occupying infinitely long shelves. Craig's Library entails, just like Hilbert's Hotel, a number of puzzling consequences.

Suppose that all the books in the library – that is, infinitely many books – are colored either with yellow or blue and are arranged in alternating fashion. So, next to any yellow book there is a blue book and next to any blue book there is a yellow book. If the librarian puts all the books on an infinitely long shelf, we will see an infinitely long series of yellow and blue stripes. Notice that the number of yellow books equals the number of blue books – there are equally infinitely many yellow books and blue books. This is not particularly counterintuitive because if we have an even, finite number of books, then we will obtain the same result. For example, if we have 100 books that are colored yellow and blue alternately, we have 50 yellow books and 50 blue books. However, Craig's Library exhibits much stranger properties. Suppose that someone who is obsessed with the color blue borrows *all* the blue books in the library. Since he is absent-minded he fails to return the books by the due date. After receiving many reminders from the library he finally returns all the blue books. Should the librarians be happy? They should, because all the blue books have come back to the library. However, the number of books in the library has remained the same before the borrower checked out the blue books and after he returned them. This is because the number of all yellow books is equivalent to the number of all yellow books *plus* the number of all blue books, which corresponds to the fact that $\aleph_0 + \aleph_0 = \aleph_0$. We do not obtain such peculiar results when it comes to finite numbers. If we remove 5 books from a collection of 100 books, there remain, of course, 95 books. If we put back the 5 books, then, of course, there will be 100 books again.

Craig maintains that this example, like the example of Hilbert's Hotel, suggests that while infinity is a coherent mathematical notion, there cannot be infinitely many objects in the actual world. The best we could do is to create items that are potentially infinite. For example, we can create a potentially infinitely large hotel by continually adding rooms or a potentially infinitely large library by continually extending bookshelves and adding books. We can never, however, have a hotel or a library that is *actually* infinite. From these observations, Craig concludes that premise (2.11), that an actual infinity cannot exist, is true.

Premise (2.12) says that an infinite temporal regress of events is an actual infinity. This premise is much more straightforward than premise (2.11). Consider any event that is taking place right now; for example, the event consisting of your reading this book. This event has not been taking place eternally. It was caused by another event and that event was caused by some other event, and so on. If the universe is eternal, then an infinite temporal chain of events represents an actual infinity because it contains infinitely many actual events. This means that the chain is comparable with Hilbert's Hotel and Craig's Library.

From premises (2.11) and (2.12) Craig derives intermediate conclusion (2.13), according to which an infinite temporal regress of events cannot exist. Given that an actual infinity cannot exist and that an infinite temporal regress of events is, just like Hilbert's Hotel and Craig's Library, an actual infinity, it follows by a simple inference that an infinite temporal regress of events cannot exist.

From intermediate conclusion (2.13) Craig concludes, as final conclusion (2.14) says, that the universe began to exist. Recall that the purpose of this sub-argument is to derive premise (2) of the *Kalām* cosmological argument, a premise according to which the universe began to exist. Conclusion (2.14) coincides with that premise.

Let us recap what we have seen so far. Premise (1) of the *Kalām* cosmological argument says that whatever begins to exist has a cause of its existence. Craig says that this premise is true because: (i) it is intuitively obvious; (ii) the negation of it entails an absurdity; and (iii) there is overwhelming inductive evidence of its truth. Premise (2) of the argument says that the universe began to exist. Since this premise is less obvious than premise (1), Craig introduces a sub-argument to demonstrate its truth. The sub-argument purports to show that the universe did begin to exist by claiming that if the universe did not begin to exist, then there has to be an actually infinite temporal regress of events, which, as Hilbert's Hotel and Craig's Library suggest, is not possible. From premises (1) and (2) Craig derives the conclusion that the universe has a cause of its existence.

Craig's defense of the *Kalām* cosmological argument could stop here, but he introduces additional sub-arguments for premise (2) in order to strengthen the argument as much as possible.

Sub-argument B: argument based on the impossibility of the formation of an actual infinity by successive addition

Craig formulates the second sub-argument as follows:

(2.21)   A collection formed by successive addition cannot be actually infinite.

(2.22)   The temporal series of past events is a collection formed by successive addition.

(2.23)   Therefore, the temporal series of past events cannot be actually infinite.

(2.24)   Therefore, the universe began to exist.

It is important to note that, unlike sub-argument A, sub-argument B does not say whether an actual infinity can exist. Let us then assume that an actual infinity, such as a bag with infinitely many marbles in it, can exist. What premise (2.21) entails is that one cannot make a bag of infinitely many marbles by putting marbles one after another into the bag. The number of marbles in the bag comes closer and closer to infinitely many but there will never be a time when you can say, 'I have finished my task. I have collected infinitely many marbles in the bag!' Even if there can be an actual infinity, Craig says, we cannot create it by adding finite objects one after another.

Consider another example. Suppose that you enter your friend's room and she shouts, '…, minus three, minus two, minus one, and zero. Phew! I have finished counting infinity.' This does not make sense. If she started counting from infinitely far in the past, why did she finish counting now rather than one hour ago, one day ago, or even one year ago? Infinity here means beginningless. If there is no finite item to begin with, then it is impossible to reach an end. This example, which shows the impossibility of counting infinity or 'traversing' infinity, also motivates premise (2.21).

Craig appeals to yet another example to motivate premise (2.21). The example, the 'Tristram Shandy paradox', is named after a character in *The Life and Opinions of Tristram Shandy, Gentleman*, a novel by Laurence Sterne. In this novel Tristram Shandy writes an autobiography but since he is a slow writer it takes him a year to write about each day of his life. Now an interesting question arises: if Tristram Shandy lives eternally, can he ever complete his autobiography? Suppose that an actual infinity can exist and that Tristram Shandy can complete the autobiography. It is then puzzling why he completed the autobiography on day X, rather than one day before, or even

100 years before, that day. Given that he had been writing for an infinite amount of time leading up to day X, he would also have been writing for an infinite amount time leading up to any day at all, up to and including day X. Pick any day in the finite past, and he would have been writing for an infinite amount of time prior to that day. This is very peculiar because it entails that no matter how far back in the past we go we never find him writing the autobiography, which contradicts the initial assumption that he had been writing it from eternity! The absurdity of this example seems to show, again, that a collection formed by successive addition cannot be actually infinite; we cannot obtain a series of actually infinitely many days by adding days one after another.

Premise (2.22) says that the temporal series of past events is a collection formed by successive addition. This premise is much more straightforward than premise (2.21). What (2.22) says is that the temporal series of past events can be obtained by adding past events one after another. That is, such a temporal series is analogous to a collection of marbles that is obtained by adding marbles one after another.

From premises (2.21) and (2.22) Craig derives intermediate conclusion (2.23), according to which the temporal series of past events cannot be actually infinite. Again, this sub-argument does not assume that an actual infinity can or cannot exist. It says that, even if an actual infinity can exist, the temporal series of past events is not an actual infinity. From this intermediate conclusion Craig derives the final conclusion (2.23), according to which the universe began to exist, which, again, coincides with premise (2) of the *Kalām* cosmological argument.

Sub-argument C: argument based on big bang cosmology

We have seen two sub-arguments for premise (2), a premise according to which the universe began to exist. What is common to these sub-arguments is that they appeal to the unique nature of infinity, which was confirmed by Cantor in a mathematically rigorous manner. This means that the two sub-arguments are both largely conceptual. Craig's third sub-argument for premise (2) is radically different from the above two because it is based mostly on empirical observations. It asserts that whether or not the above two sub-arguments are sound, the universe must have begun to exist because the big bang theory suggests that the universe is only finitely old; more specifically, it is approximately 15 billion years old. The big bang theory offers a cosmological ground for premise (2).

It is legitimate for Craig to appeal to the big bang theory because it is the most successful and most widely accepted theory of the origin of the universe. It is not that he appeals to it merely because it conveniently under-pins premise (2) of the *Kalām* cosmological argument. While we cannot exclude the possibility that a future empirical observation or a discovery in theoretical physics will refute the big bang theory, at this point no alterna-tive theory has as much explanatory capacity as the big bang theory does.

Premise (2) of the *Kalām* cosmological argument is more controver-sial than premise (1). However, as sub-argument C says, contemporary cosmology now offers strong scientific support for it. The *Kalām* cosmo-logical argument is more powerful than ever – much more powerful than the medieval Islamic theologians who invented the argument could have imagined.

As we saw above, premise (1) of the *Kalām* cosmological argument – what-ever begins to exist has a cause of its existence – seems intuitively obvious. We have also seen that premise (2) – the universe began to exist – is supported by at least three powerful sub-arguments. If any of the sub-argu-ments is sound, then premise (2) is true. From these two premises, conclu-sion (3) – the universe has a cause of its existence – follows. But how is the conclusion relevant to the existence of God? Craig maintains that the cause of the universe entailed by the *Kalām* cosmological argument has to be God, or at least something very similar to what theists call God.

First, Craig says, the cause has to be timeless, spaceless, and immaterial because time, space, and materials all came into existence when the universe began to exist. Second, the cause must also be changeless because there cannot be a change before time and space came into existence. Third, the cause must also be self-existent or uncaused because otherwise an infinite regress has to follow. Fourth, the cause also has to have enormous power because it brought about such a magnificent event as the big bang. Fifth, and finally, the cause has to be 'personal' rather than 'natural'. Craig justifies this claim as follows. Let us assume that the cause of water's freezing is a temperature below zero degrees centigrade and that the actual temperature remains below zero degrees centigrade from eternity. It then follows that if there is a glass of water from eternity it has to be frozen from eternity. In general, if a cause is given, then there must be an appropriate effect, and if the cause exists from eternity, then there must also be an effect from eternity. This means that if the cause of the universe exists from eternity, then the universe must exist from eternity as well. However, premise (2) of the *Kalām* cosmological argument says that the universe does not exist from eternity; it began to exist in the finite past. So, on the one hand, we have to think that the universe exists eternally and changelessly because its cause exists eternally (at least in some sense)[32] and changelessly. On the other hand, however, we have to think also that the universe began to exist only in the finite past. Craig solves this dilemma by appealing to the notion of a personal cause. He says that what the above consideration entails is that in the finite past a personal being that is timeless, spaceless, immaterial, changeless, self-existent, and extremely powerful created the universe. Craig says that it is appropriate to regard this being as a person because it chose to bring about freely a certain condition, which was not present until then. In this way, we can consistently hold that while the cause is eternal, the effect, that is, the existence of the universe, is not.

Craig therefore concludes that the first cause is a personal being that is timeless, spaceless, immaterial, changeless, self-existent, and extremely powerful. Although it does not immediately follow that the being in question is omniscient, omnipotent, and omnibenevolent, it seems to be compatible with and very much similar to what theists call God.

5 Objections to the *Kalām* cosmological argument

The *Kalām* cosmological argument seems to overcome various difficulties that Aquinas's First and Second Ways face. We saw earlier, for example, that the two ways fail to explain why there cannot be an infinite regress of motions and causes. The *Kalām* cosmological argument, through its sub-argument A, appears to respond to this objection persuasively. It says that that there cannot be an infinite regress, in particular, an infinite temporal regress of events, because such a regress is an actual infinity, which cannot exist. To take another example, as we saw above, the two ways attract an objection which asks why God does not need a cause of His existence while all other objects do need causes of their existence. The *Kalām* cosmological argument responds to such an objection by pointing out that premise (1) applies only to whatever *begins* to exist while God, as the cause of the universe, does not begin to exist. Given that God is self-existent, He does not require a cause of His existence. Furthermore, the argument is strengthened by contemporary cosmology and the mathematics of infinity. Hence, in several respects, the *Kalām* cosmological argument is more powerful than Aquinas's First and Second Ways. Yet it faces a number of objections in its own right.

Objection 1: premise (1) is false

Premise (1) of the *Kalām* cosmological argument says that whatever begins to exist has a cause of its existence. Although this premise is intuitively plausible one might try to refute it by claiming as follows: we can conceive of a situation in which, say, a particle pops into existence without any cause. There is nothing logically impossible in such a situation. A particle's popping into existence is not comparable to logically impossible situations such as someone's drawing a square circle or making one plus one equal five. If a particle's popping into existence is not logically impossible, then premise (1) is false; it is not the case that whatever begins to exist has a cause of its existence. Moreover, there is scientific evidence for such a claim. According to quantum mechanics, things could materialize without any cause at the subatomic level. Since quantum mechanics is widely accepted among scientists, premise (1) should be given up.

In response to this objection, Craig says that premise (1) is not something that requires a proof because it is one of many things that are so self-evidently true that they do not demand any evidence.[33] Consider, for example, a skeptical hypothesis that people around us, such as our friends and family members, do not have any feeling. If we pinch them they behave as if they feel pain. According to this hypothesis, however, they do not actually experience any pain. Consider another skeptical hypothesis, that everything around us is an illusion. According to this hypothesis, we are mere 'brains in vats', isolated brains that a mad scientist keeps in vats and stimulates electronically to create sensations. These hypotheses are logically possible and they might even be impossible to refute. Most philosophers agree, however, that we do not need to prove that these hypotheses are false in order to be justified in believing their falsity. This is because it is self-evidently true that people around us have feelings and that we are not brains in a vat. Craig says that, similarly, we are justified in believing premise (1) because it is self-evidently true that whatever begins to exist has a cause of its existence.

It is important to note that Craig agrees with the above objection that it is *logically* possible that a particle comes into existence uncaused – just as it is logically possible that people around us do not have feeling or that everything around us is an illusion. However, he says that that is irrelevant to premise (1) because the mere logical possibility does not entail that things can come into existence without any cause in the actual world. Whether or not it is logically possible, it certainly is absurd to believe that things like a motorcycle or the White House can pop into existence in reality without any cause. If so, it is even more absurd to believe that *the entire universe* can pop into existence without any cause – perhaps such a belief is the most absurd thing we could hold. Craig points out that premise (1) is so obviously true that even the skeptic David Hume endorsed it. In a letter he sent to John Stewart in February 1754, Hume wrote, 'But allow me to tell you that I never asserted so absurd a Proposition as that *anything might arise without a cause*.'[34]

What does Craig say about quantum mechanics? Craig makes two points here. First, among scientists there is no consensus about the thesis that things could materialize without any case. This idea is derived from the so-called Copenhagen interpretation of quantum mechanics. Craig points out that many great physicists today are unsatisfied with this indeterministic interpretation of quantum mechanics and, hence, that they seek more deterministic theories. Einstein was probably the best-known scientist who felt uncomfortable with the indeterministic aspects of quantum mechanics. Observing these aspects he famously remarked, 'God doesn't play dice with the universe.' Second, and more importantly, Craig claims that even if the Copenhagen interpretation is correct, it does not follow that things can come into existence out of *nothing*. The quantum vacuum is not absolute nothingness but 'a sea of fluctuating energy, an arena of violent activity that has a rich physical structure and can be described by physical laws'.[35] Hence, the Copenhagen interpretation does not entail that things can spring into being uncaused from nothing.[36] Craig, therefore, concludes that premise (1) of the *Kalām* cosmological argument withstands this line of objection.

Objection 2: premise (2.11) of sub-argument A is false

Premise (2) of the *Kalām* cosmological argument says that the universe began to exist. As we saw above, since this premise is much more controversial than premise (1), Craig provides several independent sub-arguments for premise (2). Recall sub-argument A:

Sub-argument A: argument based on the impossibility of an actual infinity.

(2.11)   An actual infinity cannot exist.
(2.12)   An infinite temporal regress of events is an actual infinity.
(2.13)   Therefore, an infinite temporal regress of events cannot exist.
(2.14)   Therefore, the universe began to exist.

If premises (2.11) and (2.12) are true, intermediate conclusion (2.13) follows, and, consequently, conclusion (2.14) follows. However, both premises (2.11) and (2.12) attract objections.

Some critics reject (2.11) by saying that an actual infinity *can* exist because infinity is a coherent concept.[37] It is impossible for either a four-sided triangle or a married bachelor to exist, for example, because the concepts 'four-sided triangle' and 'married bachelor' are self-contradictory. In other words, they cannot exist in reality because it is *logically* impossible for them to exist. On the other hand, a flying pig and a pink elephant *can* exist, even though they do not exist in reality, because the concepts 'flying pig' and 'pink elephant' are coherent. In other words, they can exist in reality because it is logically possible for them to exist. Now, the critics say, the concept of infinity is coherent because Cantor's set theory, which defines infinity, is a consistent mathematical system. It is then logically possible for an actual infinity to exist and, hence, an actual infinity can exist in reality, just like a flying pig and a pink elephant can exist in reality. Therefore, the critics conclude, (2.11) is false.

Craig's response to the objection to premise (2.11) is similar to his response to the above objection to premise (1) of the main argument. He agrees that the concept of infinity is coherent and that it is logically possible for an actual infinity to exist. However, he rejects the idea that its being *logically* possible for an actual infinity to exist entails that it is *ontologically* (or metaphysically) possible for an actual infinity to exist. This is because, according to Craig, ontological possibility does not always coincide with logical possibility. Since ontological possibility is narrower than logical possibility, he says, the mere fact that it is logically possible for something to exist does not entail that it is ontologically possible for that thing to exist. Therefore, Craig concludes, the fact that the concept of infinity is coherent does not mean that an actual infinity can exist in reality.[38]

It is not very clear, however, exactly what Craig means by ontological possibility. Is it the possibility of actualizing something physically, or is it the possibility of actualizing something given the laws of nature in the actual world? Whether or not the objection in question is successful, it seems to reveal that sub-argument A is more subtle than it initially appears. In particular, it is based on a specific notion of possibility.

Objection 3: premise (2.12) of sub-argument A is false

Let us move on to premise (2.12), according to which an infinite temporal regress of events is an actual infinity. In response to this premise one might argue that an infinite temporal regress of events is *not* an actual infinity because past events do not exist now. According to premise (2.12), if the universe does not have a beginning then there is a temporal series that contains infinitely many past events. This means that (2.12) assumes that a temporal series is analogous to, say, a chain of train cars, and that past events, which constitute a series, are analogous to individual train cars. One might claim, however, that such a picture is misleading because on one theory of time, only present events exist. If past events do not exist, there cannot be a temporal series that contains past events and present events simultaneously. We cannot construct a temporal series of events because we cannot gather and connect past and present events to form a temporal series in the way in which we gather and connect individual train cars to form a chain of train cars. Events in time are analogous to unusual train cars that vanish as time goes by. We cannot connect past and present events because when present events occur past events have already 'vanished'.

In response to the above objection, Robert Prevost claims as follows: even if past events do not exist, they could leave permanent records, which would not vanish as time goes by.[39] That is, even if an infinite temporal regress of *events* is not an actual infinity, an infinite regress of past *records* is certainly an actual infinity, and this is sufficient to construct sub-argument A.

The objection to (2.12) in question is based on a specific theory of time called 'presentism', according to which only present objects exist and past (and future) objects do not. One could reject the objection if presentism is shown to be false. In fact some philosophers have put forward alternatives to presentism, such as the growing block theory and eternalism. The growing block theory says that past and present objects exist but future objects do not, which means that a temporal series of events extends further and further as time goes by, just like a growing block expands further and further as time goes by. Eternalism says that past, present, and future objects exist, which means that a temporal series of past, present, and future events is already 'there'. If either eternalism or the growing block theory is correct, then the objection to (2.12) fails.

Whether or not the objection to (2.12) in question is successful, it seems to reveal, again, that sub-argument A is more subtle than it initially appears to be. In particular, it seems to rely on a specific theory of time – something such as the growing block theory or eternalism.

Objection 4: premise (2.21) of sub-argument B is false

Recall sub-argument B for premise (2) of the Kalām cosmological argument:

> Sub-argument B: argument based on the impossibility of the formation of an actual infinity by successive addition.

(2.21)   A collection formed by successive addition cannot be actually infinite.

(2.22)   The temporal series of past events is a collection formed by successive addition.

(2.23)   Therefore, the temporal series of past events cannot be actually infinite.

(2.24)   Therefore, the universe began to exist.

Just like sub-argument A, sub-argument B consists of two premises, (2.21) and (2.22), and if they are both true intermediate conclusion (2.23) follows and, consequently, conclusion (2.24) follows. However, both (2.21) and (2.22) attract objections.

Consider premise (2.21) first. Recall the scenario in which a person finishes counting infinitely many numbers by shouting '... minus three, minus two, minus one, zero!' The absurdity of this scenario motivates (2.21). One cannot reach infinity by successively adding or subtracting items. This means that if the universe is infinitely old, then today should never 'arrive' today. Conversely, if the universe is infinitely old but today does 'arrive' today, it is a pure mystery why it has to 'arrive' today rather than yesterday, just as it is inexplicable why the above person finishes counting infinity now rather than at some other time.

J. L. Mackie, however, objects to (2.21), arguing that such reasoning 'expresses a prejudice against an actual infinity'.[40] The prejudice on which Mackie thinks (2.21) is based is the idea that an infinite temporal series has an infinitely distant starting point. In particular, according to Mackie, Craig thinks that counting or traversing infinity is impossible because he assumes erroneously that there are infinitely distant points to start with in the above scenarios. Mackie argues to the contrary that there must not be any starting point at all, precisely because what we are concerned with here is infinity.

In response to Mackie, Craig says that premise (2.21) does not involve any prejudice against infinity. It does not assume that an actual infinity can or cannot exist. All it says is that an actual infinity cannot be formed by successive addition (and subtraction), and, according to Craig, this does not require the prejudice that there is an infinitely distant starting point. On the contrary, Craig says, (2.21) can be construed as saying that the very beginningless character of an infinite temporal series, which Mackie emphasizes, shows the impossibility of its formation by successive addition.[41]

If we think that the example of a person's counting infinity appears to suggest that there is an infinite negative natural number with which the person must start, then we can motivate (2.21) by appealing to the other example that we saw above. Consider, that is, a scenario in which a person tries to make a bag of actually infinitely many marbles by adding marbles one after another. It seems that there will be no point at which the person completes this task, and this motivates (2.21) without presupposing the existence of an infinitely remote starting point. The person's starting point in this scenario is clearly finite, in particular zero, and his goal corresponds to an actually infinitely large natural number. So the objection to (2.21) in question does not seem to succeed.

Objection 5: premise (2.22) of sub-argument B is false

Premise (2.22) says that the temporal series of past events is a collection formed by successive addition. Oppy says that this premise is based on the idea that 'the series of past events was laid down "one lump after another"'.[42] That is, using a metaphor, the temporal series of past events is like beads on a string. This is manifest, according to Oppy, in the use of the terms 'successive' and 'addition'. The idea that the world is fundamentally discrete in all respects in this way is called 'strict finite metaphysics'. Oppy claims that premise (2.22) can be rejected on the ground that there is no good reason to accept strict finite metaphysics; or, more specifically, it can be rejected on the ground that there is no good reason to accept the idea that the past has been laid down in finite 'lumps'. It might be more reasonable to think that time is continuous rather than discrete.

In response to Oppy, David S. Oderberg says that premise (2.22) does not need to presuppose strict finite metaphysics.[43] According to Oderberg, the idea that time is continuous rather than discrete does not exclude the formation of the series of past events by successive addition. A paradigm example of strict finite metaphysics with respect to time is the theory that a 'chronon', a quantum or discrete individual unit of time, exists. According to this theory, just as energy in electromagnetic waves can exist only in discrete packets, perhaps time can also exist in discrete packets. This theory suggests that the moments of time might follow each other like beads on a string. Oderberg, however, says that the *Kalām* cosmological argument does not need to assume this kind of theory. One way of supporting Oderberg's point is to say that while time itself might be continuous temporal *events* do not need to be continuous.[44] There could be *discrete* events throughout a *continuous* flow of time. Since (2.21) talks only about the temporal series of past *events* rather than about time itself it does not seem to force proponents of the *Kalām* cosmological argument to accept strict finite metaphysics.

We have reviewed various objections to sub-arguments A and B for premise (2) of the *Kalām* cosmological argument. Sub-argument A is more contentious than it initially appears because it is based on a specific notion of possibility and a specific theory of time, each of which is controversial on its own. Sub-argument B, which is free from these specificities, seems in this respect more plausible than sub-argument A. It should be noted, however, that many more objections have been introduced to refute both sub-arguments.[45] Notice that both sub-arguments involve the concept of infinity. It is inevitable that arguments that involve infinity become controversial because the concept of infinity and its applications have always provoked controversy. One might then think that sub-argument C is less controversial because it is free from the concept of infinity. Let us look now at the most common objection to sub-argument C.

Objection 6: sub-argument C is untenable

Again, premise (2) of the *Kalām* cosmological argument says that the universe began to exist. Sub-argument C tries to establish this premise by appealing to the big bang theory. The theory states, on the basis of empirical and theoretical considerations, that the universe did begin to exist approximately 15 billion years ago. One might claim, however, that sub-argument C fails because there are powerful alternatives to the big bang theory, which suggest that the universe did *not* begin to exist.

Let us consider the two most prominent alternatives. The first is the steady state theory. Hermann Bondi, Thomas Gold, and Fred Hoyle, who were skeptical of the big bang theory, proposed an alternative theory called the 'steady state theory' in 1948. As we saw earlier, the big bang theory says that the universe came into existence as a state of massive density and temperature called a 'singularity'. The entire universe itself was extremely hot and compressed to smaller than a pinhead. Over time, according to the big bang theory, it has expanded into the vast and cooler universe that we inhabit now and, moreover, the transformation of the universe is ongoing. This means that the state of the universe has been changing continuously throughout its history.

The steady state theory agrees with the big bang theory that the universe is expanding. It denies, however, that the big bang took place and that the state of the universe has been changing over time. The steady state theory assumes the 'perfect cosmological principle', which says that on a large scale the universe is both homogeneous and isotropic in space and time. This means that the universe has no beginning or end in time and that on the grand scale the universe looks the same from any spatio-temporal point within it. How can the state of the universe remain unchanged if it has been expanding? The steady state theory responds to this question by saying that the density of the universe remains the same because matter is continuously created; according to one calculation, a few hundred new atoms are created every year. Thus the universe is eternal and its state remains the same throughout time.

The steady state theory is probably the best-known alternative to the big bang theory. In fact it attracted many supporters in the mid-twentieth century. However, very few scientists defend it today. In his textbook *The Big Bang* the astronomer Joseph Silk remarks, 'Observational evidence, the harsh and final arbiter between any rival theories, eventually caused the demise of steady state cosmology … [S]teady state cosmology was overthrown in 1965 by the discovery of the *cosmic microwave background radiation*, which provided irrefutable evidence for an early, hot phase of the universe.'[46] The cosmic microwave background radiation is, as we saw earlier, one of the strongest pieces of evidence for the big bang theory. This evidence shows that the universe was once much hotter than it is now, suggesting that the steady state theory cannot be true. That is, contrary to what the steady state theory says, the state of the universe has changed and has been changing over time.

As Craig says, the steady state theory was not introduced because there are empirical observations that motivate it. It was introduced rather because some cosmologists wanted to avoid what they thought was a religious idea, namely that the universe came into existence in the finite past.[47] Ironically, in order to avoid such an idea the steady state theory had to introduce another idea which many find even more unbelievable: Matter regularly and continuously comes into existence out of nothing. Silk concludes, 'The steady state theory is now little more than a footnote of considerable historical interest in the development of modern cosmology.'[48]

Let us now consider the second alternative to the big bang theory, the oscillating universe theory. On the one hand, empirical data suggest that there was a big bang. On the other hand, many cosmologists want to avoid the implication of the big bang theory that the universe came into existence in the finite past. How can we resolve this dilemma? Some scientists try to avoid the temporal finitude of the universe by introducing the so-called oscillating (or cyclic) universe theory, according to which the universe alternates the phases of expansion and contraction, going through a big bang and a 'big crunch' alternately. In this way, we can hold that the universe is eternal without denying that that the big bang occurred.

According to the standard big bang theory, the universe will continue to expand. This means that eventually the universe will reach a state of maximum entropy. That is, at a certain point there will not be any movement of energy or life at all in the universe because all available energy has already moved to areas with less energy. This state is called 'heat death'.

The oscillating universe theory says, however, that there will be no heat death because the universe will stop its expansion before reaching that state. When the universe stops expanding it will start contracting. The contraction will be very slow at the beginning. However, as the speed accelerates the universe will grow hotter and brighter until it reaches the big crunch. The big crunch will eventually cause another big bang, which will eventually lead to another big crunch, and this alternation of expansion and contraction will continue.

The oscillating universe theory is a unique alternative to the big bang theory because it does not deny that the big bang took place. It accepts most of the available evidence for the big bang theory but nevertheless denies that the universe is finitely old and that it keeps expanding. This theory is also convenient because it avoids such difficult questions as 'what caused the big bang?', 'what is the ultimate consequence of the big bang?', and so on.

The oscillating universe theory, however, faces a number of objections. Craig, for example, claims that the theory is false because the finitude of the past has been proved.[49] According to the Penrose–Hawking singularity theorem, under very generalized conditions an initial cosmological singularity is inevitable, even for inhomogeneous and non-isotropic universes. This means that, as the big bang theory says, the universe is indeed only finitely old. There was a beginning of time and space. Moreover, proponents of the oscillating universe theory commonly predict that each cycle of oscillation increases in length. That is, a new cycle is always longer than the previous one. This means, conversely, that, even if the oscillating universe theory is true, there is no infinite past because each cycle becomes shorter and shorter as we go back in time. Second, Craig also maintains that there are no known laws of physics that allow the contraction of the universe and there are no empirical data that are consistent with or point to its contraction. In other words, in order for the oscillating universe theory to be correct, the known laws of physics would have to be revised and all sorts of existing empirical data would have to be rejected.[50] Craig concludes that the oscillating universe theory is an untenable alternative to the big bang theory, and that it was introduced, just like the steady state theory, merely to satisfy the desire to avoid the temporal finitude of the universe.

There are many other alternatives to the big bang theory but it is safe to say that the standard big bang theory is currently the most widely accepted account of the origin of the universe. In this sense it seems that sub-argument C appears to be the least controversial sub-argument for premise (2) of the Kalām cosmological argument that we have seen.

Again, Craig's formulation of the Kalām cosmological argument is the following:

1   Whatever begins to exist has a cause of its existence.
2   The universe began to exist.
3   Therefore, the universe has a cause of its existence.

We have discussed a number of objections to both premises (1) and (2) and concluded that the big bang theory might constitute a particularly strong sub-argument for premise (2). It should be noted, however, that there are at least two further critical responses to the Kalām cosmological argument. These responses were not covered by the above discussion because they do not necessarily focus on only one of the premises of the argument. They rather question the overall legitimacy or strength of the argument.

First, if sub-argument C for premise (2) is correct in saying that the big bang theory is true, then the universe began to exist. However, as the big bang theory says, the way in which the universe came into existence is fundamentally different from the way in which ordinary objects, such as tables, clouds, and particles, come into existence. On the one hand, when ordinary objects come into existence, time and space pre-exist. On the other hand, however, when the universe came into existence time and space did not pre-exist. (This is controversial but it is what Craig's own interpretation of the big bang theory entails.) They all came into existence simultaneously.

This suggests that the beginning of the universe is a unique event, if it is appropriate to call it an 'event' at all. It is the only event in the history of everything in which the existence of time and space did not precede the event itself. Given this fundamental difference one might question whether premise (1), which applies to the existence of ordinary objects, applies equally to the existence of the universe. Hence, one might conclude that there is a tension between sub-argument C for premise (2) and premise (1).

Second, Craig's formulation of the *Kalām* cosmological argument as rendered above seems misleading because conclusion (3) – the universe has a cause of its existence – does not represent the *real* conclusion of the argument. As an argument for the existence of God, the real conclusion of the *Kalām* cosmological argument has to be that God, or at least something very similar to God, exists. Indeed, as we have seen, Craig concludes that the cause of the universe entailed by the argument is a personal being that is timeless, spaceless, immaterial, changeless, self-existent, and extremely powerful. Yet even if conclusion (3), which appears relatively uncontroversial, is established it is a further question whether Craig's derivation of the real conclusion succeeds. Hence, one might accept the whole argument presented above while disputing the very conclusion that God, or a being very similar to God, exists.

6 Infinity and the meaning of life

In the film *Annie Hall*, Woody Allen performs the role of Alvy Singer, a neurotic comedian from Brooklyn. In a scene from his childhood, the young Alvy has the following conversation with his mother and doctor:

Doctor: Why are you depressed, Alvy?
Alvy's Mom: Tell Dr. Flicker.
                    (*Young Alvy sits, his head down – his mother answers for him.*)
Alvy's Mom: It's something he read.
Doctor: Something he read, huh?
Alvy at Nine: (*His head still down*) The universe is expanding.
Doctor: The universe is expanding?
Alvy at Nine: Well, the universe is everything, and if it's expanding, someday
                    it will break apart and that would be the end of everything!
Alvy's Mom: What is that your business?
                    (*She turns back to the doctor.*)
Alvy's Mom: He stopped doing his homework!

Alvy at Nine: What's the point?

Alvy's Mom: What has the universe got to do with it? You're here in Brooklyn! Brooklyn is not expanding!

Doctor: It won't be expanding for billions of years yet, Alvy. And we've gotta try to enjoy ourselves while we're here![51]

Alvy, his mother, and the doctor obviously misconstrue the big bang theory. The theory does not say that every object will expand or break apart as the universe itself expands. So, contrary to what they seem to think, Brooklyn will not break apart as the universe expands. However, there is also something right about Alvy's claim. If the big bang theory is correct, then the universe keeps expanding. This entails that one day the universe will reach a state of maximum entropy, that is, heat death. As mentioned above, under this condition there will be no energy to sustain any motion or life. Thus the big bang theory suggests not only the finitude of the universe but also, as Alvy seems to think correctly, the finitude of the future with respect to motion and life. Alvy appears to anticipate here the perennial philosophical view that life is meaningless if our existence is finite. One of the philosophers who defends such a view is none other than William Lane Craig himself.[52]

Craig says that mortality makes life absurd because it prevents us from having any ultimate significance. We might be able to save the lives of sick children or influence powerful politicians to make the world better, but that would not endow life with any *ultimate* significance; at most it would create a *relative* significance. Sooner or later we will die and the people who have been saved or influenced by us will also die. Not only them, but their families, friends, and acquaintances will die too. Moreover, our planet, our solar system, and our galaxy will vanish eventually. Even if we accomplish something that appears significant to us, it will not make any difference at all on a cosmic scale. Craig, therefore, concludes that if we are mortal, then life is meaningless.

Craig's point is nicely illustrated by another Woody Allen film, *Hannah and Her Sisters*. In that movie Allen performs the role of a television producer called Mickey Sachs. Mickey is obsessed with the idea that he has a brain tumor and he submits himself to a medical examination. The doctor tells Mickey that he has to take another examination because there is a grey area on the X-ray. Mickey becomes panicked and unable to sleep. After a more careful examination, however, the doctor tells Mickey that a brain tumor was not found and that there is absolutely nothing he needs to worry about.

Mickey is very happy – but only for a short period. When he leaves the hospital he realizes that he, and everyone, is going to die sooner or later anyway. He has the following conversation with his assistant Gail.

Mickey: Do you realize what a thread we're all hanging by?

Gail: Mickey, you're off the hook. You should be celebrating.

Mickey: (*Walking around to the front of his desk, gesturing*) Can you understand how meaningless everything is? Everything! I'm talking about nnnn – our lives, the show … the whole world, it's meaningless.

Gail: (*Gesturing*) Yeah … but you're not dying!

Mickey: No, I'm not dying now, but, but (*Gesturing*) you know, when I ran out of the hospital, I, I was so thrilled because they told me I was going to be all right. And I'm running down the street, and suddenly I stop, 'cause it hit me, all right, so, you know, I'm not going to go today. I'm okay. I'm not going to go tomorrow. (*Pointing*) But eventually, I'm going to be in that position.

Gail: (*Shrugging, unwrapping a stick of gum*) Tch, well, you know, eventually it, it is going to happen to all of us.

Mickey: Yes, but doesn't that ruin everything for you? That makes everything … (*Gail sighs. She pops a piece of gum into her mouth as Mickey continues to speak.*)

Mickey: (*Continuing*) … you know it, it just takes the pleasure out of everything. (*Gesturing, pointing*) I mean, you're gonna die, I'm gonna die, the audience is gonna die, the network's gonna – The sponsor. Everything!

Gail: (*Chewing*) I know, I know, and your hamster.

Mickey: (*Nodding emphatically*) Yes![53]

Mickey is trying to make essentially the same point as Craig. Many of us are not dying today or tomorrow, but absolutely *everyone* is dying sooner or later. And if death is the end for everyone, then everything appears utterly meaningless.

Craig, however, claims that our lives would not suddenly gain meaning merely by our becoming immortal. Even if we could exist forever, he says, life would not be meaningful without God. Craig provides several reasons for this claim. First, if God does not exist there is no ultimate value.[54] Without God there is no one to say what is right and what is wrong. This is disastrous because it means that we cannot say, for example, that helping a drowning child is *really* right or brutally murdering an innocent person is *really* wrong in any context. There cannot be any meaning in such a world. Second, if God does not exist there is no ultimate purpose.[55] Without God the universe lacks any purpose; everything in it is only a by-product of cosmic accidents. We came into existence merely by coincidence and no meaning is attached to our existence. On the other hand, Craig says, if God exists and He created the universe and us, there is hope for us.

Craig, therefore, concludes that life is meaningless without immortality and God. This conclusion itself does not necessarily entail that life *is* meaningful. Pessimists could agree with Craig's conclusion but hold simultaneously that life is meaningless either because we are not immortal or because God does not exist. However, if Craig is right in saying that life is meaningless without immortality and God and that at least some lives are meaningful, then at least some of us are immortal and God exists.

How does Craig's discussion of the meaning of life relate to that of the *Kalām* cosmological argument? As we have seen, in the course of developing the argument Craig maintains that the universe has a beginning, which means that the past is finite. The past cannot be infinite, according to Craig, because the infinitude of the past entails an infinite temporal series of past events, which cannot exist as it is an instance of actual infinity. In the course of developing a theistic account of the meaning of life, however, Craig maintains that we have to be immortal in order for life to be meaningful. This seems to entail that the future has to be infinite, if not timeless. One might think that Craig's position here is inconsistent because, on the one hand, he says that the past cannot be infinite but, on the other hand, he seems to say that the future has to be infinite. Such an assertion is, however, incorrect. Even if an infinite temporal series of past events is an instance of actual infinity an infinite series of future events is not an instance of actual infinity. It is rather an instance of *potential* infinity, because, contrary to past events, future events have not been actualized yet. Craig can, therefore, consistently embrace the finitude of the past and the infinitude of the future.

David Hilbert once remarked, 'The infinite! No other question has ever moved so profoundly the spirit of man; no other idea has so fruitfully stimulated his intellect; yet no other concept stands in greater need of clarification than that of the infinite.'[56] This is indeed true. Infinity is an intractable concept; it could well be beyond our full comprehension. Yet it underlies some of the most profound philosophical problems, such as the existence of God, the origin of the universe, and the meaning of life.

CONCLUSION

ADDITIONAL ARGUMENTS FOR AND AGAINST THE EXISTENCE OF GOD

We have mainly discussed three arguments for the existence of God: the ontological argument, the design argument, and the cosmological argument. Among the three, the design argument attracts the most attention today. The cosmological argument follows, with the ontological argument clearly being the least popular. However, if we rank them in accordance with their respective strengths, the order will be completely the opposite. As we have seen, the ontological argument, though many regard it as a mere philosophical gimmick, seems the most difficult to refute. The cosmological argument is quite powerful but it relies on some subtle metaphysical assumptions that are matters of dispute. The design argument is clearly the weakest because it lacks the scientific underpinning that it claims to have. There are, however, many more arguments for the existence of God, and there are also many arguments *against* the existence of God. Before closing this book let us survey some of them.

1 Further arguments for the existence of God

The so-called fine-tuning argument is unique because it combines elements of the design argument and the cosmological argument. Although it is normally classified as a version of the design argument it also relies, just as the cosmological argument does, on cosmological findings.

The fine-tuning argument[1]
Some scientists claim that the existence of life is grounded on an extremely delicate balance of initial conditions at the beginning of the universe. For example, Stephen Hawking estimates that if the rate of the universe's expansion one second after the big bang had been smaller by even one part in a hundred thousand million million, life could not have existed in the universe.[2] However, life does exist in the universe. This suggests that the universe was created by an intelligent designer.

Another version of the design argument that has attracted attention recently is the following:

The argument from consciousness[3]
How can the phenomenal aspect of perceptual experience, such as the throbbing feeling of a pain or the colorfulness of a visual sensation, be realized in the brain, which is nothing but an aggregation of billions of neurons? Attempts to provide a naturalistic answer to the question seem hopeless. Even if we study the physical structure and function of the brain we will never know why a specific brain state has to be correlated to a specific phenomenal experience. The only satisfactory answer to the question is that an intelligent being, possibly God, designed such correlations.

Some critics claim that the argument from consciousness is weak because it seeks to establish only a 'God of the gaps'. The mere fact that there are unexplained phenomena does not, according to them, entail the existence of God or an intelligent designer.

Both the fine-tuning argument and the argument from consciousness rely on scientific observations. Although they try to prove the existence of an intelligent being, which could be a supernatural agent like God, their premises mention only ordinary phenomena observed in science. The following argument follows another course by focusing specifically on extraordinary phenomena that exist beyond science:

The argument from miracles[4]
There are uncountably many reports of miraculous events in the history of humankind, some of which appear to have no naturalistic explanation and come from otherwise reliable sources. They suggest the active intervention of a supernatural being. Therefore, a supernatural being, possibly God, exists.

Many philosophers find this argument weak as a means of converting atheists to theism because atheists simply do not take miracle testimonies seriously. Nevertheless, the debate over this argument has raised a number of important philosophical questions: what is a miracle? what is the difference between rare, but ordinary, events and miraculous events? under what conditions can we trust testimonies involving miracles?

The above three arguments are all concerned with facts about the universe and events that take place in it. In other words, they focus on the realm of science and metaphysics. However, some theists purport to establish the existence of God by focusing on the realm of morality:

The moral argument[5]
If God does not exist, then there are no objective moral values. However, there *are* objective moral values. For example, it is not merely culturally or socially wrong but objectively wrong to murder innocent people. Therefore, God, as an objective moral lawgiver, exists.

This argument is relevant to our discussion of the meaning of life in Part III of this book. Dostoyevsky famously wrote that if there is no God, all things are permitted. If that is true, and if it is not the case that all things are permitted, then the existence of God follows. The moral argument is also closely related to the divine command theory, according to which an act is morally right or wrong on the basis of God's command. This theory has been a matter of controversy among philosophers. Arguably, the strongest objection to the divine command theory is the so-called Euthyphro dilemma: if an act is morally right or wrong because God says it is morally right or wrong, then it seems completely arbitrary what act is morally right or wrong. On the other hand, if God says an act is morally right or wrong because it *is* morally right or wrong, then God's commands are unnecessary. Therefore, God's commands are either arbitrary or unnecessary. The dilemma is so-called because it was originally introduced in Plato's dialogue *Euthyphro*.

Instead of trying to prove that God exists some theists try to show that their belief in God is at least justified:

The argument from religious experience[6]
Some beliefs, such as that the presence of this book is not an illusion created by a mad scientist, are 'properly basic'. That is, these beliefs are so basic that we do not need proofs in order to be justified in believing them. Even if it is impossible for us to prove that these beliefs are true it

is nevertheless rational for us to hold them. Since belief in God is properly basic for theists, they are justified in believing that God exists. Even if it is impossible for theists to prove that God exists it is nevertheless rational for them to hold such a belief.

In Part III we discussed the idea that some beliefs are so self-evidently true that they do not demand any evidence. In Part II we discussed the idea that being rationally justified in believing proposition p does not always entail or require that p is true. The above argument from religious experience utilizes these ideas. This is a unique argument because it defends theism without trying to prove the existence of God.

Another argument that is somewhat comparable to the argument from religious experience is the following:

Pascal's wager[7]
Should we believe in God? If we believe in God but He does not exist, then we will have wasted time when reading the Bible and praying to God. This is bad but only in a limited sense. If we believe in God and He does exist, then we can go to heaven. This is infinitely good. On the other hand, if we do not believe in God and He does not exist, then we save some time by not reading the Bible and praying to God. This is good but only in a limited sense. Yet if we do not believe in God and He does exist, then we will go to hell. This is infinitely bad. Therefore, we should believe in God.

This is a simplified formulation of 'Pascal's wager', which was originally introduced by Blaise Pascal in his *Pensées*. Critics find that this argument has at best a limited impact because it applies only to a particular Christian concept of God. Indeed many Christian theists would reject the idea that we should believe in God on the basis of this kind of cost–benefit analysis.

2 Arguments against the existence of God

Let us move on to consider some arguments *against* the existence of God. How can we show that God does not exist? Many, if not most, traditional theists ascribe three main attributes to God: omniscience, omnipotence, and omnibenevolence. Some of them ascribe additional attributes to God, such as timelessness, changelessness, immutability, simplicity, and incorporeality. This suggests that we can try to show that God does not exist by demonstrating that there cannot be a being that has these attributes. In what follows, we will see many such examples. For the sake of simplicity, let us focus on omniscience, omnipotence, and omnibenevolence and set aside other attributes.

The paradox of the stone[8]
Either God can create a stone that He cannot lift or He cannot create a stone that He cannot lift. If He can create a stone that He cannot lift, then He is not omnipotent. If He cannot create a stone that He cannot lift, then, again, He is not omnipotent. Hence, God cannot be omnipotent (no being can be). If God cannot be omnipotent, then He does not exist.

The paradox of the stone tries to show that God does not exist by appealing to the idea that the concept of omnipotence is internally incoherent or self-contradictory.

The argument from knowledge de se[9]
Suppose that I suddenly realize that I am making a mess by spilling sugar on the floor. I can express what I come to know as:

(1)   *I* am making a mess.

God can certainly know what is expressed as follows:

(2)   Yujin Nagasawa is making a mess.

What I know in knowing (1) is, however, different from what I know, or God knows, in knowing (2) because I can know (1) without knowing (2), or vice versa. For example, I can know that Yujin Nagasawa is making a mess without realizing that *I* am Yujin Nagasawa. If God knows everything knowable, then He must know what I know in knowing (1) as well as what I know in knowing (2). However, no one but I can know what I know in knowing (1). Therefore, an omniscient God does not exist.

Just as the paradox of the stone undermines God's omnipotence by showing that the concept of omnipotence is internally incoherent or self-contradictory, the argument from knowledge *de se* undermines God's omniscience by showing that the concept of omniscience is internally incoherent or self-contradictory. Let us call these arguments that purport to show that the concept of at least one of God's attributes is internally incoherent Type-A arguments.[10]

Suppose that theists can refute all Type-A arguments and succeed in demonstrating that the concepts of omniscience, omnipotence, and omnibenevolence are all internally coherent. Does that mean the existence of God is thereby secured? The answer is 'No'.

> ### The argument from God's inability to sin[11]
> If God is omnibenevolent, He should be unable to perform morally wrong or sinful actions, such as brutally torturing hundreds of innocent children. Still, if God is omnipotent, He must be able to perform such an action; after all even we humans can do so in principle. Therefore, God cannot be omnipotent and omnibenevolent at the same time, which means that God does not exist.

> ### The argument from concept possession[12]
> If God is omniscient, then He must understand fully what fear and frustration are. However, an omnipotent God cannot grasp the concepts of fear and frustration fully because He, who is omnipotent, cannot experience what it is like to suffer fear and frustration. Therefore, God cannot be omnipotent and omniscient at the same time, which means that God does not exist.

The argument from God's inability to sin and the argument from concept possession attempt to show that even if Type-A arguments are not successful, that is, even if each of the concepts of God's attributes is internally coherent, there appears to be some mutual inconsistency among them. In particular, the argument from God's inability to sin purports to show that the concepts of omnibenevolence and omnipotence are mutually inconsistent. That is, no being can have these two attributes simultaneously. Similarly, the argument from concept possession purports to show that the concepts of omniscience and omnipotence are mutually inconsistent. That is, no being can have these two attributes simultaneously. Call arguments of this type Type-B arguments.

Suppose that theists can refute all Type-A and Type-B arguments and succeed in demonstrating that the concepts of omniscience, omnipotence, and omnibenevolence are all internally coherent and mutually consistent. Does that mean that the existence of God is thereby secured? The answer is, again, 'No'.

The logical argument from evil[13]

It seems obvious that, as a matter of contingent fact, there is evil in the actual world. However, if God is omniscient, omnipotent, and omnibenevolent, there must be no evil. If God is omniscient, then He must know that there is evil in the actual world. If God is omnipotent, then He must be able to eliminate evil from the actual world. If He is omnibenevolent, then He must be willing to eliminate evil from the actual world. Therefore, the existence of evil in the actual world logically entails the non-existence of God.

The argument from divine hiddenness[14]

If God is omniscient, omnipotent and omnibenevolent, then He must bring about a state of affairs in which His existence is manifest to everyone in the actual world. It is not the case, however, that His existence is manifest to everyone in the actual world. Even many people who want to believe in God cannot clearly see that He exists. Therefore, God does not exist.

The above Type-C arguments attempt to show that even if Type-A and Type-B arguments are not successful, that is, even if God's attributes *are* internally coherent and mutually consistent, the set of these attributes is mutually inconsistent with a certain contingent fact. The logical argument from evil purports to show that the set of God's attributes is mutually inconsistent with the fact that there is evil in the actual world. Similarly, the argument from divine hiddenness purports to show that the set of God's attributes is mutually inconsistent with the fact that the existence of God is not manifest to everyone in the actual world.

Some atheists find the logical argument from evil too strong. Perhaps the existence of evil in the actual world is not *logically* inconsistent with the existence of God. Nevertheless some of them think that the existence of evil constitutes good evidence for the non-existence of God.

The evidential argument from evil[15]

Perhaps it is logically possible that evil and God coexist. However, the existence of evil still suggests that we are justified in believing that God does not exist. Consider a parallel example. Suppose that a prime suspect for murder has been arrested. There is overwhelming evidence that he is guilty. Here we are justified in believing that he is guilty, even if it might be *logically possible* that he did not commit the crime (e.g., it might be logically possible that an extraterrestrial that looks identical to the suspect killed the victim).

Atheists could similarly reformulate the problem of divine hiddenness in terms of evidence, rather than logical possibility. In Part II we saw an atheistic position called 'friendly atheism'. Friendly atheists typically accept the evidential argument from evil, as opposed to the logical argument from evil. They maintain that while they are justified in believing that God does not exist, there might be theists who are justified in believing that God does exist. This is possible because, as mentioned above, being rationally justified in believing proposition p does not always entail or require that p is true. Some unfriendly atheists, on the other hand, accept the evidential argument from evil, saying that while they are justified in believing that God does not exist there are no theists who are justified in believing that God does exist.

As we saw above, the argument from religious experience for the existence of God is more modest than most other arguments for the existence of God because it does not try to prove the existence of God; instead, it tries to prove that theists are justified in believing the existence of God. Similarly, the evidential argument from evil is more modest than many other arguments against the existence of God because it does not try to prove the non-existence of God; instead, it tries to prove that atheists are justified in believing in the non-existence of God.

What sort of significance can be attributed to arguments for and against the existence of God? If any of the arguments for the existence of God is sound, then it follows, of course, that God exists (or at least that we are justified in believing that God exists). This would be a great discovery; it would possibly be the greatest discovery in human history. On the other hand, if any of the arguments against the existence of God is sound, then it follows, of course, that God does not exist (or at least that we are justified in believing that God does not exist). While this might be a disappointment to some people, it would still be an important discovery. It would settle, at least at a certain level, disputes among theists and atheists that have persisted for more than 2,000 years. What if, then, none of the arguments is sound? That should not discourage us from studying these arguments further because it remains true that they represent some of the most ingenious attempts to explore the existence of God and the ultimate level of reality. Investigating exactly how they fail surely helps us chart a wiser course when we pursue the answers to deep metaphysical questions.

NOTES

Part I

1 H. Wang, *Reflections on Kurt Gödel*, Cambridge, Massachusetts: MIT Press, 1987, p. 18.
2 For biographical particulars about Gödel see ibid. and J. W. Dawson, Jr., *Logical Dilemmas: The Life and Work of Kurt Gödel*, Wellesley, Massachusetts: A. K. Peters, 1997.
3 J. Ferguson, 'Theistic Arguments in the Greek Philosophers', *Hibbert Journal* 51, 1953: 156–64; J. Barnes, *The Ontological Argument*, London: Macmillan, 1972.
4 For biographical particulars about Anselm see G. E. Evans, 'Anselm's Life, Works, and Immediate Influence', in Brian Davies and Brian Leftow (eds.), *The Cambridge Companion to Anselm*, Cambridge: Cambridge University Press, 2004, pp. 5–31.
5 Anselm, *Anselm's Proslogion* [1077–8], trans. M. J. Charlesworth, Notre Dame, Indiana: University of Notre Dame Press, 1979, p. 103.
6 Ibid.
7 Ibid.
8 Ibid.
9 As is common practice, this book uses the pronoun 'He' to refer to God. This should not, however, be taken to imply that God has a gender.
10 J. L. Barrett, *Why Would Anyone Believe in God?*, Lanham, Maryland: Altamira Press, 2004, pp. 77–8 and 83–4.
11 Ibid., p. 86.
12 New International Version. See also Psalm 53:1.
13 B. Pascal, *Great Shorter Works of Pascal* [originally seventeenth century], trans. E. Caillet and J. C. Blankenagel, Philadelphia: Westminster Press, 1948, p. 117.
14 B. Pascal, *Pensées* [1670], trans. W. F. Trotter. Online. Available HTTP: <http://oregonstate.edu/instruct/phl302/texts/pascal/pensees-contents.html> (accessed March 8, 2010), Section 4, 273.

15 Ed Regis, *Who Got Einstein's Office? Eccentricity and Genius at the Institute for Advanced Study*, Cambridge, Massachusetts: Perseus Publishing, 1987, p. 58.

16 A. Aczel, *Descartes' Secret Notebook*, New York: Broadway Books, 2005, p. 34.

17 R. Descartes, *Philosophical Writings of Descartes* [originally seventeenth century], vol. 1, ed. J. Cottingham, R. Stoothoff, and D. Murdoch, Cambridge: Cambridge University Press, 1985.

18 This description of Descartes's dreams relies on: Aczel, *Descartes' Secret Notebook*, pp. 57–60, and A. Gabbey and R. E. Hall, 'The Melon and the Dictionary: Reflections on Descartes's Dreams', *Journal of the History of Ideas* 59, 1998: 651–68, at pp. 652–4.

19 A. Petocz, *Freud, Psychoanalysis, and Symbolism*, Cambridge: Cambridge University Press, 1999, p. 135; S. Gaukroger, *Descartes: An Intellectual Biography*, Oxford: Oxford University Press, 1995, p. 109.

20 Descartes's key phrase '*Cogito, ergo sum*' is most commonly translated 'I think, therefore I am'. However, most Descartes scholars think that the translation should be more nuanced, for example, 'I am thinking, therefore I exist.'

21 R. Descartes, *Meditations of First Philosophy* [1641], in *Descartes: Philosophical Writings*, trans. and ed. E. Anscombe and P. T. Geach, rev. edn., Sunbury-on-Thames, Middlesex: Nelson, 1970, p. 67.

22 A. C. Grayling, *Descartes*, London: Free Press, 2005.

23 G. Wood, *Living Dolls*, London: Faber and Faber, 2002, pp. 3–4.

24 K. Benesch, *Romantic Cyborgs: Authorship and Technology in the American Renaissance*, Amherst: University of Massachusetts Press, 2002, p. 203.

25 Descartes, *Meditations of First Philosophy*, p. 103.

26 Ibid., pp. 104–5.

27 G. W. Leibniz, *New Essays Concerning Human Understanding* [1690], trans. A. G. Langley, New York: Macmillan, 1896; reprinted in part in A. Plantinga (ed.), *The Ontological Argument from St. Anselm to Contemporary Philosophers*, Garden City, New York: Anchor, 1965, p. 54. Page references refer to this reprint.

28 Ibid.

29 K. J. Harrelson, *The Ontological Argument from Descartes to Hegel*, Amherst, New York: Prometheus Books, 2009, p. 144.

30 Descartes, *Philosophical Writings of Descartes*, vol. 2, p. 91.

31 Harrelson, *The Ontological Argument*, p. 144.

32 B. Russell, *The Autobiography of Bertrand Russell*, vol. 1, *1872–1914*, London: George Allen and Unwin, 1967, p. 63.

33 B. Russell, *A History of Western Philosophy* [1945], rev. edn., London: Routledge, 2004, p. 536.

34 T. M. Drange, 'Review of Jordan Howard Sobel's *Logic and Theism*', *The Secular Web*, 2006. Online. Available HTTP: <http://www.infidels.org/library/modern/theodore_drange/sobel.html> (accessed March 8, 2010).

35 B. Russell, *Why I Am Not a Christian and Other Essays on Religion and Related Subjects*, London: George Allen and Unwin, 1957, p. 148.

36 C. McGinn, *Logical Properties*, Oxford: Oxford University Press, 2000; B. Miller, *The Fullness of Being: A New Paradigm for Existence*, Notre Dame, Indiana: University of Notre Dame Press, 2002.

37 N. Malcolm, 'Anselm's Ontological Argument', *Philosophical Review* 69, 1960: 41–62, at p. 46.

38 Ibid., p. 45.

39 A. Schopenhauer, *The Fourfold Root of the Principle of Sufficient Reason* [1813], rev. edn., trans. K. Hillebrand, London: George Bell and Sons, 1897, reprinted in part in Plantinga (ed.) *The Ontological Argument*, p. 65. Page references to this reprint.

40 Plantinga (ed.), *The Ontological Argument*, p. xii.

41 Schopenhauer, *The Fourfold Root of the Principle of Sufficient Reason*, p. 65.

42 P. Millican, 'The One Fatal Flaw in Anselm's Argument', *Mind* 113, 2004: 437–76.

43 Ibid., pp. 460–3.

44 See Plantinga (ed.), *The Ontological Argument*, p. 47. Caterus, another contemporary of Descartes, also tries to undermine the ontological argument, by providing a parallel argument for the existence of an 'existing lion' (p. 39).

45 G. Oppy, 'Gödelian Ontological Argument', *Analysis* 56, 1996: 226–30.

46 Millican, 'The One Fatal Flaw in Anselm's Argument', p. 463.

47 A. Plantinga, *God, Freedom, and Evil*, London: George Allen and Unwin, 1974, p. 91.

48 Ibid., pp. 90–1. Critics might claim that just as there are not intrinsic maxima for an island's properties there are not intrinsic maxima for properties that are ascribed to God such as knowledge, power, and benevolence. So, for example, according to this objection, there is no such thing as omniscience because for any body of knowledge there is always another body of knowledge that is larger. This objection is different from Gaunilo's because it says effectively that Anselm's concept of God as that-than-which-no-greater-can-be-thought, which is meant to subsume omniscience, omnipotence, and omnibenevolence, is incoherent in the first place. For a response to this objection see ibid., p. 91.

49 A. Cock, 'The Ontological Argument for the Existence of God', *Proceedings of the Aristotelian Society* 18, 1917–18: 363–84.

50 Thanks to Philip Goff on this point.

51 Anselm, *Monologion* [1076], in B. Davies and G. R. Evans (eds.), *Anselm of Canterbury: The Major Works*, Oxford: Oxford University Press, 1998, p. 13.

52 C. K. Grant, 'The Ontological Disproof of the Devil', *Analysis* 17, 1957: 71–2.

53 Harrelson, *The Ontological Argument*, p. ix.

54 Hartshorne had already introduced the second version of the ontological argument in 1941 in his book *Man's Vision of God*, but he was not explicit about the fact that it is found in Chapter 3 of the *Proslogion*. See Hartshorne, 'The Necessarily Existent', in *Man's Vision of God*, New York: Harper and Row, 1941; reprinted, in part, in Plantinga (ed.), *The Ontological Argument*, pp. 123–35.

55 B. Leftow, 'Anselm's Neglected Argument', *Philosophy* 77, 2002: 331–47.

56 G. Nakhnikian, 'St. Anselm's Four Ontological Arguments', in W. H. Capitan (ed.), *Art, Mind, and Religion*, Pittsburgh: University of Pittsburgh Press, 1967; F. Sontag, 'The Meaning of "Argument" in Anselm's Ontological Proof', *Journal of Philosophy* 64, 1967: 459–86.

57 K. Barth, *Anselm: Fide Quaerens Intellectum* [1931], trans. I. W. Robertson, Richmond, Virginia: John Knox Press, 1960. This interpretation is implausible because, as we saw earlier, in the preface to the *Proslogion* Anselm states explicitly that his goal is the following: 'to find one single argument that for its proof required no other save itself, and that by itself would suffice to prove that God really exists, that He is the supreme good needing no other and it is He whom all things have need of for their being and well-being, and also to prove whatever we believe about the Divine Being'.

58 Malcolm, 'Anselm's Ontological Argument', p. 45.

59 C. Hartshorne, 'Thoughts on the Development of My Concept of God', *Personalist Forum* 14, 1998: 77–82; C. Hartshorne, 'Twenty Opinions from Five Times Twenty Years', *Personalist Forum* 14, 1998: 75–6.

60 H. F. Vetter, 'Introduction and Acknowledgements', in C. Hartshorne, *A New World View*, ed. H. F. Vetter, 2003. Online. Available HTTP: <http://www.harvardsquarelibrary.org/Hartshorne/> (accessed March 8, 2010).

61 C. Hartshorne, *Born to Sing: An Interpretation and World Survey of Bird Song*, Bloomington, Indiana: Indiana University Press, 1973.

62 D. Dombrowski, 'Charles Hartshorne', in E. N. Zalta (ed.), *Stanford Encyclopedia of Philosophy*, 2005. Online. Available HTTP: <http://plato.stanford.edu/entries/hartshorne/> (accessed March 8, 2010).

63 R. Kirk, *Zombies and Consciousness*, Oxford: Oxford University Press, 2005.

64 A. Plantinga, *The Nature of Necessity*, Oxford: Clarendon Press, 1974, pp. 65–9.

65 Plantinga, *God, Freedom, and Evil*, pp. 85–112.

66 J. Hick, 'Necessary Being', *Scottish Journal of Theology* 14, 1961: 353–69.

67 A. Pruss, 'The Ontological Argument and the Motivational Centers of Lives', *Religious Studies* 46, 2010: 233–49.

68 T. Buras and M. Cantrell, 'Natural Desire and the Existence of God', unpublished manuscript, 2009.

69 J. N. Findlay, 'Can God's Existence be Disproved?', *Mind* 37, 1948: 176–83.

70 C. Hartshorne, *Anselm's Discovery: A Re-Examination of the Ontological Proof for God's Existence*, La Salle, Illinois: Open Court, 1965.

71 T. Bayne and Y. Nagasawa, 'The Grounds of Worship', *Religious Studies* 42, 2006: 299–313.

72 A PDF of Morgenstern's document on the Gödel citizenship hearing can be found on Jeffrey Kegler's website: <http://morgenstern.jeffreykegler.com/> (accessed March 8, 2010).

73 Wang, *Reflections on Kurt Gödel*, p. 18.

74 G. Oppy, *Arguing about Gods*, Cambridge: Cambridge University Press, 2006, p. 70. See also C. A. Anderson, 'Some Emendations of Gödel's Ontological Proof', *Faith and Philosophy* 7, 1990: 291–303.

75 J. H. Sobel, 'Gödel's Ontological Proof', in J. J. Thompson (ed.), *On Being and Saying: Essays for Richard Cartwright*, Cambridge, Massachusetts: MIT Press, 1987. See also R. M. Adams, 'Introductory Note to *1970', in S. Feferman, J. W. Dawson, Jr., W. Goldfarb, C. Parsons, and R. N. Solovay (eds.), *Kurt Gödel Collected Works*, vol. 3, *Unpublished Essays and Lectures*, New York: Oxford University Press, 1995.

76 Millican, 'The One Fatal Flaw in Anselm's Argument'.

77 Y. Nagasawa, 'Millican on the Ontological Argument', *Mind* 116, 2007: 1027–40; G. Oppy, 'More than One Flaw: Reply to Millican', *Sophia* 46, 2007: 295–304.

Part II

1 ABC News, 'Famous Atheist Now Believes in God', December 9, 2004. Online. Available HTTP: <http://abcnews.go.com/US/print?id=315976> (accessed March 8, 2010).

2 A. Flew and G. R. Habermas, 'My Pilgrimage from Atheism to Theism: An Exclusive Interview with Former British Atheist Professor Antony Flew', *Philosophia Christi* 6, 2004: 197–212. Online. Available HTTP: <http://www.biola.edu/antonyflew/flew-interview.pdf> (accessed March 8, 2010).

3 Ibid.
4 R. Carrier, 'Antony Flew Considers God ... Sort Of', *The Secular Web*, 2004. Online. Available HTTP: <http://www.secweb.org/asset.asp?AssetID=369> (accessed March 8, 2010).
5 A. Flew, 'Sorry to Disappoint, but I'm Still an Atheist!', *The Secular Web*, 2001. Online. Available HTTP: <http://www.secweb.org/asset.asp?AssetID=138> (accessed March 8, 2010).
6 W. L. Rowe, 'The Problem of Evil and Some Varieties of Atheism', *American Philosophical Quarterly* 16, 1979: 335–41, at p. 340.
7 Carrier, 'Antony Flew Considers God ... Sort Of'.
8 Ibid.
9 Online. Available HTTP: <http://www.discovery.org/csc/topQuestions.php#questionsAboutIntelligentDesign> (accessed March 8, 2010).
10 M. Oppenheimer, 'The Turning of an Atheist', *New York Times*, November 4, 2007. Online. Available HTTP: <http://www.nytimes.com/2007/11/04/magazine/04Flew-t.html?_r=1> (accessed March 8, 2010).
11 A. Flew, 'Flew Speaks Out: Professor Antony Flew Reviews *The God Delusion*', *bethinking.org*, 2008. Online. Available HTTP: <http://www.bethinking.org/science-christianity/intermediate/flew-speaks-out-professor-antony-flew-reviews-the-god-delusion.htm> (accessed March 8, 2010).
12 C. Darwin, *On the Origin of Species* [1859], Oxford: Oxford University Press, 1998, p. 154.
13 M. Behe, *Darwin's Black Box: The Biochemical Challenge to Evolution*, New York: Free Press, 2006, p. 39.
14 Ibid., pp. 70–1.
15 W. Dembski, *The Design Evolution: Answering the Toughest Questions about Intelligent Design*, Downers Grove, Illinois: Intervarsity Press, p. 276.
16 D. Kelemen, 'Why Are Rocks Pointy? Children's Preference for Teleological Explanations of the Natural World', *Developmental Psychology* 35, 1999: 1440–53.
17 D. Kelemen, 'British and American Children's Preferences for Teleo Functional Explanations of the Natural World', *Cognition* 88, 2003: 201–21.
18 D. Kelemen, 'Are Children "Intuitive Theists"? Reasoning about Purpose and Design in Nature', *Psychological Science* 15, 2004: 295–301.
19 E. M. Evans, 'Cognitive and Contextual Factors in the Emergence of Diverse Belief Systems: Creation versus Evolution', *Cognitive Psychology* 42, 2001: 217–66.
20 For overviews of the cognitive science of religion see: J. L. Barrett, *Why Would Anyone Believe in God?*, Lanham, Maryland: Altamira Press, 2004, and 'Cognitive Science of Religion: What Is It and Why Is It?', *Religion Compass* 1, 2007: 768–86.
21 W. Dembski, *No Free Lunch: Why Specified Complexity Cannot be Purchased without Intelligence*, Lanham, Maryland: Rowman and Littlefield, 2002, p. 6.
22 Ibid., pp. 289–302.
23 Ibid., p. 22.
24 M. Behe, 'The Modern Intelligent Design Hypothesis: Breaking Rules', in N. A. Manson (ed.), *God and Design: The Teleological Argument and Modern Science*, London: Routledge, 2003, p. 277.
25 Ibid.
26 The 'Wedge' document is available at <http://www.antievolution.org/features/wedge.html> (accessed March 8, 2010).

27 See '3: What Is the "Dissent from Darwin" List?'. Online. Available HTTP: <http://www.discovery.org/csc/topQuestions.php> (accessed March 8, 2010).

28 K. Chang, 'Few Biologists but Many Evangelicals Sign Anti-Evolution Petition', *New York Times*, February 21, 2006. Online. Available HTTP: <http://www.nytimes.com/2006/02/21/science/sciencespecial2/21peti.html> (accessed March 8, 2010).

29 Online. Available HTTP: <http://www.natcenscied.org/resources/articles/3541_project_steve_2_16_2003.asp> (accessed March 8, 2010).

30 Online. Available HTTP: <http://shovelbums.org/component/option,com_mospetition/Itemid,506/> (accessed March 8, 2010).

31 K. Chang, 'Ask Science', *New York Times*, February 21, 2006. Online. Available HTTP: <http://www.nytimes.com/2006/02/21/science/22askscience.html> (accessed March 8, 2010).

32 Ibid.

33 The National Center for Science Education, 'Analysis of the Discovery Institute's "Bibliography of Supplementary Resources for Ohio Science Instruction"', 2002. Online. Available HTTP: <http://ncseweb.org/creationism/general/analysis-discovery-institutes-bibliography> (accessed March 8, 2010).

34 *Washington Post*, 'Transcript of Roundtable Interview', August 2, 2005. Online. Available HTTP: <http://www.washingtonpost.com/wp-dyn/content/article/2005/08/02/AR2005080200899.html> (accessed March 8, 2010).

35 D. C. Dennett, 'Show Me the Science', *New York Times*, August 28, 2005. Online. Available HTTP: <http://www.nytimes.com/2005/08/28/opinion/28dennett.html> (accessed March 8, 2010).

36 Voice of America News, 'Evolution Debate under Way in Pennsylvania Courtroom', September 27, 2005. Online. Available HTTP: <http://www.voanews.com/english/archive/2005-09/2005-09-27-voa38.cfm?CFID=13696071&CFTOKEN=20763182> (accessed March 10, 2010).

37 J. Witt, 'Evolution News and Views, "Did Edwards vs. Aguillard Spawn Intelligent Design? No"', *Evolution News and Views*, 2005. Online. Available HTTP: <http://www.evolutionnews.org/2005/09/did_edwards_vs_aguillard_spawn_intellige.html> (accessed March 8, 2010).

38 I. Kant, *Critique of Pure Reason* [1781], trans. N. K. Smith, London: Macmillan, 1929, p. 520.

39 Plato, *The Laws* [360 BCE], trans. T. J. Saunders, Harmondsworth: Penguin Books, 1970, pp. 526–7.

40 Cicero, *The Nature of Gods* [45 BCE], trans. H. C. P. McGregor, London: Penguin Books, 1972, pp. 158–9.

41 Ibid., pp. 161–2.

42 T. Aquinas, *Disputed Questions on Truth (Quaestiones Disputatae de Veritate)* [1256–9], trans. R. W. Mulligan, Chicago: Henry Regnery Co., 1952; excerpt reprinted in B. Davies (ed.), *Philosophy of Religion: A Guide and Anthology*, Oxford: Oxford University Press, 2000, pp. 251–2. Page references are to this reprint.

43 Ibid.

44 W. Paley, *The Principles of Moral and Political Philosophy* [1785], Boston School Edition, Boston: Benjamin B. Mussey, 1852, pp. 150–3.

45 M. D. Eddy and D. Knight, 'Introduction', in W. Paley, *Natural Theology* [1802], Oxford: Oxford University Press, 2006, pp. ix–xxix, at p. xiii.

46 Paley, *The Principles of Moral and Political Philosophy*, p. 18.

47 Paley, *Natural Theology*, p. 7.

48 Ibid.

49 Ibid., p. 280.

50 R. Chambers, *The Book of Days*, London: W. & R. Chambers, 1832, p. 197.

51 F. Darwin (ed.), *The Life and Letters of Charles Darwin, Including an Autobiographical Chapter*, London: John Murray (1887), vol. 1, p. 41.

52 J. H. Burton, *Life and Correspondence of David Hume*, Edinburgh: William Tait, 1846, p. 31.

53 O. A. Johnson, *The Mind of David Hume: A Companion to Book I of A Treatise of Human Nature*, Urbana, Illinois: University of Illinois Press, 1995, p. 8.

54 D. Hume, *An Enquiry Concerning Human Understanding* [1748], Oxford: Oxford University Press, 2008, p. 109.

55 J. Wain (ed.), *The Journals of James Boswell: 1762–1795*, New Haven, Connecticut: Yale University Press, 1994, pp. 247–9.

56 Paley, *Natural Theology*, p. 280.

57 D. Stoljar, *Ignorance and Imagination: The Epistemic Origin of the Problem of Consciousness*, New York: Oxford University Press, 2006, p. 51.

58 W. Dembski, 'An Information-Theoretic Design Argument', in F. J. Beckwith, W. L. Craig, and J. P. Moreland (eds.), *To Everyone an Answer: A Case for the Christian Worldview*, Downers Grove, Illinois: Intervarsity Press, 2004, p. 79; T. Aquinas, *Summa Contra Gentiles* [1258–64], in A. C. Pegis (ed.), *Basic Writings of Saint Thomas Aquinas*, Notre Dame, Indiana: University of Notre Dame Press, 1955, vol. 1, p. 61 (Book 3, Chapter 38).

59 Behe, 'The Modern Intelligent Design Hypothesis', p. 277.

60 B. Russell, *Why I Am Not a Christian and Other Essays on Religion and Related Subjects*, London: George Allen and Unwin, 1957, pp. 3–4.

61 P. Curd, and R. D. McKirahan, Jr. (eds.), *A Presocratics Reader: Selected Fragments and Testimonia*, Indianapolis: Hackett, 1995, p. 13.

62 Ibid.

63 Ibid., pp. 13–14.

64 A. O. Lovejoy, *The Great Chain of Being: A Study of the History of an Idea*, Cambridge, Massachusetts: Harvard University Press, 1936.

65 E. Darwin, *Zoonomia; or, the Laws of Organic Life* [1794], 3rd edn., London: Thomas and Andrews, 1809, p. 397.

66 Paley, *Natural Theology*, p. 224.

67 Ibid., p. 225.

68 L. Huxley (ed.), *Life and Letters of Thomas Henry Huxley* [1900], Charleston, South Carolina: BiblioBazaar, 2006, vol. 1, p. 189.

69 J. Huxley, *Evolutionary Humanism*, Buffalo, New York: Prometheus Books, 1992, p. 288.

70 Darwin to J. D. Hooker, January 11, 1844.

71 Darwin to John Fordyce, May 7, 1879.

72 Darwin to F. A. McDermott, November 24, 1880.

73 R. Dawkins, *The Blind Watchmaker*, London: W. W. Norton, 1985, p. 5.

74 Darwin (ed.), *Life and Letters of Charles Darwin*, p. 310.

75 *Kizmiller et al. v. Dover Area School Board*, Middle District of Pennsylvania, December 20, 2005.

76 Online. Available HTTP: <http://ncsc.com/creationism/legal/cdesign-proponentsists> (accessed March 10, 2010).

77 *Kizmiller et al.* v. *Dover Area School Board*, Middle District of Pennsylvania, December 20, 2005.

78 Ibid.

79 P. Draper, 'Natural Selection and the Problem of Evil', *The Secular Web*, 2007. Online. Available HTTP: <http://www.infidels.org/library/modern/paul_draper/evil.html> (accessed March 8, 2010).

Part III

1 E. A. Poe, *Eureka: A Prose Poem* [1849], Amherst, New York: Prometheus Books, 1997.

2 R. B. Edwards, *What Caused the Big Bang?*, New York: Rodopi, 1994, p. 20.

3 Ibid., p. 1.

4 M. Gleiser, *The Dancing Universe: From Creation Myths to the Big Bang*, New York: Penguin Books, 1997, p. 287.

5 *Time*, 'Religion: Behind Every Door: God', December 3, 1951. Online. Available HTTP: <http://www.time.com/time/magazine/article/0,9171,889395,00.html> (accessed March 8, 2010).

6 Ibid.

7 Aristotle, *Physics* 6.9 239b9–13 = 29A25; P. Curd and R. D. McKirahan, Jr. (eds.), *A Presocratics Reader: Selected Fragments and Testimonia*, Indianapolis: Hackett, 1995, p. 75.

8 F. Cajori, *A History of Mathematics*, 5th edn., New York: Chelsea Publishing Company, 1991, p. 446.

9 Some scholars question the authenticity of this quotation from Poincaré. See J. Gray, 'Did Poincaré Say "Set Theory Is a Disease"?', *Mathematical Intelligencer* 13, 1991: 19–22.

10 J. W. Dauben, *Georg Cantor: His Mathematics and Philosophy of the Infinite*, Princeton, New Jersey: Princeton University Press, 1990, p. 298.

11 J. W. Dauben, 'Georg Cantor and the Battle for Transfinite Set Theory' [1993], *Journal of the ACMS*, Inaugural Issue 2004. Online. Available HTTP: <http://www.acmsonline.org/Dauben-Cantor.pdf> (accessed March 8, 2010).

12 J. W. Dauben, 'Georg Cantor and Pope Leo XIII: Mathematics, Theology, and the Infinite', *Journal of the History of Ideas* 38, 1977: 85–108, at p. 106.

13 Ibid.

14 A. S. Riginos, *Platonica: The Anecdotes Concerning the Life and Writings of Plato*, New York: Columbia University Press, 1976, p. 41.

15 A. N. Whitehead, *Process and Reality*, New York: Free Press, 1979, p. 39.

16 Plato, *The Laws* [360 BCE], trans. T. J. Saunders, Harmondsworth, Middlesex: Penguin Books, 1970, p. 412.

17 W. L. Craig, *The Cosmological Argument from Plato to Leibniz*, New York: Harper and Row, 1980, p. 1.

18 Plato, *Laws*, p. 413.

19 Ibid., p. 428.

20 A. Kenny, *Aquinas*, New York: Hill and Wang, 1980, p. 26.

21 B. Davies, *The Thought of Thomas Aquinas*, Oxford: Oxford University Press, 1993, p. 9.

22 T. Aquinas, *Summa Contra Gentiles* [1258–64], in A. C. Pegis (ed.), *Basic Writings of Saint Thomas Aquinas*, Notre Dame, Indiana: University of Notre Dame Press, 1955, vol. 1, p. 22.

23 Ibid.

24 Ibid., p. 23.

25 For further objections to the Third Way, see: G. Oppy, *Arguing about Gods*, Cambridge: Cambridge University Press, 2006, pp. 104–5.

26 Ibid, p. 105.

27 H. H. Goldstein, *The Computer: From Pascal to Von Neumann*, Princeton, New Jersey: Princeton University Press, 1980, p. 8.

28 For a contemporary defense of this view see: A. Plantinga, *God, Freedom, and Evil*, London: George Allen and Unwin, 1974.

29 G. W. Leibniz, *Monadology* [1714], trans. G. R. Montgomery, Mineola, New York: Dover Publications, 2005, p. 52.

30 Ibid., p. 53.

31 For Craig's defence of the *Kalām* cosmological argument see: P. Copan and W. L. Craig, *Creation out of Nothing: A Biblical, Philosophical, and Scientific Exploration*, Grand Rapids, Michigan: Baker Academic, 2004; W. L. Craig, *The Kalām Cosmological Argument*, London: Macmillan, 1979; W. L. Craig and W. Sinnott-Armstrong, *God? A Debate between a Christian and an Atheist*, Oxford: Oxford University Press, 2004; W. L. Craig and Q. Smith, *Theism, Atheism, and Big Bang Cosmology*, Oxford: Clarendon Press, 1993.

32 One might think that because Craig says that the cause of the universe is timeless he cannot say that it is also eternal, because eternity is normally understood as time without an end. He seems to think, however, that timelessness and eternity are not incompatible. He says that even though the cause is timeless it is also 'in some sense eternal'. See W. L. Craig, *Reasonable Faith: Christian Truth and Apologetics*, rev. edn., Wheaton, Illinois: Crossway Books, 1994, p. 117.

33 W. L. Craig, 'Graham Oppy on the *Kalām* Cosmological Argument', *Sophia* 32, 1993: 1–11, at p. 6.

34 J. Y. T. Greig, *The Letters of David Hume*, 2 vols., Oxford: Clarendon Press, 1932, p. 66.

35 L. Strobel, *The Case for a Creator*, Grand Rapids, Michigan: Zondervan, 2004, p. 101.

36 W. L. Craig, 'The Cosmological Argument', in P. Copan and C. Meister (eds.), *Philosophy of Religion: Classic and Contemporary Issues*, Oxford: Blackwell, 2008, p. 89.

37 J. L. Mackie, *The Miracle of Theism: Arguments for and against the Existence of God*, Oxford: Clarendon Press, 1982, pp. 93–5. See also: G. Oppy, 'Craig, Mackie, and the *Kalām* Cosmological Argument', *Religious Studies* 27, 1991: 189–97, at pp. 194–5.

38 Craig, 'Graham Oppy on the *Kalām* Cosmological Argument'.

39 R. Prevost, 'Classical Theism and the *Kalām* Principle', in W. L. Craig and M. S. McLeod (eds.), *The Logic of Rational Theism: Exploratory Essays*, Lewiston, New York: Edwin Mellen Press, 1990, p. 116, n. 7. See also: M. R. Nowacki, *The Kalām Cosmological Argument for God*, Amherst, New York: Prometheus Books, 2007, pp. 116 and 146, n. 60.

40 Mackie, *The Miracle of Theism*, p. 93.

41 W. L. Craig, 'Professor Mackie and the *Kalām* Cosmological Argument', *Religious Studies* 20, 1984: 367–75, at p. 369.

42 G. Oppy, 'More than a Flesh Wound', *Ars Disputandi* 2, 2002. Online. Available HTTP: <http://www.arsdisputandi.org/index.html?http://www.arsdisputandi.org/publish/articles/000067/index.html> (accessed March 8, 2010).

43 D. Oderberg, 'The *Kalām* Cosmological Argument neither Bloodied nor Bowed', *Philosophia Christi* Series 3, 2001: 193–6.

44 Nowacki, *The Kalām Cosmological Argument for God*, p. 124.

45 Ibid., ch. 2.

46 J. Silk, *The Big Bang*, 5th edn., New York: Owl Books, 2001, pp. 6–7.

47 Copan and Craig, *Creation out of Nothing*, p. 226.

48 Silk, *The Big Bang*, p. 7.

49 Copan and Craig, *Creation out of Nothing*, p. 226.

50 Craig, *Reasonable Faith*, pp. 103–4.

51 W. Allen and M. Brickman, *Annie Hall*, 1977. Online. Available HTTP: <http://www.script-o-rama.com/movie_scripts/a/annie-hall-script-screenplay-woody.html> (accessed March 8, 2010).

52 Craig, *Reasonable Faith*, ch. 2.

53 W. Allen, *Hannah and Her Sisters*, 1986. Online. Available HTTP: <http://www.script-o-rama.com/movie_scripts/h/hannah-and-her-sisters-script.html> (accessed March 8, 2010).

54 Craig, *Reasonable Faith*, pp. 60–1.

55 Ibid., pp. 62–5.

56 W. L. Schaaf (ed.), *Mathematics, Our Great Heritage: Essays on the Nature and Cultural Significance of Mathematics*, New York: Harper and Brothers, 1948, p. 147.

Conclusion

1 J. D. Barrow and F. J. Tipler, *The Anthropic Cosmological Principle*, Oxford: Oxford University Press, 1988; B. Carr (ed.), *Universe or Multiverse?*, Cambridge: Cambridge University Press, 2007; J. Leslie, *Universes*, new edn., London: Routledge, 1996.

2 W. L. Craig and W. Sinnott-Armstrong, *God? A Debate between a Christian and an Atheist*, Oxford: Oxford University Press, 2004, p. 9.

3 R. M. Adams, 'Flavors, Colors and God', in his *The Virtue of Faith*, Oxford: Clarendon Press, 1987, pp. 243–60; J. P. Moreland, *Consciousness and the Existence of God: A Theistic Argument*, London: Routledge, 2008.

4 R. M. Burns, *The Great Debate on Miracles*, Lewisburg, Pennsylvania: Bucknell University Press, 1981; J. Earman, *Hume's Abject Failure: The Argument against Miracles*, Oxford: Oxford University Press, 2000; R. Swinburne, *The Concept of Miracle*, London: Macmillan Press, 1970.

5 R. M. Adams, *Finite and Infinite Goods*, Oxford: Oxford University Press, 2002; P. Quinn, *Divine Commands and Moral Requirements*, Oxford: Oxford University Press, 1978; W. J. Wainwright, *Religion and Morality*, Aldershot: Ashgate, 2005; E. J. Wielenberg, *Value and Virtue in a Godless Universe*, Cambridge: Cambridge University Press, 2005.

6 W. P. Alston, *Perceiving God: The Epistemology of Religious Experience*, Ithaca, New York: Cornell University Press, 1991; A. Plantinga, 'Reason and Belief in God', in A. Plantinga and N. Wolterstorff (eds.), *Faith and Rationality: Reason and Belief in God*, Notre Dame, Indiana: University of Notre Dame Press, 1983, pp. 16–93; A. Plantinga, *Warranted Christian Belief*, Oxford: Oxford University Press, 2000.

7 A. Hájek, 'Waging War on Pascal's Wager', *Philosophical Review* 113, 2003: 27–56; J. Jordan (ed.), *Gambling on God*, Lanham, Maryland: Rowman and Littlefield, 1994; J. Jordan, *Pascal's Wager: Pragmatic Arguments and Belief in God*, Oxford: Oxford

University Press, 2007; N. Rescher, *Pascal's Wager: A Study of Practical Reasoning in Philosophical Theology*, Notre Dame, Indiana: University of Notre Dame Press, 1985.

8 M. Martin and R. Monnier (eds.), *The Impossibility of God*, Amherst, New York: Prometheus Books, 2003; G. I. Mavrodes, 'Some Puzzles Concerning Omnipotence', *Philosophical Review* 72, 1963: 221–3; J. H. Sobel, *Logic and Theism: Arguments for and against Beliefs in God*, Cambridge: Cambridge University Press, 2003.

9 P. Grim, 'Against Omniscience: The Case from Essential Indexicals', *Noûs* 19, 1985: 151–80; P. Grim, 'The Being that Knew Too Much', *International Journal for Philosophy of Religion* 47, 2000: 141–54; Y. Nagasawa, *God and Phenomenal Consciousness: A Novel Approach to Knowledge Arguments*, Cambridge: Cambridge University Press, 2008, ch. 2.

10 For a more detailed classification of Type-A, Type-B and Type-C arguments against the existence of God see: Y. Nagasawa, 'A New Defence of Anselmian Theism', *Philosophical Quarterly* 58, 2008: 577–96.

11 W. Morriston, 'Omnipotence and Necessary Moral Perfection: Are They Compatible?', *Religious Studies* 37, 2001: 143–60; W. Morriston, 'Omnipotence and the Anselmian God', *Philo* 4, 2001: 7–20; N. Pike, 'Omnipotence and God's Ability to Sin', *American Philosophical Quarterly* 6, 1969: 208–16.

12 T. Alter, 'On Two Alleged Conflicts between Divine Attributes', *Faith and Philosophy* 19, 2002: 47–57; D. Blumenfeld, 'On the Compossibility of the Divine Attributes', *Philosophical Studies* 34, 1978: 91–103.

13 M. M. Adams and R. M. Adams (eds.), *The Problem of Evil*, Oxford: Oxford University Press, 1990; J. Hick *Evil and the God of Love*, New York: Harper and Row, 1966, rev. edn., 1978; J. L. Mackie, 'Evil and Omnipotence', *Mind* 64, 1955: 200–12; M. L. Peterson (ed.), *The Problem of Evil: Selected Readings*, Notre Dame, Indiana: University of Notre Dame Press, 1992; A. Plantinga, *God, Freedom, and Evil*, London: George Allen and Unwin, 1974; W. L. Rowe (ed.), *God and the Problem of Evil*, Oxford: Blackwell, 2001.

14 D. Howard-Snyder, *Divine Hiddenness: New Essays*, Cambridge: Cambridge University Press, 2001; P. K. Moser, *The Elusive God: Reorienting Religious Epistemology*, Cambridge: Cambridge University Press, 2008; J. L. Schellenberg, *Divine Hiddenness and Human Reason*, Ithaca, New York: Cornell University Press, 2006.

15 D. Howard-Snyder (ed.), *The Evidential Argument from Evil*, Bloomington and Indianapolis: Indiana University Press, 1996; M. Martin and R. Monnier (eds.), *The Improbability of God*, Amherst, New York: Prometheus Books, 2006; W. L. Rowe, 'The Problem of Evil and Some Varieties of Atheism', *American Philosophical Quarterly* 16, 1979: 335–41; N. Trakakis, *The God beyond Belief: In Defence of William Rowe's Evidential Argument from Evil*, Dordrecht: Springer, 2007.

FURTHER READING

General

Alter, T. and Howell, R. J. *The God Dialogues: A Philosophical Journey*, Oxford: Oxford University Press, 2010.

Craig, W. L. and Sinnott-Armstrong, W., *God? A Debate between a Christian and an Atheist*, Oxford: Oxford University Press, 2004.

Everitt, N., *The Non-Existence of God*, London: Routledge, 2004.

Le Poidevin, R., *Arguing for Atheism: An Introduction to the Philosophy of Religion*, London: Routledge, 1996.

Mackie, J. L., *The Miracle of Theism: Arguments for and against the Existence of God*, Oxford: Clarendon Press, 1982.

Oppy, G., *Arguing about Gods*, New York: Cambridge University Press, 2006.

Plantinga, A. and Tooley, M., *Knowledge of God*, Oxford: Blackwell, 2008.

Smart, J. J. C. and Haldane, J. J., *Atheism and Theism*, 2nd edn., Oxford: Blackwell, 2002.

Swinburne, R., *The Existence of God*, 2nd edn., Oxford: Oxford University Press, 2004.

Arguments for the existence of God

The ontological argument

Davies, B. and Leftow, B. (eds.), *The Cambridge Companion to Anselm*, Cambridge: Cambridge University Press, 2004.

Dombrowski, D. A., *Rethinking the Ontological Argument: A Neoclassical Theistic Response*, Cambridge: Cambridge University Press, 2006.

Harrelson, K. J., *The Ontological Argument from Descartes to Hegel*, Amherst, New York: Prometheus Books, 2009.

Hick, J. and McGill, A. (eds.), *The Many-Faced Argument: Recent Studies on the Ontological Argument for the Existence of God*, London: Macmillan, 1968.

Logan, I., *Reading Anselm's* Proslogion, Farnham: Ashgate, 2009.

Morris, T. V., *Anselmian Explorations: Essays in Philosophical Theology*, Notre Dame, Indiana: University of Notre Dame Press, 1987.

Oppy, G., *Ontological Arguments and Belief in God*, Cambridge: Cambridge University Press, 1995.

Plantinga, A. (ed.), *The Ontological Argument: From St. Anselm to Contemporary Philosophers*, Garden City, New York: Anchor Books, 1965.

The design argument

Baird, R. M. and Rosenbaum, S. E., *Intelligent Design: Science or Religion? Critical Perspectives*, Amherst, New York: Prometheus Books, 2007.

Behe, M., *Darwin's Black Box: The Biochemical Challenge to Evolution*, New York: Free Press, 2006.

Dembski, W. A., *The Design Inference: Eliminating Chance through Small Probabilities*, Cambridge: Cambridge University Press, 1998.

—— *No Free Lunch: Why Specified Complexity Cannot be Purchased without Intelligence*, Lanham, Maryland: Rowman and Littlefield, 2002.

Manson, N. A. (ed.), *God and Design: The Teleological Argument and Modern Science*, London: Routledge, 2003.

Meyer, S. C., *Signature in the Cell: DNA and the Evidence for Intelligent Design*, New York: HarperOne, 2010.

Pennock, R. T., *Intelligent Design Creationism and Its Critics: Philosophical, Theological, and Scientific Perspectives*, Cambridge, Massachusetts: MIT Press, 2001.

The cosmological argument

Copan, P. and Craig, W. L., *Creation out of Nothing: A Biblical, Philosophical, and Scientific Exploration*, Grand Rapids, Michigan: Baker Academic, 2004.

Craig, W. L., *The Cosmological Argument from Plato to Leibniz*, New York: Harper and Row, 1980.

—— *The* Kalām *Cosmological Argument*, London: Macmillan, 1979.

Craig, W. L. and Smith, Q., *Theism, Atheism, and Big Bang Cosmology*, Oxford: Clarendon Press, 1993.

Nowacki, M. R., *The Kalām Cosmological Argument for God*, Amherst, New York: Prometheus Books, 2007.

O'Connor, T., *Theism and Ultimate Explanation: The Necessary Shape of Contingency*, Oxford: Blackwell, 2008.

Pruss, A. R., *The Principle of Sufficient Reason: A Reassessment*, Cambridge: Cambridge University Press, 2006.

Rowe, W., *The Cosmological Argument*, Princeton, New Jersey: Princeton University Press, 1975.

The fine-tuning argument

Barrow, J. D. and Tipler, F. J., *The Anthropic Cosmological Principle*, Oxford: Oxford University Press, 1988.
Carr, B. (ed.), *Universe or Multiverse?*, Cambridge: Cambridge University Press, 2007.
Leslie, J., *Universes*, new edn., London: Routledge, 1996.

The argument from consciousness

Adams, R. M., 'Flavors, Colors and God', in his *The Virtue of Faith*, Oxford: Clarendon Press, 1987, pp. 243–60.
Moreland, J. P., *Consciousness and the Existence of God: A Theistic Argument*, London: Routledge, 2008.
See also Oppy, *Arguing about Gods* and Swinburne, *The Existence of God*, above.

The argument from miracles

Burns, R. M., *The Great Debate on Miracles*, Lewisburg, Pennsylvania: Bucknell University Press, 1981.
Earman, J., *Hume's Abject Failure: The Argument against Miracles*, Oxford: Oxford University Press, 2000.
Swinburne, R., *The Concept of Miracle*, London: Macmillan Press, 1970.

The moral argument

Adams, R. M., *Finite and Infinite Goods*, Oxford: Oxford University Press, 2002.
Quinn, P., *Divine Commands and Moral Requirements*, Oxford: Oxford University Press, 1978.
Wainwright, W. J., *Religion and Morality*, Aldershot: Ashgate, 2005.
Wielenberg, E. J., *Value and Virtue in a Godless Universe*, Cambridge: Cambridge University Press, 2005.
See also Swinburne, *The Existence of God*, above.

The argument from religious experience

Alston, W. P., *Perceiving God: The Epistemology of Religious Experience*, Ithaca, New York: Cornell University Press, 1991.
Plantinga, A., 'Reason and Belief in God', in A. Plantinga and N. Wolterstorff (eds.), *Faith and Rationality*, Notre Dame: University of Notre Dame Press, 1983, pp. 16–93.
—— *Warranted Christian Belief*, Oxford: Oxford University Press, 2000.

Pascal's wager

Hájek, A., 'Waging War on Pascal's Wager', *Philosophical Review* 113, 2003: 27–56.

Jordan, J. (ed.), *Gambling on God*, Lanham, Maryland: Rowman and Littlefield, 1994.

—— *Pascal's Wager: Pragmatic Arguments and Belief in God*, Oxford: Oxford University Press, 2007.

Rescher, N., *Pascal's Wager: A Study of Practical Reasoning in Philosophical Theology*, Notre Dame, Indiana: University of Notre Dame Press, 1985.

Arguments against the existence of God

The paradox of the stone

Martin, M. and Monnier, R. (eds.), *The Impossibility of God*, Amherst, New York: Prometheus Books, 2003.

Mavrodes, G. I., 'Some Puzzles Concerning Omnipotence', *Philosophical Review* 72, 1963: 221–3.

Sobel, J. H., *Logic and Theism: Arguments for and against Beliefs in God*, Cambridge: Cambridge University Press, 2003.

The argument from knowledge de se

Grim, P., 'Against Omniscience: The Case from Essential Indexicals', *Noûs* 19, 1985: 151–80.

—— 'The Being that Knew Too Much', *International Journal for Philosophy of Religion* 47, 2000: 141–54.

Nagasawa, Y., *God and Phenomenal Consciousness: A Novel Approach to Knowledge Arguments*, Cambridge: Cambridge University Press, 2008.

The argument from God's inability to sin

Morriston, W., 'Omnipotence and the Anselmian God', *Philo* 4, 2001: 7–20.

—— 'Omnipotence and Necessary Moral Perfection: Are They Compatible?', *Religious Studies* 37, 2001: 143–60.

Pike, N., 'Omnipotence and God's Ability to Sin', *American Philosophical Quarterly* 6, 1969: 208–16.

See also Martin and Monnier (eds.), *The Impossibility of God*, above.

The argument from concept possession

Alter, T., 'On Two Alleged Conflicts between Divine Attributes', *Faith and Philosophy* 19, 2002: 47–57.

Blumenfeld, D., 'On the Compossibility of the Divine Attributes', *Philosophical Studies* 34, 1978: 91–103.

See also Martin and Monnier (eds.), *The Impossibility of God* and Nagasawa, *God and Phenomenal Consciousness*, above.

The logical argument from evil

Adams, M. M. and Adams, R. M. (eds.), *The Problem of Evil*, Oxford: Oxford University Press, 1990.

Hick, J., *Evil and the God of Love*, rev. edn., New York: Harper and Row, 1978.

Mackie, J. L., 'Evil and Omnipotence', *Mind* 64, 1955: 200–12.

Peterson, M. L. (ed.), *The Problem of Evil: Selected Readings*, Notre Dame, Indiana: University of Notre Dame Press, 1992.

Plantinga, A., *God, Freedom, and Evil*, London: George Allen and Unwin, 1974.

Rowe, W. L. (ed.), *God and the Problem of Evil*, Oxford: Blackwell, 2001.

See also Mackie, *The Miracle of Theism* and Martin and Monnier (eds.), *The Impossibility of God*, above.

The argument from divine hiddenness

Howard-Snyder, D., *Divine Hiddenness: New Essays*, Cambridge: Cambridge University Press, 2001.

Moser, P. K., *The Elusive God: Reorienting Religious Epistemology*, Cambridge: Cambridge University Press, 2008.

Schellenberg, J. L., *Divine Hiddenness and Human Reason*, Ithaca, New York: Cornell University Press, 2006.

The evidential argument from evil

Howard-Snyder, D. (ed.), *The Evidential Argument from Evil*, Bloomington and Indianapolis: Indiana University Press, 1996.

Martin, M. and Monnier, R. (eds.), *The Improbability of God*, Amherst, New York: Prometheus Books, 2006.

Rowe, W. L., 'The Problem of Evil and Some Varieties of Atheism', *American Philosophical Quarterly* 16, 1979: 335–41.

Trakakis, N., *The God beyond Belief: In Defence of William Rowe's Evidential Argument from Evil*, Dordrecht: Springer, 2007.

See also Adams and Adams (eds.), *The Problem of Evil*; Peterson (ed.), *The Problem of Evil*; and Rowe (ed.), *God and the Problem of Evil*, above.

BIBLIOGRAPHY

Aczel, A., *Descartes' Secret Notebook*, New York: Broadway Books, 2005.

Adams, M. M. and Adams, R. M. (eds.), *The Problem of Evil*, Oxford: Oxford University Press, 1990.

Adams, R. M., *Finite and Infinite Goods*, Oxford: Oxford University Press, 2002.

—— 'Flavors, Colors and God', in his *The Virtue of Faith*, Oxford: Clarendon Press, 1987.

—— 'Introductory Note to *1970', in S. Feferman, J. W. Dawson, Jr., W. Goldfarb, C. Parsons, and R. N. Solovay (eds.), *Kurt Gödel Collected Works*, vol. 3, *Unpublished Essays and Lectures*, New York: Oxford University Press, 1995.

Allen, W., *Hannah and Her Sisters*, 1986. Online. Available HTTP: <http://www.script-o-rama.com/movie_scripts/h/hannah-and-her-sisters-script.html> (accessed March 8, 2010).

Allen, W. and Brickman, M., *Annie Hall*, 1977. Online. Available HTTP: <http://www.script-o-rama.com/movie_scripts/a/annie-hall-script-screenplay-woody.html> (accessed March 8, 2010).

Alston, W. P., *Perceiving God: The Epistemology of Religious Experience*, Ithaca, New York: Cornell University Press, 1991.

Alter, T., 'On Two Alleged Conflicts between Divine Attributes', *Faith and Philosophy* 19, 2002: 47–57.

Alter, T. and Howell, R. J., *The God Dialogues: A Philosophical Journey*, Oxford: Oxford University Press, 2010.

Anderson, C. A., 'Some Emendations of Gödel's Ontological Proof', *Faith and Philosophy* 7, 1990: 291–303.

Anselm, *Anselm's Proslogion* [1077–8], trans. M. J. Charlesworth, Notre Dame, Indiana: University of Notre Dame Press, 1979.

—— *Monologion* [1076], in B. Davies and G. R. Evans (eds.), *Anselm of Canterbury: The Major Works*, Oxford: Oxford University Press, 1998.

Aquinas, T., *Disputed Questions on Truth (Quaestiones Disputatae de Veritate)* [1256–9], trans. R. W. Mulligan, Chicago: Henry Regnery Co., 1952; excerpt reprinted in B. Davies (ed.), *Philosophy of Religion: A Guide and Anthology*, Oxford: Oxford University Press, 2000.

—— *Summa Contra Gentiles* [1258–64], in A. C. Pegis (ed.), *Basic Writings of Saint Thomas Aquinas*, vol. 1, Notre Dame, Indiana: University of Notre Dame Press, 1955.

Baird, R. M. and Rosenbaum, S. E., *Intelligent Design: Science or Religion? Critical Perspectives*, Amherst, New York: Prometheus Books, 2007.

Barnes, J., *The Ontological Argument*, London: Macmillan, 1972.

Barrett, J. L., 'Cognitive Science of Religion: What Is It and Why Is It?', *Religion Compass* 1, 2007: 768–86.

—— *Why Would Anyone Believe in God?*, Lanham, Maryland: Altamira Press, 2004.

Barrow, J. D. and Tipler, F. J., *The Anthropic Cosmological Principle*, Oxford: Oxford University Press, 1988.

Barth, K., *Anselm: Fide Quaerens Intellectum* [1931], trans. I. W. Robertson, Richmond, Virginia: John Knox Press, 1960.

Bayne, T. and Nagasawa, Y., 'The Grounds of Worship', *Religious Studies* 42, 2006: 299–313.

Behe, M., *Darwin's Black Box: The Biochemical Challenge to Evolution*, New York: Free Press, 2006.

—— 'The Modern Intelligent Design Hypothesis: Breaking Rules', in N. A. Manson (ed.), *God and Design: The Teleological Argument and Modern Science*, London: Routledge, 2003.

Benesch, K., *Romantic Cyborgs: Authorship and Technology in the American Renaissance*, Amherst: University of Massachusetts Press, 2002.

Blumenfeld, D., 'On the Compossibility of the Divine Attributes', *Philosophical Studies* 34, 1978: 91–103.

Buras, T. and Cantrell M., 'Natural Desire and the Existence of God', unpublished manuscript, 2009.

Burns, R. M., *The Great Debate on Miracles*, Lewisburg, Pennsylvania: Bucknell University Press, 1981.

Burton, J. H., *Life and Correspondence of David Hume*, Edinburgh: William Tait, 1846.

Cajori, F., *A History of Mathematics*, 5th edn., New York: Chelsea Publishing Company, 1991.

Carr, B. (ed.), *Universe or Multiverse?*, Cambridge: Cambridge University Press, 2007.

Carrier, R., 'Antony Flew Considers God ... Sort of', *The Secular Web*, 2004. Online. Available HTTP: <http://www.secweb.org/asset.asp?AssetID=369> (accessed March 8, 2010).

Chambers, R., *The Book of Days*, London: W. & R. Chambers, 1832.

Chang, K. 'Ask Science', *New York Times*, February 21, 2006. Online. Available HTTP: <http://www.nytimes.com/2006/02/21/science/22askscience.html> (accessed March 8, 2010).

—— 'Few Biologists but Many Evangelicals Sign Anti-Evolution Petition', *New York Times*, February 21, 2006. Online. Available HTTP: <http://www.nytimes.com/2006/02/21/science/sciencespecial2/21peti.html> (accessed March 8, 2010).

Cicero, *The Nature of Gods* [45 BCE], trans. H. C. P. McGregor, London: Penguin Books, 1972.

Cock, A., 'The Ontological Argument for the Existence of God', *Proceedings of the Aristotelian Society* 18, 1917–18: 363–84.

Copan, P. and Craig, W. L., *Creation out of Nothing: A Biblical, Philosophical, and Scientific Exploration*, Grand Rapids, Michigan: Baker Academic, 2004.

Craig, W. L., 'The Cosmological Argument', in P. Copan and C. Meister (eds.), *Philosophy of Religion: Classic and Contemporary Issues*, Oxford: Blackwell, 2008.

—— *The Cosmological Argument from Plato to Leibniz*, New York: Harper and Row, 1980.

—— *The* Kalām *Cosmological Argument*, London: Macmillan, 1979.

—— 'Graham Oppy on the *Kalām* Cosmological Argument', *Sophia* 32, 1993: 1–11.

—— 'Professor Mackie and the *Kalām* Cosmological Argument', *Religious Studies* 20, 1984: 367–75.

—— *Reasonable Faith: Christian Truth and Apologetics*, rev. edn., Wheaton, Illinois: Crossway Books, 1994.

Craig, W. L. and Sinnott-Armstrong, W., *God? A Debate between a Christian and an Atheist*, Oxford: Oxford University Press, 2004.

Craig, W. L. and Smith, Q., *Theism, Atheism, and Big Bang Cosmology*, Oxford: Clarendon Press, 1993.

Curd, P. and McKirahan, R. D., Jr. (eds.), *A Presocratics Reader: Selected Fragments and Testimonia*, Indianapolis: Hackett, 1995.

Darwin, C., *On the Origin of Species* [1859], Oxford: Oxford University Press, 1998.

Darwin, E., *Zoonomia; or, the Laws of Organic Life* [1794], 3rd edn., London: Thomas and Andrews, 1809, p. 397.

Darwin, F. (ed.), *The Life and Letters of Charles Darwin, Including an Autobiographical Chapter*, vol. 1, London: John Murray, 1887.

Dauben, J., 'Georg Cantor and the Battle for Transfinite Set Theory' [1993], *Journal of the ACMS*, inaugural issue, 2004. Online. Available HTTP: <http://www.acmsonline. org/Dauben-Cantor.pdf> (accessed March 8, 2010).

—— 'Georg Cantor and Pope Leo XIII: Mathematics, Theology, and the Infinite', *Journal of the History of Ideas* 38, 1977: 85–108.

—— *Georg Cantor: His Mathematics and Philosophy of the Infinite*, Princeton, New Jersey: Princeton University Press, 1990.

Davies, B., *The Thought of Thomas Aquinas*, Oxford: Oxford University Press, 1993.

Davies, B. and Leftow, B. (eds.), *The Cambridge Companion to Anselm*, Cambridge: Cambridge University Press, 2004.

Dawkins, R., *The Blind Watchmaker*, London: W. W. Norton, 1985.

Dawson, J. W., Jr., *Logical Dilemmas: The Life and Work of Kurt Gödel*, Wellesley, Massachusetts: A. K. Peters, 1997.

Dembski, W., *The Design Evolution: Answering the Toughest Questions about Intelligent Design*, Downers Grove, Illinois: Intervarsity Press, 2004.

—— *The Design Inference: Eliminating Chance through Small Probabilities*, Cambridge: Cambridge University Press, 1998.

Dembski, W., 'An Information-Theoretic Design Argument', in F. J. Beckwith, W. L. Craig, and J. P. Moreland (eds.), *To Everyone an Answer: A Case for the Christian Worldview*, Downers Grove, Illinois: Intervarsity Press, 2004.

—— *No Free Lunch: Why Specified Complexity Cannot be Purchased without Intelligence*, Lanham, Maryland: Rowman and Littlefield, 2002.

Dennett, D. C., 'Show Me the Science', *New York Times*, August 28, 2005. Online. Available HTTP:<http://www.nytimes.com/2005/08/28/opinion/28dennett.html> (accessed March 8, 2010).

Descartes, R., *Meditations of First Philosophy* [1641], in *Descartes: Philosophical Writings*, ed. and trans. E. Anscombe and P. T. Geach, rev. edn., Sunbury-on-Thames: Nelson, 1970.

—— *Philosophical Writings of Descartes* [originally seventeenth century], 2 vols., ed. J. Cottingham, R. Stoothoff, and D. Murdoch, Cambridge: Cambridge University Press, 1985.

Dombrowski, D., 'Charles Hartshorne', in E. N. Zalta (ed.), *Stanford Encyclopedia of Philosophy*, 2005. Online. Available HTTP: <http://plato.stanford.edu/entries/hartshorne/> (accessed March 8, 2010).

—— *Rethinking the Ontological Argument: A Neoclassical Theistic Response*, Cambridge: Cambridge University Press, 2006.

Drange, T. M., 'Review of Jordan Howard Sobel's *Logic and Theism*', *The Secular Web*, 2006. Online. Available HTTP: <http://www.infidels.org/library/modern/theodore_drange/sobel.html> (accessed March 8, 2010).

Draper, P., 'Natural Selection and the Problem of Evil', *The Secular Web*, 2007. Online. Available HTTP: <http://www.infidels.org/library/modern/paul_draper/evil.html> (accessed March 8, 2008).

Earman, J., *Hume's Abject Failure: The Argument against Miracles*, Oxford: Oxford University Press, 2000.

Eddy, M. D. and Knight, D., 'Introduction', in W. Paley, *Natural Theology* [1802], Oxford: Oxford University Press, 2006.

Edwards, R. B., *What Caused the Big Bang?*, New York: Rodopi, 1994.

Evans, E. M., 'Cognitive and Contextual Factors in the Emergence of Diverse Belief Systems: Creation versus Evolution', *Cognitive Psychology* 42, 2001: 217–66.

Evans, G. E., 'Anselm's Life, Works, and Immediate Influence', in B. Davies and B. Leftow (eds.), *The Cambridge Companion to Anselm*, Cambridge: Cambridge University Press, 2004.

Everitt, N., *The Non-Existence of God*, London: Routledge, 2004.

Ferguson, J., 'Theistic Arguments in the Greek Philosophers', *Hibbert Journal* 51, 1953: 156–64.

Findlay, J. N., 'Can God's Existence be Disproved?', *Mind* 37, 1948: 176–83.

Flew, A. 'Flew Speaks Out: Professor Antony Flew Reviews *The God Delusion*', *bethinking. org*, 2008. Online. Available HTTP: <http://www.bethinking.org/science-christianity/intermediate/flew-speaks-out-professor-antony-flew-reviews-the-god-delusion.htm> (accessed March 8, 2010).

—— 'Sorry to Disappoint, but I'm Still an Atheist!', *The Secular Web*, 2001. Online. Available HTTP: <http://www.secweb.org/asset.asp?AssetID=138> (accessed March 8, 2010).

Flew, A. and Habermas, G. R., 'My Pilgrimage from Atheism to Theism: An Exclusive Interview with Former British Atheist Professor Antony Flew', *Philosophia Christi* 6, 2004: 197–212. Online. Available HTTP: <www.biola.edu/antonyflew/flew-interview.pdf> (accessed March 8, 2010).

Gabbey, A. and Hall, R. E., 'The Melon and the Dictionary: Reflections on Descartes's Dreams', *Journal of the History of Ideas* 59, 1998: 651–68.

Gaukroger, S., *Descartes: An Intellectual Biography*, Oxford: Oxford University Press, 1995.

Gleiser, M., *The Dancing Universe: From Creation Myths to the Big Bang*, New York: Penguin Books, 1997.

Goldstein, H. H., *The Computer: From Pascal to Von Neumann*, Princeton, New Jersey: Princeton University Press, 1980.

Grant, C. K., 'The Ontological Disproof of the Devil', *Analysis* 17, 1957: 71–2.

Gray, J., 'Did Poincaré Say "Set Theory Is a Disease"?', *Mathematical Intelligencer* 13, 1991: 19–22.

Grayling, A. C., *Descartes*, London: Free Press, 2005.

Greig, J. Y. T., *The Letters of David Hume*, 2 vols., Oxford: Clarendon Press, 1932.

Grim, P., 'Against Omniscience: The Case from Essential Indexicals', *Noûs* 19, 1985: 151–80.

—— 'The Being that Knew Too Much', *International Journal for Philosophy of Religion* 47, 2000: 141–54.

Hájek, A., 'Waging War on Pascal's Wager', *Philosophical Review* 113, 2003: 27–56.

Harrelson, K. J., *The Ontological Argument from Descartes to Hegel*, Amherst, New York: Prometheus Books, 2009.

Hartshorne, C., *Anselm's Discovery: A Re-Examination of the Ontological Proof for God's Existence*, La Salle, Illinois: Open Court, 1965.

—— *Born to Sing: An Interpretation and World Survey of Bird Song*, Bloomington, Indiana: Indiana University Press, 1973.

—— 'The Necessarily Existent', in *Man's Vision of God*, New York: Harper and Row, 1941; reprinted, in part, in A. Plantinga (ed.), *The Ontological Argument from St. Anselm to Contemporary Philosophers*, Garden City, New York: Anchor, 1965.

—— 'Thoughts on the Development of My Concept of God', *Personalist Forum* 14, 1998: 77–82.

—— 'Twenty Opinions from Five Times Twenty Years', *Personalist Forum* 14, 1998: 75–6.

Hick, J., *Evil and the God of Love*, New York: Harper and Row, 1966; rev edn., 1978.

—— 'Necessary Being', *Scottish Journal of Theology* 14, 1961: 353–69.

Hick, J. and McGill, A. (eds.), *The Many-Faced Argument: Recent Studies on the Ontological Argument for the Existence of God*, London: Macmillan, 1968; new edn., 2009.

Howard-Snyder, D. *Divine Hiddenness: New Essays*, Cambridge: Cambridge University Press, 2001.

Howard-Snyder, D. (ed.), *The Evidential Argument from Evil*, Bloomington and Indianapolis: Indiana University Press, 1996.

Hume, D., *An Enquiry Concerning Human Understanding* [1748], Oxford: Oxford University Press, 2008.

Huxley, J., *Evolutionary Humanism*, Buffalo, New York: Prometheus Books, 1992.

Huxley, L. (ed.), *Life and Letters of Thomas Henry Huxley* [1900], vol. 1, Charleston, South Carolina: BiblioBazaar, 2006.

Johnson, O. A., *The Mind of David Hume: A Companion to Book I of A Treatise of Human Nature*, Urbana, Illinois: University of Illinois Press, 1995.

Jordan, J. (ed.), *Gambling on God*, Lanham, Maryland: Rowman and Littlefield, 1994.

—— *Pascal's Wager: Pragmatic Arguments and Belief in God*, Oxford: Oxford University Press, 2007.

Kant, I., *Critique of Pure Reason* [1781], trans. N. K. Smith, London: Macmillan, 1929.

Kenny, A., *Aquinas*, New York: Hill and Wang, 1980.

Kelemen, D., 'Are Children "Intuitive Theists"? Reasoning about Purpose and Design in Nature', *Psychological Science* 15, 2004: 295–301.

—— 'British and American Children's Preferences for Teleo-Functional Explanations of the Natural World', *Cognition* 88, 2003: 201–21.

—— 'Why Are Rocks Pointy? Children's Preference for Teleological Explanations of the Natural World', *Developmental Psychology* 35, 1999: 1440–53.

Kirk, Robert, *Zombies and Consciousness*, Oxford: Oxford University Press, 2005.

Le Poidevin, R., *Arguing for Atheism: An Introduction to the Philosophy of Religion*, London: Routledge, 1996.

Leftow, B., 'Anselm's Neglected Argument', *Philosophy* 77, 2002: 331–47.

Leibniz, G. W., *Monadology* [1714], trans. G. R. Montgomery, Mineola, New York: Dover Publications, 2005.

—— *New Essays Concerning Human Understanding* [1690], trans. A. G. Langley, New York: Macmillan, 1896; reprinted in part in Plantinga, A. (ed.), *The Ontological Argument from St. Anselm to Contemporary Philosophers*, Garden City, New York: Anchor, 1965.

Leslie, J., *Universes*, new edn., London: Routledge, 1996.

Logan, I., *Reading Anselm's* Proslogion, Farnham: Ashgate, 2009.

Lovejoy, A. O., *The Great Chain of Being: A Study of the History of an Idea*, Cambridge, Massachusetts: Harvard University Press, 1936.

Mackie, J. L., 'Evil and Omnipotence', *Mind* 64, 1955: 200–12.

—— *The Miracle of Theism: Arguments for and against the Existence of God*, Oxford: Clarendon Press, 1982.

Malcolm, N., 'Anselm's Ontological Argument', *Philosophical Review* 69, 1960: 41–62.

Manson, N. A. (ed.), *God and Design: The Teleological Argument and Modern Science*, London: Routledge, 2003.

Martin, M. and Monnier, R. (eds.), *The Impossibility of God*, Amherst, New York: Prometheus Books, 2003.

—— *The Improbability of God*, Amherst, New York: Prometheus Books, 2006.

Mavrodes, G. I., 'Some Puzzles Concerning Omnipotence', *Philosophical Review* 72, 1963: 221–3.

McGinn, C., *Logical Properties*, Oxford: Oxford University Press, 2000.

Meyer, S. C., *Signature in the Cell: DNA and the Evidence for Intelligent Design*, New York: HarperOne, 2010.

Miller, B., *The Fullness of Being: A New Paradigm for Existence*, Notre Dame, Indiana: University of Notre Dame Press, 2002.

Millican, P., 'The One Fatal Flaw in Anselm's Argument', *Mind* 113, 2004: 437–76.

Moreland, J. P., *Consciousness and the Existence of God: A Theistic Argument*, London: Routledge, 2008.

Morris, T. V., *Anselmian Explorations: Essays in Philosophical Theology*, Notre Dame, Indiana: University of Notre Dame Press, 1987.

Morriston, W., 'Omnipotence and the Anselmian God', *Philo* 4, 2001: 7–20.

—— 'Omnipotence and Necessary Moral Perfection: Are They Compatible?', *Religious Studies* 37, 2001: 143–60.

Moser, P. K., *The Elusive God: Reorienting Religious Epistemology*, Cambridge: Cambridge University Press, 2008.

Nagasawa, Y., *God and Phenomenal Consciousness: A Novel Approach to Knowledge Arguments*, Cambridge: Cambridge University Press, 2008.

—— 'Millican on the Ontological Argument', *Mind* 116, 2007: 1027–40.

—— 'A New Defence of Anselmian Theism', *Philosophical Quarterly* 58, 2008: 577–96.

Nakhnikian, G., 'St. Anselm's Four Ontological Arguments', in W. H. Capitan (ed.), *Art, Mind, and Religion*, Pittsburgh: University of Pittsburgh Press, 1967.

National Center for Science Education, 'Analysis of the Discovery Institute's "Bibliography of Supplementary Resources for Ohio Science Instruction"', 2002. Online. Available HTTP: <http://ncseweb.org/creationism/general/analysis-discovery-institutes-bibliography> (accessed March 8, 2010).

Nowacki, M. R., *The Kalām Cosmological Argument for God*, Amherst, New York: Prometheus Books, 2007.

O'Connor, T., *Theism and Ultimate Explanation: The Necessary Shape of Contingency*, London: Wiley-Blackwell, 2008.

Oderberg, D., 'The *Kalām* Cosmological Argument neither Bloodied nor Bowed', *Philosophia Christi* Series 3, 2001: 193–6.

Oppenheimer, M., 'The Turning of an Atheist', *New York Times*, November 4, 2007. Online. Available HTTP: <http://www.nytimes.com/2007/11/04/magazine/04Flew-t.html?_r=1> (accessed March 8, 2010).

Oppy, G., *Arguing about Gods*, Cambridge: Cambridge University Press, 2006.

—— 'Craig, Mackie, and the *Kalām* Cosmological Argument', *Religious Studies* 27, 1991: 189–97.

—— 'Gödelian Ontological Argument', *Analysis* 56, 1996: 226–30.

—— 'More than a Flesh Wound', *Ars Disputandi* 2, 2002. Online. Available HTTP: <http://www.arsdisputandi.org/index.html?http://www.arsdisputandi.org/publish/articles/000067/index.html> (accessed March 8, 2010).

—— 'More than One Flaw: Reply to Millican', *Sophia* 46, 2007: 295–304.

—— *Ontological Arguments and Belief in God*, Cambridge: Cambridge University Press, 1995.

Paley, W., *Natural Theology* [1802], Oxford: Oxford University Press, 2006.

Paley, W., *The Principles of Moral and Political Philosophy* [1785], Boston School Edition, Boston: Benjamin B. Mussey, 1852.

Pascal, B., *Great Shorter Works of Pascal* [originally seventeenth century], trans. E. Caillet and J. C. Blankenagel, Philadelphia: Westminster Press, 1948.

—— *Pensées* [1670], trans. W. F. Trotter. Online. Available HTTP: <http://oregonstate.edu/instruct/phl302/texts/pascal/pensees-contents.html> (accessed March 8, 2010).

Pennock, R.T., *Intelligent Design Creationism and Its Critics: Philosophical, Theological, and Scientific Perspectives*, Cambridge, Massachusetts: MIT Press, 2001.

Peterson, M. L. (ed.), *The Problem of Evil: Selected Readings*, Notre Dame, Indiana: University of Notre Dame Press, 1992.

Petocz, A., *Freud, Psychoanalysis, and Symbolism*, Cambridge: Cambridge University Press, 1999.

Pike, N., 'Omnipotence and God's Ability to Sin', *American Philosophical Quarterly* 6, 1969: 208–16.

Plantinga, A., *God, Freedom, and Evil*, London: George Allen and Unwin, 1974.

—— *The Nature of Necessity*, Oxford: Clarendon Press, 1974.

—— 'Reason and Belief in God', in A. Plantinga and N. Wolterstorff (eds.), *Faith and Rationality*, Notre Dame, Indiana: University of Notre Dame Press, 1983.

—— *Warranted Christian Belief*, Oxford: Oxford University Press, 2000.

Plantinga, A. (ed.), *The Ontological Argument from St. Anselm to Contemporary Philosophers*, Garden City, New York: Anchor, 1965.

Plantinga, A. and Tooley, M., *Knowledge of God*, Oxford: Blackwell, 2008.

Plato, *The Laws* [360 BCE], trans. T. J. Saunders, Harmondsworth, Middlesex: Penguin Books, 1970.

Poe, E. A., *Eureka: A Prose Poem* [1849], Amherst, New York: Prometheus Books, 1997.

Prevost, R., 'Classical Theism and the *Kalām* Principle', in W. L. Craig and M. S. McLeod (eds.), *The Logic of Rational Theism: Exploratory Essays*, Lewiston, New York: Edwin Mellen Press, 1990.

Pruss, A. R., 'The Ontological Argument and the Motivational Centers of Lives', *Religious Studies* 46, 2010: 233–49.

—— *The Principle of Sufficient Reason: A Reassessment*, Cambridge: Cambridge University Press, 2006.

Quinn, P., *Divine Commands and Moral Requirements*, Oxford: Oxford University Press, 1978.

Regis, E., *Who Got Einstein's Office? Eccentricity and Genius at the Institute for Advanced Study*, Cambridge, Massachusetts: Perseus Publishing, 1987.

Rescher, N., *Pascal's Wager: A Study of Practical Reasoning in Philosophical Theology*, Notre Dame, Indiana: University of Notre Dame Press, 1985.

Riginos, A. S., *Platonica: The Anecdotes Concerning the Life and Writings of Plato*, New York: Columbia University, 1976.

Rowe, W., *The Cosmological Argument*, Princeton, New Jersey: Princeton University Press, 1975.

Rowe, W., *God and the Problem of Evil*, Oxford: Blackwell, 2001.

—— 'The Problem of Evil and Some Varieties of Atheism', *American Philosophical Quarterly* 16, 1979: 335–41.

Russell, B., *The Autobiography of Bertrand Russell*, vol. 1, *1872–1914*, London: George Allen and Unwin, 1967.

—— *A History of Western Philosophy* [1945], rev. edn., London: Routledge, 2004.

—— *Why I Am Not a Christian and Other Essays on Religion and Related Subjects*, London: George Allen and Unwin, 1957.

Schaaf, W. L. (ed.), *Mathematics, Our Great Heritage: Essays on the Nature and Cultural Significance of Mathematics*, New York: Harper and Brothers, 1948.

Schellenberg, J. L., *Divine Hiddenness and Human Reason*, Ithaca, New York: Cornell University Press, 2006.

Schopenhauer, A., *The Fourfold Root of the Principle of Sufficient Reason* [1813], rev. edn., trans. K. Hillebrand, London: George Bell and Sons, 1897; reprinted in part in Plantinga, A. (ed.), *The Ontological Argument from St. Anselm to Contemporary Philosophers*, Garden City, New York: Anchor, 1965.

Silk, J., *The Big Bang*, 5th edn., New York: Owl Books, 2001.

Smart, J. J. C. and Haldane, J. J., *Atheism and Theism*, 2nd edn., Oxford: Blackwell, 2002.

Sobel, J. H., 'Gödel's Ontological Proof', in J. J. Thompson (ed.), *On Being and Saying: Essays for Richard Cartwright*, Cambridge, Massachusetts: MIT Press, 1987.

—— *Logic and Theism: Arguments for and against Beliefs in God*, Cambridge: Cambridge University Press, 2003.

Sontag, F., 'The Meaning of "Argument" in Anselm's Ontological Proof', *Journal of Philosophy* 64, 1967: 459–86.

Stoljar, D., *Ignorance and Imagination: The Epistemic Origin of the Problem of Consciousness*, New York: Oxford University Press, 2006.

Strobel, L., *The Case for a Creator*, Grand Rapids, Michigan: Zondervan, 2004.

Swinburne, R., *The Concept of Miracle*, London: Macmillan Press, 1970.

—— *The Existence of God*, 2nd edn., Oxford: Clarendon Press, 2004.

Time, 'Religion: Behind Every Door: God', December 3, 1951. Online. Available HTTP: <http://www.time.com/time/magazine/article/0,9171,889395,00.html> (accessed March 8, 2010).

Trakakis, N., *The God beyond Belief: In Defence of William Rowe's Evidential Argument from Evil*, Dordrecht: Springer, 2007.

Vetter, H. F., 'Introduction and Acknowledgements', in C. Hartshorne, *A New World View*, ed. H. F. Vetter, 2003. Online. Available HTTP: <http://www.harvardsquarelibrary.org/Hartshorne/> (accessed March 8, 2010).

Voice of America News, 'Evolution Debate under Way in Pennsylvania Courtroom', September 27, 2005. Online. Available HTTP: <http://www.voanews.com/english/archive/2005-09/2005-09-27-voa38.cfm?CFID=13696071&CFTOKEN=20763182> (accessed March 10, 2010).

Wain, J. (ed.), *The Journals of James Boswell: 1762–1795*, New Haven, Connecticut: Yale University Press, 1994.

Wainwright, W. J., *Religion and Morality*, Aldershot: Ashgate, 2005.

Wang, H., *Reflections on Kurt Gödel*, Cambridge, Massachusetts: MIT Press, 1987.

Washington Post, 'Transcript of Roundtable Interview', August 2, 2005. Online. Available HTTP: <http://www.washingtonpost.com/wp-dyn/content/article/2005/08/02/AR2005080200899.html> (accessed March 8, 2010).

Whitehead, A. N., *Process and Reality*, New York: Free Press, 1979.

Wielenberg, E. J., *Value and Virtue in a Godless Universe*, Cambridge: Cambridge University Press, 2005.

Witt, J., 'Evolution News and Views, "Did Edwards vs. Aguillard Spawn Intelligent Design? No"', *Evolution News and Views*, 2005. Online. Available HTTP: <http://www.evolutionnews.org/2005/09/did_edwards_vs_aguillard_spawn_intellige.html> (accessed March 8, 2010).

Wood, G., *Living Dolls*, London: Faber and Faber, 2002.

INDEX

Made in the USA
Columbia, SC
23 August 2023

22040216R00115